PREFACE.

WHEN the Publishers issued the first volume of this work, they felt that it supplied a want long realized by the Christian world, in illuminating a subject which is of great interest to the Christian mind, the relation of the Son of God to the Father, and his position in Heaven, together with the fall of man and the Mediatorship of Christ between him and his Creator.

In this second volume the author continues with renewed interest the subject of the mission of Christ, as manifested by his Miracles and Teachings. The reader will find that this book furnishes invaluable aid in studying the lessons of Christ set forth in the Gospels.

The author, as a religious writer and speaker, has labored for the public during more than twenty years. Being aided in the study of the Scriptures, and in her work as a religious teacher, by the special enlightenment of the Spirit of God, she is peculiarly qualified to present the facts of the Life and Ministry of Christ, in connection with the divine plan of human redemption, and to practically apply the lessons of Jesus to the simple duties of life.

One of the most pleasing features of this book is the plain and simple language with which the author clothes thoughts that glow with truth and beauty.

PUBLISHERS.

CONTENTS.

(7)

THE GREAT CONTROVERSY.

CHAPTER I.

THE FIRST ADVENT OF CHRIST.

THE Son of God was next in authority to the great Lawgiver. He knew that his life alone could be sufficient to ransom fallen man. He was of as much more value than man as his noble, spotless character, and exalted office as commander of all the heavenly host, were above the work of man. He was in the express image of his Father, not in features alone, but in perfection of character.

The blood of beasts could not satisfy the demands of God as an atoning sacrifice for the transgression of his law. The life of a beast was of less value than the life of the offending sinner, therefore could not be a ransom for sin. It could only be acceptable with God as a figure of the offering of his Son.

Man could not atone for man. His sinful, fallen condition would constitute him an imperfect offering, an atoning sacrifice of less value than Adam before his fall. God made man perfect and upright, and after his transgression there could be no sacrifice acceptable to God for him, unless the offering made should in value be superior to man as he was in his state of perfection and innocency.

The divine Son of God was the only sacrifice of sufficient value to fully satisfy the claims of God's perfect law. The angels were sinless, but of less value than the law of God. They were amenable to law. They were messengers to do the will of Christ, and before him to bow. They were created beings, and probationers. Upon Christ no requirements were laid. He had power to lay down his life, and to take it again. No obligation was laid upon him to undertake the work of atonement. It was a voluntary sacrifice that he made. His life was of sufficient value to rescue man from his fallen condition.

The Son of God was in the form of God, and he thought it not robbery to be equal with God. He was the only one, who as a man walked the earth, who could say to all men, Who of you convinceth me of sin? He had united with the Father in the creation of man, and he had power through his own divine perfection of character to atone for man's sin, and to elevate him, and bring him back to his first estate.

The sacrificial offerings, and the priesthood of the Jewish system, were instituted to represent the death and mediatorial work of Christ. All those ceremonies had no meaning, and no virtue, only as they related to Christ, who was himself the foundation of, and who brought into existence, the entire system. The Lord had made known to Adam, Abel, Seth, Enoch, Noah, Abraham, and the ancient worthies, especially Moses, that the ceremonial system of sacrifices and the priesthood, of themselves, were not sufficient to secure the salvation of one soul.

The system of sacrificial offerings pointed to

Christ. Through these, the ancient worthies saw Christ, and believed in him. These were ordained of Heaven to keep before the people the fearful separation which sin had made between God and man, requiring a mediating ministry. Through Christ, the communication which was cut off because of Adam's transgression was opened between God and the ruined sinner. But the infinite sacrifice that Christ voluntarily made for man remains a mystery that angels cannot fully fathom.

The Jewish system was symbolical, and was to continue until the perfect Offering should take the place of the figurative. The Mediator, in his office and work, would greatly exceed in dignity and glory the earthly, typical priesthood. The people of God, from Adam's day down to the time when the Jewish nation became a separate and distinct people from the world, had been instructed in regard to the Redeemer to come, which their sacrificial offerings represented. This Saviour was to be a mediator, to stand between the Most High and his people. Through this provision, a way was opened whereby the guilty sinner might find access to God through the mediation of another. The sinner could not come in his own person, with his guilt upon him, and with no greater merit than he possessed in himself. Christ alone could open the way, by making an offering equal to the demands of the divine law. He was perfect, and undefiled by sin. He was without spot or blemish. The extent of the terrible consequences of sin could never have been known, had not the remedy provided been of infinite value. The salvation of fallen man was procured at such an immense cost that angels marveled, and could not fully comprehend the divine mystery that the Majesty of Heaven, equal with God, should die for the rebellious race.

As the time drew near for the Son of God to make his first advent, Satan became more vigilant in preparing the hearts of the Jewish people to be steeled against the evidences he should bring of his Messiahship. The Jews had become proud and boastful. The purity of the priesthood had not been preserved, but was fearfully corrupted. They retained the forms and ceremonies of their system of worship, while their hearts were not in the work. They did not sustain personal piety and virtuous characters. And the more they were wanting in the qualifications necessary to the sacred work, as priests of the most high God, the more tenacious were they of outward show of piety, zeal, and devotion.

They were hypocritical. They loved the honors of the world, and were ambitious to become exalted through riches. In order to obtain their desire, they improved every opportunity to take advantage of the poor, especially of the widow and fatherless. They exacted heavy sums of money of those who were conscientious, on various pretenses, for the Lord's treasury, and used the means thus dishonestly obtained for their own advantage. They were themselves rigorous to outwardly keep the law. They appeared to show great respect for traditions and customs, in order to obtain money from the people to gratify their corrupt ambition.

Traditions, customs, and needless ceremonies, were repeated to the people, which God had not given them through Moses or any other one. These originated from no higher source than man.

The chief priests, scribes, and elders, forced these upon the people as the commandments of God. Their hearts were hard and unfeeling. They showed no mercy to the poor and unfortunate. Yet, at the same time, while praying in the market-places, and giving alms to be seen of men, and thus putting on the outward semblance of goodness, they were devouring widows' houses by their heavy taxes which they laid upon them. They were apparently exact in outward forms when observed of men; for they wished to give impressions of their importance. They wished the people to have exalted ideas of their zeal and devotion to religious duties, while they were daily robbing God by appropriating the offerings of the people to themselves.

The priesthood had become so corrupt that the priests had no scruples in engaging in the most dishonest and criminal acts to accomplish their designs. Those who assumed the office of high priest prior to, and at, the time of Christ's first advent, were not men divinely appointed to the sacred work. They had eagerly aspired to the office through love of power and show. They desired a position where they could have authority, and practice fraud under a garb of piety, and thereby escape detection. The high priest held a position of power and importance. He was not only counselor and mediator, but judge; and there was no appeal from his decision. The priests were held in restraint by the authority of the Romans, and were not allowed the power of legally putting any one to death. This power rested with those who bore rule over the Jews. Men of corrupt hearts sought the distinguished office of high priest, and frequently obtained it by bribery and

assassination.   The high priest, clad in his consecrated and expensive robes, with the breastplate
upon his breast, the light flashing upon the precious stones inlaid in the breastplate, presented a
most imposing appearance, and struck the conscientious, true-hearted people with admiration, reverence, and awe.   The high priest was designed
in an especial manner to represent Christ, who
was to become a high priest forever after the order of Melchisedec.   This order of priesthood
was not to pass to another, or be superseded by
another.

The Jewish nation had corrupted their religion
by useless ceremonies and customs.   This laid a
heavy tax upon the people, especially the poorer
classes.   They were also under bondage to the Romans, and required to pay tribute to them.   The
Jews were unreconciled to their bondage, and
looked forward to the triumph of their nation
through the Messiah, the powerful deliverer foretold in prophecy.   Their views were narrow.
They thought the Coming One would, at his appearing, assume kingly honors, and, by force of
arms, subdue their oppressors, and take the
throne of David.   Had they, with humble minds
and spiritual discernment, studied the prophecies,
they would not have been found in so great error
as to overlook the prophecies which pointed to
his first advent in humility, and misapply those
which spoke of his second coming with power and
great glory.   The Jewish people had been striv-
ing for power.   They were ambitious for worldly
honors.   They were proud and corrupt, and could
not discern sacred things.   They could not distinguish between those prophecies which pointed
to the first advent of Christ, and those that de-

scribed his second, glorious appearing. The power and glory described by the prophets as attending his second advent, they looked for at his first advent. Their national glory was to them their greatest anxiety. Their ambitious desire was the establishment of a temporal kingdom, which they supposed would reduce the Romans to subjection, and exalt themselves with authority and power to reign over them. They had made the proud boast to those to whom they were in subjection, that they were not to oppress them long; for their reign would soon commence, which would be more exalted and glorious than even that of Solomon.

When the time was fulfilled, Christ was born in a stable, and cradled in a manger, surrounded by the beasts of the stall. And is this indeed the Son of God, to all outward appearance a frail, helpless babe, so much resembling other infants? His divine glory and majesty were vailed by humanity, and angels heralded his advent. The tidings of his birth were borne with joy to the heavenly courts, while the great men of the earth knew it not. The proud Pharisees and scribes, with their hypocritical ceremonies, and apparent devotion to the law, knew nothing of the Babe of Bethlehem. They were ignorant of the manner of his appearing, notwithstanding all their boasted learning and wisdom in expounding the law and the prophecies in the schools of the prophets. They were devising means to advantage themselves. Their study was as to the most successful manner to obtain riches and worldly honor, and they were wholly unprepared for the revelation of the Messiah. They looked for a mighty prince, who should reign upon David's throne, and whose kingdom should endure forever. Their proud and lofty ideas of the coming of the Messiah were not in accordance with the prophecies which they professed to be able to expound to the people. They were spiritually blind, and were leaders of the blind.

In Heaven it was understood that the time had come for the advent of Christ to the world, and angels leave glory to witness his reception by those he came to bless and save. They had witnessed his glory in Heaven, and they anticipate that he will be received with honor in accordance with his character, and the dignity of his mission. As angels approach the earth, they first come to the people God had separated from the nations of the world as his peculiar treasure. They see no especial interest among the Jews, no eager waiting and watching that they may be the first to receive the Redeemer, and acknowledge his advent.

In the temple, which had been hallowed by daily sacrificial offerings, prefiguring his coming, and symbolizing his death, no preparations are being made to welcome the Saviour of the world. The Pharisees continue to repeat their long, meaningless prayers in the streets, to be heard of men, in order to obtain the reputation of great piety and devotion.

The angels from Heaven behold with astonishment the indifference of the people, and their ignorance in regard to the advent of the Prince of Life. The proud Pharisees, claiming to be God's chosen people, in their hypocritical devotions, are proclaiming the law, and exalting traditions, while men of other nations are dealing in fables, and are worshiping false gods. All alike were ignorant of the great event which prophecy had foretold would transpire.

Angels behold the weary travelers, Joseph and Mary, making their way to the city of David to be taxed, according to the decree of Cæsar Augustus. Here, in the providence of God, Joseph and Mary had been brought; for this was the place prophecy had predicted that Christ should be born. They seek a place of rest at the inn, but are turned away because there is no room. The wealthy and honorable have been welcomed, and find refreshment and room, while these weary travelers are compelled to seek refuge in a coarse building which shelters the dumb beasts.

Here the Saviour of the world is born. The Majesty of Glory, who filled all Heaven with admiration and splendor, is humiliated to a bed in a manger. In Heaven, he was surrounded by holy angels; but now his companions are the beasts of the stall. What humiliation is this! Wonder, O Heavens! and be astonished, O earth!

As there are none among the sons of men to herald the advent of the Messiah, angels must now do that work which it was the honored privilege of men to do. But the angels, with the glad tidings of the birth of the Saviour, are sent to the humble shepherds, and not to the learned Jews, who profess to be the expounders of prophecy; for they have no heart to receive it.

"And there were in the same country shepherds abiding in the field, keeping watch over their flock by night. And lo! the angel of the Lord came upon them, and the glory of the Lord shone round about them, and they were sore afraid." Humble shepherds, who are guarding their flocks by night, are the ones who joyfully re-

ceive their testimony. Suddenly the heavens are
lighted up with a brightness which alarms the
shepherds. They know not the reason of this
grand display. They do not at first discern the
myriads of angels that are congregated in the
heavens. The brightness and glory from the
heavenly host illuminate and glorify the entire
plain. While the shepherds are terrified at the
glory of God, the leading angel of the throng
quiets their fears by revealing himself to them,
saying, "Fear not; for behold I bring you good
tidings of great joy, which shall be to all people.
For unto you is born this day, in the city of David,
a Saviour, which is Christ the Lord. And this
shall be a sign unto you: ye shall find the babe
wrapped in swaddling clothes, lying in a manger.
And suddenly there was with the angel a multitude of the heavenly host, praising God, and saying, Glory to God in the highest, and on earth,
peace, good-will toward men."

As their fears are dispelled, joy takes the place
of astonishment and terror. They could not, at
first, bear the radiance of glory, which attended
the whole heavenly host, to break upon them suddenly. One angel only appears to the gaze of the
watching shepherds to dissipate their fears, and
make known their mission. As the light of the
angel encircles them, the glory rests upon them,
and they are strengthened to endure the greater
light and glory attending the myriads of heavenly
angels. "And it came to pass, as the angels
were gone away from them into Heaven, the shepherds said one to another, Let us now go even
unto Bethlehem, and see this thing which is come
to pass, which the Lord hath made known unto us.
And they came with haste, and found Mary and

Joseph, and the babe lying in a manger. And when they had seen it, they made known abroad the saying which was told them concerning this child. And all they that heard it, wondered at those things which were told them by the shepherds. But Mary kept all these things, and pondered them in her heart. And the shepherds returned, glorifying and praising God for all the things that they had heard and seen, as it was told unto them."

The shepherds are filled with joy, and as the bright glory disappears, and the angels return to Heaven, they are all aglow with the glad tidings, and hasten in search of the Saviour. They find the infant Redeemer, as the celestial messengers had testified, wrapped in swaddling clothes, and lying in the narrow confines of a manger.

The events which had but just transpired, have made indelible impressions upon their minds and hearts, and they are filled with amazement, love, and gratitude for the great condescension of God to man in sending his Son into the world. The shepherds spread the joyful tidings everywhere, of the wondrous glory they had seen, and the celestial praises they had heard from the lips of the heavenly host.

The King of glory stooped low to take humanity; and angels, who had witnessed his splendor in the heavenly courts, as he was worshiped by all the heavenly hosts, were disappointed to find their divine Commander in a position of so great humiliation.

The Jews had separated themselves so far from God by their wicked works, that angels could not communicate to them the tidings of the advent of the infant Redeemer. God chooses the wise men of the East to do his will.

"Now when Jesus was born in Bethlehem of Judea in the days of Herod the king, behold, there came wise men from the East to Jerusalem, saying, Where is he that is born King of the Jews? for we have seen his star in the east, and are come to worship him." These men were not Jews; but they had been waiting for the predicted Messiah. They had studied prophecy, and knew the time was at hand when Christ would come; and they were anxiously watching for some sign of this great event, that they might be among the first to welcome the infant heavenly King, and worship him. These wise men were philosophers, and had studied the works of God in nature. In the wonders of the heavens, in the glories of the sun, moon, and stars, they traced the finger of God. They were not idolaters. They lived up to the dim light which shone upon them. These men were regarded by the Jews as heathen; but they were more pure in the sight of God than the Jews who had been privileged with great light, and who made exalted professions, yet did not live up to the light God had given them. These wise men had seen the heavens illuminated with light, which enshrouded the heavenly host who heralded the advent of Christ to the humble shepherds. And after the angels returned to Heaven, a luminous star appeared, and lingered in the heavens.

This light was a distant cluster of flaming angels, which appeared like a luminous star. The unusual appearance of the large, bright star which they had never seen before, hanging as a sign in the heavens, attracted their attention. They were not privileged to hear the proclamation of the angels to the shepherds. But the Spirit of God moved them out to seek this heavenly Visitor to a fallen world. The wise men directed their course where the star seemed to lead them. And as they drew nigh to the city of Jerusalem, the star was enshrouded in darkness, and no longer guided them. They reasoned that the Jews could not be ignorant of the great event of the advent of the Messiah, and they made inquiries in the vicinity of Jerusalem.

The wise men are surprised to see no unusual interest upon the subject of the coming of the Messiah. They fear that after all they may not have read the prophecies correctly. Uncertainty beclouds their minds, and they become anxious. They hear the priests repeating and enforcing their traditions, and expounding the law, and exalting their religion, and their own piety. They point to their phylacteries, and the borders of their garments, upon which the precepts of the law and their traditions are inscribed, as evidences of their devotion, while they denounce the Romans and the Greeks as heathen and sinners above all men. The wise men leave Jerusalem not as confident and hopeful as when they entered it. They marvel that the Jews are not interested and joyful in prospect of this great event of the advent of Christ.

The churches of our time are seeking worldly aggrandizement, and are as unwilling to see the light of the prophecies, and receive the evidences of their fulfillment, which show that Christ is soon to come, as were the Jews in reference to his first appearing. They were looking for the temporal and triumphant reign of Messiah in Jerusalem. Professed Christians of our time are expecting the temporal prosperity of the church, in the conversion of the world, and the enjoyment of the temporal millennium.

The wise men plainly stated their errand. They were in search of Jesus, the king of the Jews, for they had seen his star in the east, and had come to worship him.

The city of Jerusalem was thrown into great excitement by the sayings of the wise men. The news was immediately carried to Herod. He was exceedingly troubled, yet disguised the discomfiture, and received the men with apparent courtesy.

The advent of Christ was the greatest event which had taken place since the creation of the world. The birth of Christ, which gave joy to the angels of Heaven, was not welcome to the kingly powers of the world. Suspicion and envy were aroused in king Herod, and his wicked heart was planning his dark purposes for the future. The Jews manifested a stupid indifference to the story of the wise men. But Herod is intensely interested and excited. He summons the scribes, and the chief priests, and urges upon them to search carefully prophetic history, and tell him where the infant king was to be born. The careless indifference and apparent ignorance of the scribes and chief priests, as they turn to their books for the words of prophecy, irritate the fully aroused king. He thinks they are trying to conceal from him the real facts in regard to the birth of the Messiah. He authoritatively commands them to make close search in relation to their expected king.

"And when he had gathered all the chief priests and scribes of the people together, he demanded of them where Christ should be born.

And they said unto him, In Bethlehem of Judea; for thus it is written by the prophet, And thou Bethlehem, in the land of Juda, art not the least among the princes of Juda; for out of thee shall come a Governor, that shall rule my people Israel. Then Heród, when he had privily called the wise men, inquired of them diligently what time the star appeared. And he sent them to Bethlehem, and said, Go and search diligently for the young child; and when ye have found him, bring me word again, that I may come and worship him also."

Although Herod received the wise men with apparent respect, yet the intimation by them of the birth of a king to reign in Jerusalem, excited his envy and hatred against the infant whom he thought might prove his rival, and drive him, or his descendants, from the throne. A storm of opposition and satanic fury took possession of Herod, and he determined to destroy this infant king. Yet he put on a calm exterior, and requested a private interview with the wise men. He then inquired particularly the exact time the star appeared. He apparently hailed the supposition of the birth of Christ with joy, expressing a desire to be immediately informed by the wise men, that he might be among the first to show him true honor by worshiping him also. The wise men were not able to read the heart of the tyrant Herod; but God, who is acquainted with every emotion of the soul, with the intents and purposes of the heart, was not deceived by his hypocritical pretenses. His power will protect and preserve the precious infant Saviour from Satan's devices, until his mission on earth is accomplished. "When they had heard the king, they departed;

and lo! the star which they saw in the east went
before them, till it came and stood over where
the young child was. When they saw the star,
they rejoiced with exceeding great joy."

After the wise men had left Jerusalem, they
again saw, to their great joy, the guiding star in
the heavens, which directed them to the birthplace
of our Saviour. "And when they were come
into the house, they saw the young child with
Mary his mother, and fell down, and worshiped
him. And when they had opened their treasures,
they presented unto him gifts; gold, and frank-
incense, and myrrh." The wise men found no
loyal guard to debar their entrance to the presence of Christ. The honorable of the world are
not in attendance. In place of the people who
should have welcomed with grateful homage the
Prince of Life, he is surrounded with dumb beasts.

The glory of God attending the angelic host,
had scarcely disappeared from the plains of Bethlehem when the malice of envious Herod was
aroused in opposition to the infant Saviour. This
king understood that Christ was to reign over a
temporal kingdom, and he was utterly averse to
the idea of a Jewish king. The chief priests and
scribes had professed to understand the prophecies in reference to the appearing of Christ. They
had repeated to the people the prophecies which
relate to the second appearing of Christ in power
and great glory, to put down all authority, and
to rule over the whole earth. They had in a
boastful, resentful manner, asserted that Christ
was to be a temporal prince, and that every kingdom and nation was to bow in submission to his
authority.

These priests had not searched the prophecies with an eye single to the glory of God, or with a desire to conform their lives to the high standard marked out by the prophets. They searched the Scriptures to find ancient prophecies which they could in some way interpret to sustain their lofty pride, and to show with what contempt God regarded all the nations of the world except the Jews. They declared that the power and authority they were then compelled to respect and obey, would soon come to an end; for Messiah would take the throne of David, and, by force of arms, restore the Jews to their liberty, and to their exalted privileges. The understanding of the Jews was darkened. They had no light in themselves. They were seeing the prophecies through their own perverse understanding. Satan was leading them on to their own ruin. And Herod was determined to defeat the purposes of the Jews, and to humble these proud boasters, by destroying Christ as soon as he should be found.

After the mission of the wise men had been accomplished, they were purposing to return, and bear the joyful news to Herod of the success of their journey. But God sent his angel in the night season to turn the course of the wise men. In a vision of the night they were plainly told not to return to Herod. They obeyed the heavenly vision. "And being warned of God in a dream that they should not return to Herod, they departed into their own country another way. And when they were departed, behold the angel of the Lord appeareth to Joseph in a dream, saying, Arise, and take the young child and his mother, and flee into Egypt, and be thou there until I bring thee word; for Herod will seek the young child to destroy him. When he arose, he took the young child and his mother by night, and departed into Egypt."

The Lord moved upon the wise men to go in search of Jesus, and he directed their course by a star. This star, leaving them when near Jerusalem, led them to make inquiries in Judah; for they thought it was not possible for the chief priests and scribes to be ignorant of this great event. The coming of the wise men made the whole nation acquainted with the object of their journey, and directed their attention to the important events which were transpiring. God well knew that the advent of his Son to earth would stir the powers of darkness. Satan did not want that light should come into the world. The eye of God was upon his Son every moment. The Lord had fed his prophet Elijah by a miracle when upon a long journey. He could obtain food from no other source. He rained manna from Heaven for the children of Israel. The Lord provided a way for Joseph to preserve his own life, and the life of Jesus, and that of the mother, by their fleeing into Egypt. He provided for the necessities of their journey, and for their sojourn in Egypt, by moving upon the wise men of the East to go in search of the infant Saviour, and to bear him valuable offerings as a token of honor. The Lord is acquainted with the hearts of all men. He directed the course of Joseph into Egypt, that he might there find an asylum from the wrath of a tyrannical king, and the life of the infant Saviour be preserved. The earthly parents of Jesus were poor. The gifts brought to them by the wise men sustained them while in the land of strangers.

Herod waited anxiously for the return of the

wise men; for he was impatient to carry out his
determined purpose to destroy the infant King of
Israel. After he had waited long for the knowledge he desired, he feared his purpose might be
thwarted. He reasoned thus: Could those men
have read the dark deed he premeditated?
Could they have understood his design, and purposely avoided him? This he thought was insult
and mockery. His impatience, envy, and hatred,
increased. He was stirred by his father, the devil,
to seek the accomplishment of his purpose by a
most cruel act. If he should fail in carrying out
his murderous intent by pretense and subtlety, he
would, by power and authority, strike terror to
the hearts of all the Jews. They should have an
example of what their king would meet, should they
seek to place one upon the throne in Jerusalem.

And here was a favorable opportunity to humble
the pride of the Jews, and bring upon them a calamity which should discourage them in their ambition to have a separate government, and become
the glory of the whole earth, as they had proudly
boasted. Herod issued a proclamation to a large
body of soldiers, whose hearts were hardened by
crime, war, and bloodshed, to go throughout
Bethlehem and all the coasts thereof, and massacre all the children from two years old and
under. Herod designed in this cruel act to
accomplish a double purpose: first, to exercise,
by this bold act, his power and authority over
the Jews; and, second, to silence their proud
boastings in regard to their king, and also make his
own kingdom secure, by murdering the infant
prince whom he envied and feared. This cruel work
was accomplished. The sword of unfeeling soldiers carried destruction everywhere. The horror

and distress of parents were beyond description.
The wailing cries of bereaved mothers, as they
clasped their expiring infants to their breasts,
rose above the coarse jests and imprecations of
the soldiers, while they cried to Heaven for venge-
ance on the tyrant king.

All this terrible calamity was suffered of God,
to humble the pride of the Jewish nation. Their
crimes and wickedness had been so great that the
Lord permitted the wicked Herod to thus punish
them. Had they been less boastful and ambitious,
their lives pure, their habits simple and sincere,
God would have preserved them from being thus
humiliated and afflicted by their enemies. God
would, in a signal manner, have made the wrath
of the king harmless to his people, had they been
faithful and perfect before him. But he could not
especially work for them, for their works were abhorred by him.

The Jews had excited the envy and hatred of
Herod against Christ, through their false interpretation of the prophets. They taught that Christ
was to reign over an earthly empire, in unsurpassed glory. Their proud boasting presented
the Saviour of the world, and his mission to the
earth, altogether in a false light. Their lofty
ideas and their proud boasting did not result as
Satan had at first purposed they should, in the
destruction of the infant Saviour, but rebounded
back upon themselves, filling their homes with
mourning. Jeremiah, in prophetic vision, says:
"In Rama was there a voice heard, lamentation
and weeping, and great mourning, Rachel weeping
for her children, and would not be comforted, because they are not." But Herod did not long
survive his cruel work. He died a fearful death.

He was compelled to yield to a power he could not turn aside or overcome.

After Herod was cut off from the earth, the angel again warned Joseph to return to the land of Israel. He was desirous to make his home in Judah or Bethlehem; but when he heard that the son of the tyrannical Herod reigned upon his father's throne, he was afraid that the purposes of the father might be carried out by the son in murdering Christ. While in his perplexity, not knowing where to locate, the Lord, through his angel, again selected for him a place of safety. "And he came and dwelt in a city called Nazareth; that it might be fulfilled which was spoken by the prophets, He shall be called a Nazarene."

This was the reception the Saviour met as he came to a fallen world. He left his heavenly home, his majesty, and riches, and high command, and took upon himself man's nature, that he might save the fallen race. Instead of men glorifying God for the honor he had conferred upon them in thus sending his Son in the likeness of sinful flesh, by giving him a place in their affections, there seemed to be no rest nor safety for the infant Saviour. Jehovah could not trust to the inhabitants of the world his Son, who came into the world that through his divine power he might redeem fallen man. He who came to bring life to man, met, from the very ones he came to benefit, insult, hatred, and abuse. God could not trust his beloved Son with men while carrying on his benevolent work for their salvation, and final exaltation to his own throne. He sent angels to attend his Son and preserve his life, till his mission on earth should be accomplished, and he should die by the hands of the very men he came to save.

CHAPTER II.

THE LIFE OF CHRIST.

FROM his childhood, Jesus conformed his life strictly to the Jewish laws. He manifested great wisdom in his youth. The grace and power of God were upon him. The word of the Lord, by the mouth of the prophet Isaiah, describes the office and work of Christ, and shows the sheltering care of God over his Son in his mission to earth, that the relentless hatred of men, inspired by Satan, should not be permitted to thwart the design of the great plan of salvation.

"Behold my servant, whom I uphold; mine elect, in whom my soul delighteth; I have put my Spirit upon him. He shall bring forth judgment to the Gentiles. He shall not cry, nor lift up, nor cause his voice to be heard in the street. A bruised reed shall he not break, and the smoking flax shall he not quench. He shall bring forth judgment unto truth. He shall not fail nor be discouraged, till he have set judgment in the earth."

The voice of Christ was not heard in the street, in noisy contention with those who were opposed to his doctrine. Neither was his voice heard in the street in prayer to his Father, to be heard of men. His voice was not heard in joyful mirth. His voice was not raised to exalt himself, and to gain the applause and flattery of men. When engaged in teaching, he withdrew his disciples away from the noise and confusion of the busy city to some retired place more in harmony with the lessons of humility, piety, and virtue, which

he would impress upon their minds.   He shunned
human praise, and preferred solitude and peaceful retirement to the noise and confusion of mortal life.   His voice was often heard in earnest,
prevailing intercessions to his Father ; yet for
these exercises he chose the lonely mountain, and
frequently spent whole nights in prayer for strength
to sustain him under the temptations he should
meet, and to accomplish the important work he
came to do for the salvation of man.   His petitions were earnest and mingled with strong cries
and tears.   And notwithstanding the labor of
soul during the night, he ceased not his labor
through the day.   In the morning he would quietly resume his work of mercy and disinterested
benevolence.   The life of Christ was in marked
contrast to that of the Jews, and for this very reason they wished to destroy him.

The chief priests, and scribes, and elders, loved
to pray in the most public places ; not only in the
crowded synagogues, but in the corners of the
streets, that they might be seen of men, and
praised for their devotion and piety.   Their acts of
charity were done in the most public manner, and
for the purpose of calling the attention of the
people to themselves.   Their voices were indeed
heard in the streets, not only in exalting themselves, but in contention with those who differed
with them in doctrine.   They were resentful and
unforgiving, proud, haughty, and bigoted.   The
Lord, through his faithful prophet, shows the life
of Christ in marked contrast to the hypocritical
chief priests, scribes, and Pharisees.

The parents of Jesus yearly visited Jerusalem,
in accordance with the Jewish law.   Their son,
Jesus, then twelve years old, accompanied them.

In returning to their home, after they had gone
a day's journey, their anxiety was aroused, as they
missed Jesus. He had not been seen of them
since they left Jerusalem. They supposed he
was with the company. Inquiry and search were
made among their acquaintances and relatives for
their much-loved son; but no trace could be
found of him. They hastened back to Jerusalem,
their hearts heavy with sorrow. For one day of
neglect they lost their son, Jesus, from their company, which cost them three days of anxious
search, with sorrowful hearts, before they found
him. This should be a lesson to those who are
following Christ. If they neglect watchfulness
and prayer, and become careless, they may, in
one day lose Christ; but it may take many days
of anxious, sorrowful search to find him again,
and to enjoy the peace of mind and consolation of
his grace that they lost through vain talking,
jesting, joking, and evil speaking, or even neglect
of prayer.

"And it came to pass, that after three·days
they found him in the temple, sitting in the midst
of the doctors, both hearing them, and asking
them questions. And all that heard him were astonished at his understanding and answers. And
when they saw him, they were amazed; and his
mother said unto him, Son, why hast thou thus
dealt with us? behold, thy father and I have
sought thee sorrowing. And he said unto them,
How is it that ye sought me? wist ye not that I
must be about my Father's business? And they
understood not the saying which he spake unto
them. And he went down with them, and came
to Nazareth, and was subject unto them; but his
mother kept all these sayings in her heart. And

Jesus increased in wisdom and stature, and in favor with God and man."

The doctors, and expounders of the law, always taught the people publicly upon especial occasions. It was upon one of these occasions that Jesus gave manifest proofs of superior wisdom, penetration, and mature judgment. The people were more surprised because the parents of Christ were poor, and he had not received the advantages of education. The question passed from lip to lip, Whence has this youth such wisdom, having never learned? While the parents of Christ were in search of him, they saw large numbers flocking to the temple; and as they entered it, the well-known voice of their son arrested their attention. They could not get sight of him for the crowd; but they knew that they were not mistaken, for no voice was like his, marked with solemn melody. The parents gazed in astonishment at the scene. Their son, in the midst of the grave and learned doctors and scribes, was giving evidence of superior knowledge by his discreet questions and answers. His parents were gratified to see him thus honored. But the mother could not forget the grief and anxiety she had suffered because of his tarry at Jerusalem, and she, in a reproving manner, inquired why he had thus dealt with them, relating her fears and sorrow on his account.

Said Jesus, " How is it that ye sought me?" This pointed question was to lead them to see that if they had been mindful of their duty, they would not have left Jerusalem without him. He then adds, " Wist ye not that I must be about my Father's business?" While they had been unmindful of the responsible charge intrusted to them, Jesus was engaged in the work of his Father. Mary knew that Christ did not refer to his earthly father, Joseph, but to Jehovah. She laid these things to heart, and profited by them.

In returning from Jerusalem with the crowd, talking and visiting engrossed their minds, and Jesus was forgotten for an entire day. His absence was not observed until the close of the day. Joseph and Mary had been honored of God in an especial manner, in being intrusted with the responsible charge of the Saviour. Angels had heralded his birth to the shepherds, and God had directed the course of Joseph, to preserve the life of the infant Saviour. But the confusion of much talk had led to the neglect of their sacred trust, and Jesus was not brought to mind for an entire day, by those who should not have forgotten him for a moment. They returned their weary way, sad and fearful, to Jerusalem. They recalled the terrible massacre of innocent children by the cruel Herod in hope of destroying the king of Israel. When their anxiety was relieved by finding Jesus, they did not acknowledge their own neglect of duty, but their words reflected on Christ—"Why hast thou thus dealt with us? behold, thy father and I have sought thee sorrowing." Jesus, in most respectful language, inquires, "How is it that ye sought me?" But these words modestly reflect back the censure upon themselves, in reminding them that, if they had not permitted themselves to be engrossed with matters of no special importance, they would not have had the trouble of searching for him. He then justifies his course: "Wist ye not that I must be about my Father's business?" While he was engaged in the work he came to the earth to perform, they had neg-

lected the work his Father had especially intrusted
to them. They could not fully comprehend the
words of Christ; yet Mary, in a great measure,
understood their import, and laid them away in
her heart to ponder over in the future.

It was so natural for the parents of Christ to
look upon him as their own child, as parents com-
monly regard their children, that they were in
danger of losing the precious blessing which daily
attended them in the presence of Jesus, the world's
redeemer. As Christ was daily with them, his
life in many respects as other children, it was difficult to keep before them his sacred mission, and
the daily blessing of having committed to their
charge and parental care, for a while, the Son of
God, whose divinity was vailed with humanity.
His tarry in Jerusalem was designed of him as a
gentle reminder to them of their duty, lest they
should become indifferent in a greater degree, and
lose the sense of the high favor God had conferred
upon them.

Not one act in the life of Christ was unimpor-
tant. Every event of his life was for the benefit
of his followers in future time. This circumstance
of the tarry of Christ in Jerusalem teaches an important lesson to those who should believe on him.
Many had come a great distance to keep the passover, instituted that the Hebrews might keep ·
in memory their wonderful deliverance from
Egypt. This ordinance was designed to call their
minds from their world-loving interests, and from
their cares and anxieties in relation to temporal
concerns, and to review the works of God. They
were to call to mind his miracles, his mercies and
loving-kindness, to them, that their love and reverence for him might increase, and lead them to

ever look to him, and trust in him in all their trials, and not turn to other gods.

The observance of the passover possessed a mournful interest to the Son of God. He saw in the slain lamb a symbol of his own death. The people who celebrated this ordinance were instructed to associate the slaying of the lamb with the future death of the Son of God. The blood, marking the door-posts of their houses, was the symbol of the blood of Christ which was to be efficacious for the believing sinner, in cleansing him from sin, and sheltering him from the wrath of God which was to come upon the impenitent and unbelieving world, as the wrath of God fell upon the Egyptians. But none could be benefited by this special provision made by God for the salvation of man unless they should perform the work the Lord left them to do. They had a part to act themselves, and by their acts to manifest their faith in the provision made for their salvation.

Jesus was acquainted with hearts. He knew that, as the crowd returned in company from Jerusalem, there would be much talking and visiting which would not be seasoned with humility and grace, and the Messiah and his mission would be nearly forgotten. It was his choice to return from Jerusalem with his parents alone; for in being retired, his father and mother would have more time for reflection, and for meditation upon the prophecies which referred to his future sufferings and death. He did not wish that the painful events which they were to experience in his offering up his life for the sins of the world, to be new and unexpected to them. He was separated from them in their return from Jerusalem. After the celebration of the passover, they sought him sor-

rowing three days. When he should be slain for
the sins of the world, he would be separated from
them, lost to them, for three days. But after that,
he would reveal himself to them, and be found of
them, and their faith rely upon him as the redeemer
of the fallen race, the advocate with the Father in
their behalf.

Here is a lesson of instruction to all the followers
of Christ. He designed that none of these lessons
should be lost, but be written for the benefit of
future generations. There is necessity of care-
fulness of words and actions when Christians are
associated together, lest Jesus be forgotten of them,
and they pass along careless of the fact that Jesus
is not among them. When they are aroused to
their condition, they discover that they have jour-
neyed without the presence of Him who could give
peace and joy to their hearts, and days are occupied in returning, and searching for him whom
they should have retained with them every moment. Jesus will not be found in the company of
those who are careless of his presence, and who
engage in conversation having no reference to
their Redeemer, in whom they profess their hopes
of eternal life are centered. Jesus shuns the company of such, so also do the angels who do his
commands. These heavenly messengers are not
attracted to the crowd where minds are diverted
from heavenly things. These pure and holy spirits cannot remain in the company where Jesus'
presence is not desired and encouraged, and his
absence not marked. For this reason, great mourning, grief, and discouragement exist. Through
lack of meditation, watchfulness, and prayer, they
have lost all that is valuable. The divine rays of
light emanating from Jesus are not with them,

cheering them with their loving, elevating influence. They are enshrouded in gloom, because their careless, irreverent spirit has separated Jesus from their company, and driven the ministering angels from them.

Many who attend meetings of devotion, and have been instructed by the servants of God, and been greatly refreshed and blessed in seeking Jesus, have returned to their homes no better than they left them, because they did not feel the importance of praying and watching thereunto, as they returned to their homes. They frequently feel inclined to complain of others, because they realize their loss. Some murmur against God, and do not reproach themselves as being the cause of their own darkness, and sufferings of mind. These should not reflect upon others. The fault is in themselves. They talked and jested, and visited away the heavenly Guest, and themselves they have only to blame. It is the privilege of all to retain Jesus with them. If they do this, their words must be select, seasoned with grace. The thoughts of their hearts must be disciplined to meditate upon heavenly and divine things.

The love of God, manifested toward fallen man in the gift of his beloved Son, amazed the holy angels. "God so loved the world that he gave his only begotten Son, that whosoever believeth in him should not perish, but have everlasting life." The Son was the brightness of the Father's glory, and the express image of his person. He possessed divine excellence and greatness. He was equal with God. It pleased the Father that in him all fullness should dwell. He "thought it not robbery to be equal with God." Yet he "made himself of no reputation, and took upon him the form of a servant, and was made in the likeness of men. And being found in fashion as a man, he humbled himself, and became obedient unto death, even the death of the cross.''

In Christ were united the human and the divine. His mission was to reconcile God to man, and man to God. His work was to unite the finite with the Infinite. This was the only way in which fallen men could be exalted, through the merits of the blood of Christ, to be partakers of the divine nature. Taking human nature fitted Christ to understand the nature of man's trials, and all the temptations wherewith he is beset. Angels, who were unacquainted with sin, could not sympathize with man in his peculiar trials.

Before Christ left Heaven and came into the world to die, he was taller than any of the angels. He was majestic and lovely. But when his ministry commenced, he was but little taller than the common size of men then living upon the earth. Had he come among men with his noble, heavenly form, his outward appearance would have attracted the minds of the people to himself, and he would have been received without the exercise of faith.

It was in the order of God that Christ should take upon himself the form and nature of fallen man, that he might be made perfect through suffering, and himself endure the strength of Satan's fierce temptations, that he might understand how to succor those who should be tempted. The faith of men in Christ as the Messiah was not to rest on the evidences of sight, and they believe on him because of his personal attractions, but because of the excellence of character found in him, which never had been found, neither could be, in another. All who loved virtue, purity, and holiness, would be drawn to Christ, and would see sufficient evidence of his being the Messiah foretold by prophecy that should come. Those who thus trusted in the word of God, would receive the benefits of the teachings of Christ, and finally of his atonement.

Christ came to call the attention of all men to his Father, teaching them repentance toward God. His work was to reconcile man to God. Although Christ did not come as he was expected, yet he came just as prophecy had marked out that he would come. Those who wished to believe, had sufficient grounds for their faith by referring to prophecy which predicted the coming of the Just One, and described the manner of his coming.

The ancient Jewish church were the highly favored people of God, brought out of Egypt and acknowledged as his own peculiar treasure. The many and exceeding great and precious promises to them as a people, were the hope and confidence of the Jewish church. Herein they trusted, and believed their salvation sure. No other people professed to be governed by the commandments of God. Our Saviour came first to his own people, but they received him not.

The self-righteous, unbelieving Jews expected their Saviour and King would come into the world clothed with majesty and power, compelling all Gentiles to yield obedience to him. They did not expect any humiliation and suffering would be manifested in him. They would not receive the meek and lowly Jesus, and acknowledge him to be the Saviour of the world. Had he appeared in splendor, and assumed the authority of the world's great men, instead of taking the form of a servant, they would have received and worshiped him.

CHAPTER III.

LIFE AND MISSION OF JOHN.

ABOUT the time of the birth of John, the Jews were in a deplorable condition. And in order to keep down insurrection, they were allowed to have a separate government, in name, while the Romans virtually ruled them. The Jews saw that their power and liberty were restricted, and that, in reality, they were under the Roman yoke. The Romans claimed the right to appoint men to the priesthood, and to remove them from office at will. Thus was there a door opened for the priesthood to become corrupt. The priests, not being divinely appointed, abused their office, and were unfaithful in their ministrations. Men of corrupt morals, with money and influence, obtained the favor of those in power, and succeeded in attaining to the priesthood. The whole country felt . their oppression, and revolt and dissension were the result of this state of things.

The pious Jews were looking, believing, and earnestly praying, for the coming of the Messiah. God could not manifest his glory and power to his people through a corrupt priesthood. The set time to favor his people had come. The faith of the Jews had become clouded, in consequence of their departure from God. Many of the leaders of the people brought in their own traditions, and enforced them upon the Jews, as the commandments of God. The pious Jews believed, and trusted in God that he would not leave his people in this condition, to be a reproach to the heathen.

He had, in time past, raised them up a deliverer when in their distress they had called upon him. From the predictions of the prophets, they thought the time appointed of God had arrived when Messiah would come. And when he should come, they would have a clear revelation of the divine will, and that their doctrines would be freed from the traditions and needless ceremonies which had confused their faith. The pious, aged Jews waited day and night for the coming Messiah, praying that they might see the Saviour before they died. They longed to see the cloud of ignorance and bigotry dispelled from the minds of the people.

"Zacharias and Elizabeth were both righteous before God walking in all the commandments and ordinances of the Lord blameless." They were far advanced in years. Zacharias ministered in the holy office of the priesthood. "And it came to pass that while he executed the priest's office before God in the order of his course, according to the custom of the priest's office, his lot was to burn incense when he went into the temple of the Lord. And the whole multitude of the people were praying without at the time of incense. And there appeared unto him an angel of the Lord standing on the right side of the altar of incense."

And when Zacharias saw the angel of God, he was surprised and troubled. This conscientious, God-fearing soul questioned whether he had himself offended God, and that this divine messenger had come to reprove, or in judgment, to condemn. The heavenly messenger cheered him with these words:

"Fear not, Zacharias, for thy prayer is heard; and thy wife Elizabeth shall bear thee a son, and thou shalt call his name John. And thou shalt have joy and gladness; and many shall rejoice at his birth. For he shall be great in the sight of the Lord, and shall drink neither wine nor strong drink; and he shall be filled with the Holy Ghost. And many of the children of Israel shall he turn to the Lord their God. And he shall go before him in the spirit and power of Elias, to turn the hearts of the fathers to the children, and the disobedient to the wisdom of the just; to make ready a people prepared for the Lord."

In the above words the angel Gabriel enjoined upon Zacharias that John should be brought up with strictly temperate habits. This was to secure to him physical, mental, and moral health, that he should be qualified for the important mission of making ready a people for the Lord. In order to accomplish this great work, the Lord must work with him. The Spirit of God would be with John if he should be obedient to the requirement of the angel.

A great work was before John, and in order for him to have a sound physical constitution, and mental and moral power, to do this work, he must control appetite and passion. John was to lead out as a reformer, and by his abstemious life, and plain dress, rebuke the intemperate habits, and the sinful extravagance, of the people. The indulgence of appetite in luxurious food, and the use of wine, were lessening physical strength, and weakening the intellect, so that crime and grievous sins did not appear sinful. The angel Gabriel gave special directions to the parents of John in regard to temperance. A lesson was given upon health reform by one of the exalted angels from the throne of Heaven. John was to reform the children of Israel, and turn them to the Lord.

He had the promise that God would work with
him. He was "to turn the hearts of the fathers to
the children, and the disobedient to the wisdom of
the just, to make ready a people prepared for the
Lord."

John was a representative of the people of God
in the last days, to whom God has committed important and solemn truths. The world at large
are given to gluttony and the indulgence of base
passions. The light of health reform is opened
before the people of God at this day, that they
may see the necessity of holding their appetites
and passions under control of the higher powers of
the mind. This is also necessary, that they may
have mental strength and clearness, to discern the
sacred chain of truth, and turn from the bewitch-
ing errors and pleasing fables, that are flooding
the world. Their work is to present before the
people the pure doctrine of the Bible. Hence
health reform finds its place in the preparatory
work for the second appearing of Christ.

Zacharias was as much astonished at the words
of the angel, as he was at his appearance. He
had so humble an opinion of himself that he thought
it could not be possible that he was thus to be
honored of the Lord. He inquired, Whereby
shall I know this? for I am an old man, and my
wife well stricken in years. Zacharias for a moment forgot the unlimited power of God, and that
nothing was impossible with him. He did not call
to mind the case of Abraham and Sarah, and the
fulfillment of the promise of God to them.

Zacharias received a confirmation of the angel's
message, "Behold, thou shalt be dumb, and not
able to speak, until the day that these things
shall be performed, because thou believest not

my words which shall be fulfilled in their season."
He was soon made to realize the verity of the divine mission. The angel had no sooner departed than he was struck dumb.

The particular office of Zacharias was to pray in behalf of the people, for pardon of public and national sins, and to earnestly pray for the coming of the long-expected Saviour whom they believed must redeem his people. When Zacharias attempted to pray, he could not utter a word. The people waited long for the appearance of Zacharias, to learn whether God had given them any visible token of his approbation. They began to fear from his long tarry that God had manifested his displeasure. When Zacharias came out of the temple, his countenance was shining with the light which the heavenly angel had reflected upon him. But he could not speak to the people. He made signs to them that an angel had appeared to him in the temple, and because of his unbelief he was deprived of the power of speech, until the prediction of the angel should be fulfilled.

Soon after the birth of John, "the tongue of Zacharias was loosed, and he spake and praised God. And fear came on all that dwelt round about them; and all these sayings were noised abroad throughout all the hill country of Judea. And all that heard them, laid them up in their hearts, saying, What manner of child shall this be? And the hand of the Lord was with him; and his father Zacharias was filled with the Holy Ghost, and prophesied. And the child grew, and waxed strong in spirit, and was in the deserts until the day of his showing unto Israel."

The prophet John separated himself from his friends and kindred, and made his home in the wilderness. He denied himself of the ordinary comforts of life. His food was simple. His clothing was a garment made of hair-cloth, confined about the waist with a leather girdle. His parents had in a most solemn manner dedicated him to God from his birth.

The life of John, although passed in the wilderness, was not inactive. His separation from society did not make him gloomy and morose, neither was he unreconciled with his lonely life of hardship and privation. It was his choice to be secluded from the luxuries of life, and from depraved society. Pride, envy, jealousy, and corrupt passions seemed to control the hearts of men. But John was separated from the influence of these things, and, with discerning eye and wonderful discrimination, read the characters of men. He lived in the quiet retreat of the wilderness, and occasionally he mingled in society; but would not remain long where the moral atmosphere seemed to be polluted. He feared that the sight of his eyes and the hearing of his ears would so pervert his mind that he would lose a sense of the sinfulness of sin. A great work was before him, and it was necessary that he should form a character unbiased by any surrounding influence. It was necessary that his physical, mental, and moral conditions should be of that high and noble type that would qualify him for a work which required firmness and integrity, that when he should appear among men he could enlighten them, and be instrumental in giving a new direction to their thoughts, and awakening them to the necessity of forming righteous characters. John would bring the people up to the standard of divine perfection. He studied the peculiarities of minds, that he might know how to adapt his instructions to the people.

John did not feel strong enough to stand the great pressure of temptation he would meet in society. He feared his character would be molded according to the prevailing customs of the Jews, and he chose the wilderness as his school, in which his mind could be properly educated and disciplined from God's great book of nature. In the wilderness, John could the more readily deny himself and bring his appetite under control, and dress in accordance to natural simplicity. And there was nothing in the wilderness that would take his mind from meditation and prayer. Satan had access to John, even after he had closed every avenue in his power through which he would enter. But his habits of life were so pure and natural that he could discern the foe, and had strength of spirit and decision of character to resist him.

The book of nature was open before John with its inexhaustible store of varied instruction. He sought the favor of God, and the Holy Spirit rested upon him, and kindled in his heart a glowing zeal to do the great work of calling the people to repentance, and to a higher and holier life. John was fitting himself, by the privations and hardships of his secluded life, to so control all his physical and mental powers that he could stand among the people as unmoved by surrounding circumstances as the rocks and mountains of the wilderness that had surrounded him for thirty years.

The state of public affairs when John's work commenced, was unsettled. Discord and insurrection were prevailing, when the voice of John was first lifted up, like the sound of a trumpet pealing forth from the wilderness, thrilling the hearts of all who heard with a new and strange power. John fearlessly denounced the sins of the people, saying, "Repent ye; for the kingdom of Heaven is at hand." Multitudes answered to the voice of the prophet, and flocked to the wilderness. They saw, in the singular dress and appearance of this prophet, a resemblance to the description of the ancient seers, and the opinion prevailed that he was one of the prophets risen from the dead.

It was the purpose of John to startle and arouse the people, and cause them to tremble because of their great wickedness. In simplicity and plainness he pointed out the errors and crimes of men. A power attended his words, and, relcutant as the people were to hear the denunciation of their unholy lives, yet they could not resist his words. He flattered none; neither would he receive flattery of any. The people, as if with common consent, came to him repenting, and confessing their sins, and were baptized of him in Jordan.

Kings and rulers came to the wilderness to hear the prophet, and were interested, and deeply convicted as he fearlessly pointed out their particular sins. His discernment of character and spiritual sight read the purposes and hearts of those who came to him, and he fearlessly told, both rich and poor, the honorable and the lowly, that without repentance of their sins, and a thorough conversion, although they might claim to be righteous, they could not enjoy the favor of God, and have part in the kingdom of the Messiah, whose coming he announced.

In the spirit and with the power of Elijah, John denounced the corruptions of the Jews, and raised

his voice in reproving their prevailing sins. His
discourses were plain, pointed, and convincing.
Many were brought to repentance of their sins,
and, as evidence of their repentance, were baptized of him in Jordan. This was the preparatory
work for the ministry of Christ. Many were
convicted because of the plain truths uttered by
this faithful prophet; but, by rejecting the light,
they became enshrouded in deeper darkness, so
that they were fully prepared to turn from the
evidences attending Jesus, that he was the true
Messiah.

As John looked forward to the ministry and miracles of Christ, he appealed to the people, " saying, Repent ye; for the kingdom of Heaven is at
hand." He was successful in his ministry. Persons of all rank, high and low, rich and poor,
submitted to the requirements of the prophet, as
necessary for them in order to participate in the
kingdom he came to declare. Many of the scribes
and Pharisees came to him, confessing their sins,
and were baptized of him in Jordan. The confes-
sions made by the Pharisees astonished the prophet;
for they had exalted themselves as better than other
men, and had maintained a high opinion of their
own piety and worthiness. As they sought to obtain
remission of their sins, and revealed the secrets of
their lives, which had been covered from the eyes
of men, the prophet was amazed. " But when he
saw many of the Pharisees and Sadducees come
to his baptism, he said unto them, O generation of
vipers, who hath warned you to flee from the wrath
to come? Bring forth, therefore, fruits meet for
repentance. And think not to say within yourselves, We have Abraham to our father; for I say

unto you, that God is able of these stones to raise
up children unto Abraham.''

The whole Jewish nation seemed to be affected
by the mission of John. The threatenings of God
on account of their sins, repeated by the prophet,
for a time alarmed them. John knew that they
cherished the idea that, because they were of the
seed of Abraham, they were securely established
in the favor of God, while their course of action
was abhorred of him. Their conduct was, in many
respects, even worse than that of the heathen nations to whom they felt so much superior. The
prophet faithfully presented to them the ability of
God to raise up those who would take their place,
and would become more worthy children of Abraham. He told them plainly that God was not dependent upon them to fulfill his purposes ; for he
could provide ways and means independent of
them to carry forward his great work which was
to be accomplished in purity and righteousness.
John further adds : '' And now also the ax is laid
unto the root of the trees ; therefore every tree
which bringeth not forth good fruit is hewn down,
and cast into the fire.'' He impresses upon them
that the value of the tree is ascertained by the
fruit it produces. Though a tree may bear an
exalted name, yet if it produces no fruit, or if its
fruit is unworthy of the name, the name will avail
nothing in saving the tree from destruction. '' Of
thorns men do not gather figs, nor of a bramble-
bush gather they grapes.''

The prophet of God was impressed by the holy
Spirit that many of the Pharisees and Sadducees
who asked baptism had no true convictions of their
sins. They had selfish motives. They thought that
if they should become friends of the prophet, they

would stand a better chance to be personally favored of the coming Prince. In their blindness they believed that he was to set up a temporal kingdom, and bestow honors and riches upon his subjects.

John rebuked their selfish pride and avarice. He warned them of their unbelief, and condemned their hypocrisy. He told them that they had not fulfilled the conditions of the covenant on their part, which would entitle them to the promises God made to a faithful and obedient people. Their proud boasts of being children of Abraham did not make them really such. Their exhibitions of pride, their arrogance, jealousy, selfishness, and cruelty, stamped their characters as a generation of vipers, rather than the children of obedient and just Abraham. Their wicked works had disqualified them to claim the promises God made to the children of Abraham. John assured them that God would raise up children unto Abraham from the very stones, to whom he could fulfill his promise, rather than to depend on the natural children of Abraham who had neglected the light God had given them, and had become hardened by selfish ambition and wicked unbelief. He told them that if they were really the children of Abraham, they would do the works of their father Abraham. They would have Abraham's faith, love, and obedience. But they did not bear this fruit. They had no claim to Abraham as their father, or the promises God made to the seed of Abraham. " Every tree which bringeth not forth good fruit is hewn down, and cast into the fire." While they were professing to be God's commandment-keeping people, their works denied their faith, and without true repentance for their sins they would have no part in the kingdom of Christ. Justice, benevolence, mercy, and the love of God would characterize the lives of his commandment-keeping people. Unless these fruits were seen in their daily life, all their profession was of no more value than chaff which would be devoted to the fire of destruction.

The Jews had deceived themselves by misinterpreting the words of the Lord through his prophets, of his eternal favor to his people Israel.

" Thus saith the Lord, which giveth the sun for a light by day, and the ordinances of the moon and of the stars for a light by night, which divideth the sea when the waves thereof roar; the Lord of hosts is his name: If those ordinances depart from before me, saith the Lord, then the seed of Israel also shall cease from being a nation before me forever. Thus saith the Lord: If heaven above can be measured, and the foundations of the earth searched out beneath, I will also cast off all the seed of Israel for all that they have done, saith the Lord." Jer. 31:35-37.

These words the Jews applied to themselves. And because God had shown them so great favor and mercy, they flattered themselves that, notwithstanding their sins and iniquities, he would still retain them as his favored people, and shower especial blessings upon them. They misapplied the words of Jeremiah, and depended for their salvation upon being called the children of Abraham. If they had indeed been worthy of the name of Abraham's children, they would have followed the righteous example of their father Abraham, and would have done the works of Abraham.

This has been the danger of the people of God in all ages; and especially is this the danger of those living near the close of time. We are cited by the apostle to the unbelief, blindness, rebellion, and repeated sins of the Hebrews, as a warning. Paul plainly states that " all these things happened unto them for ensamples; and they are written for our admonition, upon whom the ends of the world are come." If, in these last days of peril, for the encouragement of persons in responsible positions, God in mercy gives them a testimony of favor, they frequently become lifted up, and lose sight of their frailties and weaknesses, and rely upon their own judgment, flattering themselves that God cannot accomplish his work without their especial aid. They trust in their own wisdom; and the Lord permits them, for a time, to apparently prosper, to reveal the weakness and folly of the natural heart. But the Lord will, in his own time, and in his own way, bring down the pride and folly of these deceived ones, and show to them their true condition. If they will accept the humiliation, and by confession and sincere repentance, turn unto the Lord, perfecting holiness in the fear of God, he will renew his love to them. But if they shut their eyes to their own sins, as did the Jews, and choose their own ways, the Lord will give them up to blindness of mind, and hardness of heart, that they cannot discern the things of the Spirit of God.

God cannot do much for man, because he misinterprets his blessings, and concludes that he is favored on account of some goodness in himself. It is not safe to speak in the praise of mortals; for they cannot bear it. Satan has the special work to do of flattering poor souls, and he needs not the help of the Lord's servants in this matter. How few realize the weakness of human nature

and the subtlety of Satan. Many in these last
days are preparing themselves for affliction and
sorrow, or for complete separation from the favor
of God, because of their pride and self-righteousness. They will fall through self-exaltation.

The prophet John impressed upon the people
the necessity of their profession being accompanied
with good works. Their words and actions would
be their fruit, and would determine the character
of the tree. If their works were evil, the truth
of God would testify against them. God would
in no wise excuse sin in a people who had been
enlightened, even if he had, in their days of faith-
fulness and purity, loved them, and given them
especial promises. These promises and blessings
were always upon condition of obedience upon
their part.

The Lord pronounced, by the mouth of Moses,
blessings upon the obedient, and curses upon the
disobedient. "Ye shall make you no idols," was
the command of God. "Ye shall keep my Sabbaths, and reverence my sanctuary. I am the
Lord. If ye walk in my statutes, and keep my
commandments, and do them ; then I will give you
rain in due season, and the land shall yield her
increase, and the trees of the field shall yield
their fruit." Many and great blessings are enu-
merated, which God would bestow ; and then, above
all the other blessings, he promised, "I will set
my tabernacle among you ; and my soul shall not
abhor you. And I will walk among you, and will
be your God, and ye shall be my people." "But
if ye will not hearken unto me, and will not do all
these commandments ; and if ye shall despise my
statutes, or if your soul abhor my judgments, so
that ye will not do all my commandments, but

that ye break my covenant, I also will do this
unto you: I will even appoint over you terror,
consumption, and the burning ague, that shall con-
sume the eyes, and cause sorrow of heart; and ye
shall sow your seed in vain; for your enemies
shall eat it. And I will set my face against you,
and ye shall be slain before your enemies. They
that hate you shall reign over you, and ye shall
flee when none pursueth you."

The Jews were experiencing the fulfillment of
the threatened curse of God for their departure
from him, and for their iniquity; yet they did not
lay these things to heart, and afflict their souls before God. A people that hated them ruled over
them. They were claiming the blessings God had
promised to confer upon them should they be obedient and faithful. But at the very time they
were suffering under the curse of God because of
disobedience. John declared to them that unless
they bore fruit, they would be hewn down and
cast into the fire.

He specified the fruit they were required to bear
in order to become the subjects of Christ's kingdom; which were works of love, mercy, and benevolence. They must have virtuous characters.
These fruits would be the result of genuine repentance and faith. If blessed with plenty, and
they saw others destitute, they should divide with
them. They must be workers. "He that hath
two coats, let him impart to him that hath none;
and he that hath meat, let him do likewise. Then
came also publicans to be baptized, and said unto
him, Master, what shall we do? And he said unto
them, Exact no more than that which is appointed
you. And the soldiers likewise demanded of him,
saying, And what shall we do? And he said unto

them, do violence to no man, neither accuse any
falsely; and be content with your wages."

John gave his disciples lessons in practical godliness. He showed them that true goodness, hon-
esty, and fidelity, must be seen in their daily life,
and that they should be actuated by unselfish
principles, or they would be no better than common sinners.

Unless others should be made better within the
sphere of their influence, they would be like the
fruitless tree. Their wealth was not to be used
merely for selfish purposes. They were to relieve
the wants of the destitute, and to make free-will
offerings to God to advance the interests of his
cause. They should not abuse their privileges, to
oppress, but should shield the defenseless, redress
the wrongs of the injured, and thus give a noble
example of benevolence, compassion, and virtue,
to those who were inferior and dependent. If they
made no change in their conduct, but continued
to be extravagant, selfish, and void of principle,
they would correctly represent the tree bearing no
good fruit. This lesson is applicable to all Christians. The followers of Christ should evidence to
the world a change in their life for the better, and
by their good works show the transforming influence of the Spirit of God upon their hearts.
But there are many who bear no fruit to the glory
of God; they give no evidence of a radical change
in their life. Although they make high profession, they have not felt the necessity of obtaining
a personal experience for themselves, by engaging
in Christian duties with hearts of love, intensified
by their new and holy obligations, feeling no
weight of their responsibility in doing their Master's work with readiness and diligence.

The people thought that John might be the promised Messiah. His life was so unselfish, marked with humility and self-denial. His teachings, exhortations, and reproofs, were fervent, sincere, and courageous. In his mission, he turned not to the right or to the left to court the favors or applause of any. He did not aspire to worldly honor or worldly dignity, but was humble in heart and life, and did not assume honors that did not belong to him. He assured his followers that he was not the Christ.

John, as a prophet, stood forth as God's representative, to show the connection between the law and prophets, and the Christian dispensation. His work and ministry pointed back to the law and the prophets, while he, at the same time, pointed the people forward to Christ, as the Saviour of the world. He raised his voice and cried to the people, " Behold the Lamb of God, which taketh away the sin of the world."

Multitudes followed this singular prophet from place to place, and many sacrificed all to obey his instruction. Kings, and the noble of the earth, were attracted to this prophet of God, and heard him gladly. As John saw that the attention of the people was directed to him, thinking that he might be the Coming One, he sought every opportunity to direct the attention of the people to One mightier than himself.

CHAPTER IV.

THE MISSION OF CHRIST.

CHRIST'S life had been so retired and secluded at Nazareth that John had not a personal acquaintance with him, and he did not positively know that he was the Messiah. He was acquainted with the circumstances of his birth, and he believed him to be the promised One. The secluded life of Christ for thirty years at Nazareth, in which he gave no special evidence of his Messiahship, suggested doubts to John whether he was indeed the One for whose coming he was to prepare the way. John, however, rested the matter in faith, fully believing that God would in due time make it plain. The Lord had shown him that the Messiah would be pointed out to him by a distinct sign; when this should be done, then John could present him to the world as the long-expected Messiah, the Lamb of God, that was to take away the sin of the world.

John had heard of the sinless character and spotless purity of Christ. His life was in harmony with what the Lord had revealed to him respecting one that was among them whose life was without the taint of sin. John had also seen that he should be the example for every repenting sinner. When Christ presented himself for baptism, John recognized him at once as the superior one revealed to him. He discerned, in the person and deportment of Christ, a character above every other man he had ever seen. The very atmosphere of his presence was holy and awe-inspiring. Although he knew him not as the Messiah, yet

never had such a holy influence been realized by
John from any one as when in the presence of
Christ. He felt the superiority of Christ at once,
and shrank from performing the rite of baptism
to one whom he knew to be sinless. Many had
come to him to receive the baptism of repentance,
confessing their sins and crimes; but John could
not understand why the only sinless one upon the
earth should ask for an ordinance implying guilt,
virtually confessing, by the symbol of baptism,
pollution to be washed away. He remonstrated
with Christ, acknowledging his superiority, and
refused to administer the ordinance, saying, " I
have need to be baptized of thee, and comest thou
to me?" With firm and gentle authority Jesus
waives the refusal of John and his plea of unworthiness, saying, " Suffer it to be so now; for
thus it becometh us to fulfill all righteousness."

Christ came not confessing his own sins; but
guilt was imputed to him as the sinner's substitute. He came not to repent on his own account;
but in behalf of the sinner. As man had transgressed the law of God, Christ was to fulfill every
requirement of that law, and thus show perfect
obedience. " Lo, I come to do thy will, O God !"
Christ honored the ordinance of baptism by submitting to this rite. In this act he identified himself with his people as their representative and
head. As their substitute, he takes upon him
their sins, numbering himself with the transgressors, taking the steps the sinner is required to
take, and doing the work the sinner must do. His
life of suffering and patient endurance after his
baptism were an example to converted sinners of
what they should endure and patiently suffer in
consequence of their transgressions and sins.

John finally yielded to the request of Christ, notwithstanding his feelings of unworthiness to baptize him, and performed the service.   He led the
Saviour of the world down into the river Jordan
in the presence of a large concourse of people,
and buried him in the water.

After Christ rose up from the water and from
the hand of John, he walked out to the bank of
Jordan, and bowed in the attitude of prayer.   The
eyes of John were fastened upon Christ with the
deepest interest and amazement.   His heart was
stirred with emotion as he looked upon him thus
bowed as a suppliant.   Christ's hands were raised
upward, and his gaze seemed to penetrate Heaven.
As the believer's example, his sinless humanity
supplicated support and strength from his Heavenly Father, as he was about to commence his public
labors as the Messiah.   Jesus poured out his soul
in earnest prayer.   A new and important era was
opening before him.   His former peaceful, quiet
life is to here end.   He had been happy in a life
of industry and toil, while fulfilling the duties de-
volving on a son.   He was an example to those in
childhood, youth, and manhood.   His deportment
showed that he felt the importance and solemnity
of the hour.   He knew that trials, toils, conflicts,
sufferings, and death, were in the path his feet had
entered.   He felt the weight of the responsibilities he must bear.   He was about to engage in
new and arduous duties.   A sense of the sinfulness of men, and the hardness of their hearts,
which separated them from God, convinced him
that but few would discern his merciful mission,
and accept the salvation he came from Heaven to
bring them.

Never before had angels listened to such a

prayer as Christ offered at his baptism, and they were solicitous to be the bearers of the message from the Father to his Son. But, no; direct from the Father issues the light of his glory. The heavens were opened, and beams of glory rested upon the Son of God, and assumed the form of a dove, in appearance like burnished gold. The dove-like form was emblematical of the meekness and gentleness of Christ. While the people stood spell-bound with amazement, their eyes fastened upon Christ, from the opening heavens came these words: "This is my beloved Son, in whom I am well pleased." The words of confirmation that Christ is the Son of God was given to inspire faith in those who witnessed the scene, and to sustain the Son of God in his arduous work. Notwithstanding the Son of God was clothed with humanity, yet Jehovah, with his own voice, assures him of his sonship with the Eternal. In this manifestation to his Son, God accepts humanity as exalted through the excellence of his beloved Son.

As John had now witnessed the heavenly dove resting upon Jesus, which was the promised token of the Messiah, he stretched forth his hand, and with assurance proclaimed before the multitude, "Behold the Lamb of God, which taketh away the sin of the world!" From this time John had no doubt in regard to Jesus being the true Messiah.

After this, Jesus withdrew into the wilderness, to be tempted of the devil forty days. His long fast ended, the victory won, he returns to the banks of the Jordan, mingling again with the disciples of John, yet giving no outward evidence of his special work, and taking no measures to bring himself to notice.

Men were sent from the highest authority in Jerusalem to inquire in regard to the great agitation John was creating. He was calling whole cities and towns to listen to his voice of warning; and they would know the prophet's authority for thus claiming the attention of the people, and turning the world upside down. These messengers challenged John to tell them certainly if he was the Messiah. John confessed, I am not the Christ. And they asked him, What then? Art thou Elias? And he saith, I am not. Art thou that prophet? And he answered, No. Then said they unto him, Who art thou? that we may give an answer to them that sent us. What sayest thou of thyself? He said, I am the voice of one crying in the wilderness. Make straight the way of the Lord, as said the prophet Esaias. John is then questioned as to his authority for baptizing, and thus agitating the people, when he does not claim to be Christ, or Elias, neither that prophet. The words, "That prophet," has reference to Moses. The Jews had been inclined to the belief that Moses would be raised from the dead, and taken to Heaven. They did not know that Moses had already been resurrected.

When John came, baptizing with water, the Jews thought that he might be the prophet Moses risen from the dead; for he seemed to have a thorough knowledge of the prophecies, and to understand the history of the Hebrews and their wanderings in the wilderness in consequence of their unjust murmurings and continual rebellion. They also called to mind the peculiar circumstances of John's birth, and wonderful manifestation of God to Zacharias, his father, in the temple, by the visitation of the angel from the presence of God, and the power of speech, being taken from Zacharias, because he did not believe the words of the angel, and the unloosing of his tongue at the birth of John. These important facts had in the past thirty years been measurably forgotten. But when John appeared as a prophet, the manifestation of the Spirit of God at his birth was called to mind.

When the messengers from the highest authority in Jerusalem were communing with John in reference to his mission and work, he could have taken honor to himself, had he been so disposed. But he would not assume honors that did not belong to him. While conversing with the messengers, suddenly his eye kindled, his countenance lighted up, and his whole being seemed stirred with deep emotion, as he discovered the person of Jesus in the concourse of people. He raised his hand, pointing to Christ, saying, There standeth One among you whom ye know not. I have come to prepare the way before him whom ye now see. He is the Messiah. He it is who coming after me is preferred before me, whose shoe's latchet I am not worthy to unloose.

"The next day John seeth Jesus coming unto him, and saith, Behold the Lamb of God, which taketh away the sin of the world! This is he of whom I said, After me cometh a man which is preferred before me; for he was before me. And I knew him not; but that he should be made manifest to Israel, therefore am I come baptizing with water. And John bare record, saying, I saw the Spirit descending from Heaven like a dove, and it abode upon him. And I knew him not. But he that sent me to baptize with water, the same said unto me, Upon whom thou shalt see the Spirit descending, and remaining on him, the same is he which baptizeth with the Holy Ghost. And I saw and bare record, that this is the Son of God. Again, the next day after, John stood, and two of his disciples ; and looking upon Jesus as he walked, he saith, Behold the Lamb of God !" And the two disciples heard him speak, and they followed Jesus. Then Jesus turned and saw them following, and saith unto them, What seek ye ? The disciples confessed that they were seeking Christ, and that they desired to become acquainted with him, and to be instructed by him at his home. These two disciples were charmed with the deeply impressive, yet simple and practical, lessons of Christ. Their hearts had never been so moved before. Andrew, Simon Peter's brother, was one of these disciples. He was interested for his friends and relatives, and was anxious that they also should see Christ, and hear for themselves his precious lessons. Andrew went in search of his brother Simon, and with assurance claimed to have found Christ, the Messiah, the Saviour of the world. He brought his brother to Jesus, and as soon as Jesus looked upon him, he said, Thou art Simon, the son of Jona ; thou shalt be called Cephas, which is by interpretation a stone. The next day Christ selected another disciple, Philip, and bade him follow him. Philip fully believed that Christ was the Messiah, and began to search for others to bring them to listen to the teachings of Christ, which had so charmed him. Then Philip found Nathanael. He was one of the number who heard John proclaim, " Behold the Lamb of God, which taketh away the sin of the world."

He felt deeply convicted, and retired to a grove, concealed from every human eye, and there meditated upon the announcement of John, calling to his mind the prophecies relating to the coming of the Messiah and his mission. He queried thus: Could this indeed be the Messiah for whom they had so long waited, and were so desirous to see? Hope sprang up in the heart of Nathanael that this might be the one that would save Israel. He bowed before God and prayed that if the person whom John had declared to be the Redeemer of the world was indeed the promised deliverer, that it might be made known to him. The Spirit of the Lord rested upon Nathanael in such a special manner that he was convinced that Christ was the Messiah. While Nathanael was praying, he heard the voice of Philip calling him, saying, "We have found him, of whom Moses in the law, and the prophets did write, Jesus of Nazareth, the son of Joseph. And Nathanael said unto him, Can there any good thing come out of Nazareth? Philip saith unto him, Come and see. Jesus saw Nathanael coming to him, and saith of him, Behold an Israelite indeed, in whom is no guile! Nathanael saith unto him, Whence knowest thou me? Jesus answered and said unto him, Before that Philip called thee, when thou wast under the fig tree, I saw thee."

Nathanael's wavering faith was now strengthened, and he answered and said, "Rabbi, thou art the son of God; thou art the King of Israel. Jesus answered and said unto him, Because I said unto thee, I saw thee under the fig tree, believest thou? Thou shalt see greater things than these. And he saith unto him, Verily, verily, I say unto you, Hereafter ye shall see Heaven open, and the angels of God ascending and descending upon the Son of Man."

In these first few disciples the foundation of the Christian church was being laid by individual effort. John first directed two of his disciples to Christ. Then one of these finds a brother, and brings him to Christ. He then calls Philip to follow him, and he went in search of Nathanael. Here is an instructive lesson for all the followers of Christ. It teaches them the importance of personal effort, making direct appeals to relatives, friends, and acquaintances. There are those who profess to be acquainted with Christ for a life time who never make personal effort to induce one soul to come to the Saviour. They have left all the work with the minister. He may be well qualified for his work ; but he cannot do the work which God has left upon the members of the church. Very many excuse themselves from being interested in the salvation of those who are out of Christ, and are content to selfishly enjoy the benefits of the grace of God themselves, while they make no direct effort to bring others to Christ. In the vineyard of the Lord there is a work for all to do, and unselfish, interested, faithful workers will share largely of his grace here, and of the reward he will bestow hereafter. Faith is called into exercise by good works, and courage and hope are in accordance with working faith. The reason many professed followers of Christ have not a bright and living experience, is because they do nothing to gain it. If they would engage in the work which God would have them do, their faith would increase, and they would advance in the divine life.

Jesus was pleased with the earnest faith of Nathanael that asked for no greater evidence than the few words he had spoken. And he looked forward with pleasure to the work he was to do in relieving the oppressed, healing the sick, and in breaking the bands of Satan. In view of these blessings which Christ came to bestow, he says to Nathanael, in the presence of the other disciples, "Hereafter ye shall see heaven opened, and the angels of God ascending and descending upon the Son of Man."

Christ virtually says, On the bank of Jordan the heavens were opened before me, and the Spirit descended like a dove upon me. That scene at Jordan was but a token to evidence that I was the Son of God. If you believe in me as such, your faith shall be quickened, and you shall see that the heavens will be opened, and shall never be closed. I have opened them for you, and the angels of God, that are united with me in the reconciliation between earth and Heaven, uniting the believers on the earth with the Father above, will be ascending, bearing the prayers of the needy and distressed from the earth to the Father above, and descending, bringing blessings of hope, courage, health, and life, for the children of men.

The angels of God are ever moving up and down from earth to Heaven, and from Heaven to earth. All the miracles of Christ performed for the afflicted and suffering were, by the power of God, through the ministration of angels. Christ condescended to take humanity, and thus he unites his interests with the fallen sons and daughters of Adam here below, while his divinity grasps the throne of God. And thus Christ opens the communication of man with God, and God with man.

All the blessings from God to man are through the ministration of holy angels.

Disciples were being daily added to Christ, and people flocked from cities and villages to hear him. Many came to him for baptism; but Christ baptized none. His disciples performed this ordinance. And while Christ's disciples were baptizing large numbers, there arose a question among the Jews and the disciples of John, whether the act of baptism purified the sinner from the guilt of sin. The disciples of John answered that John baptized only unto repentance, but Christ's disciples unto a new life. John's disciples were jealous of the popularity of Christ, and said to John, referring to Christ, " He that was with thee beyond Jordan, to whom thou bearest witness, behold the same baptizeth, and all men come to him. John answered and said, A man can receive nothing except it be given him from Heaven."

In this answer John virtually says, Why should you be jealous on my account ? " Ye yourselves bear me witness that I said, I am not the Christ, but that I am sent before him. He that hath the bride is the bridegroom; but the friend of the bridegroom which standeth and heareth him, rejoiceth greatly because of the bridegroom's voice. This my joy therefore is fulfilled.

John, so far from being jealous of the prosperity of Christ's mission, rejoices as he witnesses the success of the work he came to do. He assures his disciples that his special mission was to direct the attention of the people to Christ. " He must increase; but I must decrease. He that cometh from above is above all. He that is of the earth is earthly, and speaketh of the earth. He that cometh from Heaven is above all. And what he hath seen and heard, that he testifieth; and no man receiveth his testimony."

John assured his disciples that Jesus was the promised Messiah, the Saviour of the world. As his work was closing, he taught his disciples to look to Jesus, and follow him as the great teacher. John's life, with the exception of the joy he experienced in witnessing the success of his mission, was without pleasure. It was one of sorrow and self-denial. He who heralded the first advent of Christ, was not permitted to personally hear, nor to witness the power manifested by him. John's voice was seldom heard, except in the wilderness. His life was lonely. Multitudes had flocked to the wilderness to hear the words of the wonderful prophet. He had laid the ax at the root of the tree. He had reproved sin, fearless of the consequences, and prepared the way for the ministry of Christ.

Herod was affected as he listened to the pointed testimony of John, and, with deep interest, he inquired what he must do to become his disciple. He was convicted by the plain truths uttered by John. His conscience condemned him, for a woman of vile passions had gained his affections and controlled his mind. This unprincipled woman was ambitious for power and authority, and thought if she became the wife of Herod her object would be gained. As Herod listened to the practical truths proclaimed by John, reproving the transgression of the law of God, and setting forth the future punishment which the guilty must suffer, he trembled, and greatly desired to break the chain of lust which held him. He opened his mind to John, who brought Herod to the law of God, face to face, and told him it would be im-

possible for him to have part in the kingdom of
the Messiah unless he should break away from the
unlawful connections with his brother's wife, and,
with his whole heart, obey the commandments of
God.

Herod was inclined to act upon the advice of
John, and stated to Herodias that he could not
marry her in defiance of the law of God. But
this determined woman would not be thwarted in
her designs. Intense hatred was awakened in her
heart toward John. Herod was weak in principle,
vacillating in mind, and Herodias had no great difficulty in re-establishing herself in his favor, and
holding her influence over him. Herod yielded
to the pleasures of sin, rather than submit to the
restrictions of the law of God.

When Herodias had gained influence over
Herod, she determined to be revenged upon the
prophet for his daring to reprove their course of
crime. And she influenced him to imprison John.
But Herod intended to release him. While confined in prison, John heard, through his disciples,
of the mighty works of Jesus. He could not personally listen to his gracious words; but the disciples informed him, and comforted him with a
relation of what they had seen and heard.

John having spent his life in the open air, in
active, persevering labor, enduring privations,
hardship, and toil, he had never before experienced
the trials of confined living. He therefore became
desponding, and even doubts troubled him whether
Christ was indeed the Messiah. His disciples had
brought to him accounts of the wonderful things
they had witnessed in the ministry of Christ.
But he concluded that if Christ was indeed the

Messiah, he would publicly proclaim himself as the Saviour of the world.

John had indistinct ideas of the kingdom Christ came to establish, as also had the disciples of Christ. They thought Christ would establish a temporal kingdom, and reign upon the throne of David in Jerusalem. He became impatient because Christ did not immediately make himself known, assume kingly authority, and subdue the Romans. He hoped that if Christ established his kingdom, he would be brought out of prison. He decided that if Jesus was really the Son of God, and could do all things, he would exercise his power and set him at liberty.

John sent his disciples to inquire of Christ, "Art thou he that should come, or do we look for another?" The disciples sought the presence of Christ; but they could not communicate with him immediately, because of the crowd who were bearing the sick to Jesus. The afflicted, blind, and lame were passing through the throng. The disciples of John saw the miracles of Christ, and that at his word the lifeless clay became animate, and the glow of health took the place of the pallor of death. Jesus said to the disciples of John, "Go and show John again those things which ye do hear and see. The blind receive their sight, the lame walk, the lepers are cleansed, and the deaf hear, the dead are raised up, and the poor have the gospel preached to them. And blessed is he, whosoever shall not be offended in me."

In these words John is gently reproved for his impatience. The cautious reproof returned to John was not lost upon him. He then better understood the character of Christ's mission. And with submission and faith, he yielded himself into

the hands of God, to live, or to die, as should best
advance his glory.

After the disciples of John had departed, Jesus
addressed the multitude concerning John, "What
went ye out into the wilderness for to see? A reed
shaken with the wind?" Jesus knew that a reed
trembling in the wind was the very opposite of
John's character. John could not be moved by
flattery, nor be deceived by prevailing errors.
Neither could he be turned aside from the work he
came to do by rewards, or worldly honors. He
would preserve his integrity at the expense of his
life. Steadfast as a rock stood the prophet of
God, faithful to rebuke sin and crime in all their
forms, in kings and nobles, as readily as in the un-
honored and unknown. He swerved not from
duty. Loyal to his God, in noble dignity of moral
character, he stood firm as a rock, faithful to
principle.

"But what went ye out for to see? A man
clothed in soft raiment? Behold they that wear
soft clothing are in kings' houses. But what went
ye out for to see? A prophet? Yea, I say unto
you, and more than a prophet. For this is he of
whom it is written, Behold, I send my messenger
before thy face, which shall prepare thy way before thee. Verily I say unto you, Among them
that are born of women there hath not risen a
greater than John the Baptist; notwithstanding,
he that is least in the kingdom of Heaven is
greater than he. And from the days of John the
Baptist until now, the kingdom of Heaven suffereth
violence, and the violent take it by force."

The people whom Christ addressed well knew
that the apparel worn by John was the opposite
of that worn in royal palaces. Christ virtually

asked: What motive induced you to flock to the
wilderness to hear the preaching of John? The
wilderness is not the place to find those who live
delicately, and who clothe themselves in rich, soft
apparel. Christ wished them to observe the contrast between the clothing of John and that of
the Jewish priests. The prophet wore a plain,
rough garment, possessing no beauty, but answering the purpose for which clothing was first designed. In marked contrast to the garments of
John, was the gorgeous apparel of the Jewish
priests and elders.

These officials, thinking that they would be
reverenced in accordance with their external appearance, adopted great splendor of dress, making a rich display of costly robes and dazzling
breastplates. They were more anxious to win
the admiration of men than to obtain spotless
purity of character and holiness of life, that
would gain the approval of God.

Christ admonished his disciples, and also the
multitude, to follow that which was good in the
teachings of the scribes and Pharisees, but not to
imitate their wrong examples, nor be deceived by
their ambitious pretensions.

He says, "All, therefore, whatsoever they bid
you observe, that observe and do; but do not ye
after their works; for they say, and do not. For
they bind heavy burdens, and grievous to be
borne, and lay them on men's shoulders; but
they themselves will not move them with one of
their fingers. But all their works they do to be
seen of men; they make broad their phylacteries,
and enlarge the borders of their garments, and
love the uppermost rooms at feasts, and the chief

seats in the synagogues, and greetings in the markets, and to be called of men, Rabbi, Rabbi."

John saw that these proud Jews were exalting and glorifying themselves by parading their ostentatious piety before the public. They bound portions of the law upon their foreheads and about their wrists, that all might recognize and pay deference to their assumed sanctity. True, God had commanded the children of Israel to place a ribbon of blue in the border of their garments, upon which the ten commandments, in brief, should be embroidered. This was to continually remind them of their duty to love God supremely, and their neighbor as themselves. But the farther they had departed from their primitive purity and simplicity, and the more directly their daily lives were opposed to the law of God, the more particular were they to make broad their phylacteries, and add to the words which God had specified should be traced on the ribbon of blue. Outwardly they were expressing the deepest devotion, while their acts were in strong contrast with their profession.

CHAPTER V.

THE DEATH OF JOHN.

THE spirit of reform stirred the soul of John. The light of wisdom and the power of God were upon him. Inspiration from Heaven kindled a holy zeal that led him to denounce the Jewish priests, and pronounce the curse of God upon them. They made high pretensions to godliness while they were strangers to charity, mercy, and the love of God. They sought, by the gorgeousness of their apparel and their lofty manners, to inspire awe and command the respect of men, while they were abhorred by the Most High.

Though their hearts and lives were contrary to the will of God, they deceived themselves with the vain supposition that eternal blessings were theirs by virtue of the promises made to Abraham, the father of the faithful. They were not clothed with humility. They were destitute of the faith and piety of Abraham. They had not earned by integrity and purity of life, the moral worth which would ally them to him as his children, yet they expected to share the promises given him of the Lord. The fearless manner in which the prophet John had denounced the Pharisees and exposed their iniquity and hypocrisy, startled those who had been accustomed to seeing them honored and exalted.

His preaching had aroused intense interest everywhere. His earnest appeals and denunciations had stirred the consciences of men. People had flocked from towns, cities, and villages, attracted to the wilderness by his earnest and fervent exhortations, his courageous warnings and reproofs, such as they had never before heard. There was no outward display in the dress of John to attract, or to awaken admiration. He resembled the prophet Elijah in the coarseness of his apparel, and in his plain and simple diet. He fed upon locusts and wild honey, which the wilderness afforded, and drank the pure water flowing from the eternal hills.

Yet so great had been the crowds that listened

to him that his fame had spread throughout the land. And now that he was imprisoned, the people waited with interest to see what would be the result, never thinking that he would be visited with any severe punishment, as his life was without blame.

Herod's purpose to release John from prison was delayed from time to time through fear of displeasing Herodias, who was determined he should be put to death. While he was delaying, she was active, planning how to be revenged in the most effectual manner on the prophet, because he had ventured to tell the truth, and reprove their unlawful life. She knew that although Herod kept John in prison, he designed to release him, for he honored and feared him, and believed that he was a true prophet of God. John had made known to Herod the secrets of his heart and life, and his reproofs had struck terror to the guilty conscience of the king.

In many things Herod had reformed his dissolute life. But the use of luxurious food and stimulating drink was constantly enervating his moral as well as physical powers, and warring against the earnest appeals of the Spirit of God, which had struck conviction to his heart, and was urging him to put away his sins. Herodias was acquainted with the weak points in the character of Herod. She knew that under ordinary circumstances, while his intelligence controlled him, she could not compass the death of John.

She had tried, but unsuccessfully, to gain the consent of Herod to have John slain. Her revengeful spirit was now at work to accomplish her inhuman design by strategy. She knew that the only way to accomplish her purpose would be through the gratification of the king's intemperate appetite. So she covered her hatred as best she could, looking forward to the royal birthday, which she knew would be an occasion of gluttony and intoxication. The king's love of luxurious food and wine would give her an opportunity to throw him off his guard. She would entice him to indulge his appetite, which would arouse passions of the baser order, subvert the finer sensibilities, produce a recklessness of consequences, and an inability to exercise his proper judgment and decision.

She was acquainted with the effect of these carnivals upon the intellect and morals. She knew that the unnatural exhilaration of the spirits induced by intemperance lowers the moral standard of the mind, making it impossible for holy impulses to enter the heart and govern the excited passions, that festivities and amusements, dances, and free use of wine, cloud the senses, and remove the fear of God; therefore she prepared everything to flatter his pride and vanity, and indulge his passions. She made the most costly preparations for feasting, and voluptuous dissipation.

When the great day arrived, and the king with his lords was feasting and drinking in the banqueting hall, Herodias sent her daughter, dressed in a most enchanting manner, into the royal presence. Salome was decorated with costly garlands and flowers, sparkling jewels and flashing bracelets. With little covering, and less modesty, she danced for the amusement of the royal guests. To their perverted senses, she seemed a vision of beauty and loveliness, and charmed away the last remnants of self-respect and propriety. Instead of being governed by enlightened reason, refined taste, and sensitive conscience, the baser qualities of the mind held the guiding reins. Virtue and principle had no controlling power.

The mind of Herod was in a whirl. His faculties were confused, judgment and reverence were dethroned. He saw only the hall of pleasure, with his reveling guests, the banquet table, sparkling wine and flashing lights, and the young girl in her voluptuous beauty dancing before him. In the recklessness of the moment he was desirous to make some display which would exalt him still higher before the great men of his kingdom; and he rashly promised, and confirmed his promise with an oath, to give the daughter of Herodias whatever she might ask.

The object for which she had been sent into the royal presence was now gained. Having obtained so wonderful a promise, she ran to her mother, desiring to know what she should ask. The mother's answer was ready—the head of John the Baptist in a charger. Salome was shocked. She did not understand the hidden revenge in her mother's heart, and at first refused to present such an inhuman request; but the determination of the wicked mother prevailed. Moreover, she bade her daughter make no delay, but hasten to prefer her request before Herod would have time for reflection. Accordingly Salome returned to Herod with her terrible petition: "I will that thou give me, by and by, in a charger, the head of John the Baptist. And the king was exceeding sorry; yet for his oath's sake, and for their sakes which sat with him, he would not reject her."

Herod was astonished and confounded. The riotous mirth ceased, for his guests were thrilled with horror at this inhuman request. An ominous silence settled down upon the scene of revelry. The king, though drunken and confused, endeavored to summon reason to his aid.

He had been exalted for constancy and superior judgment, and he did not wish to appear fickle or rash in character. The oath had been made in honor of his guests, and had one of them offered a word of remonstrance against the fulfillment of his promise, he would gladly have saved the life of John. He gave them opportunity to speak in the prisoner's behalf. They had traveled long distances to the mountains in the wilderness to listen to his powerful discourses, and they knew he was a man without crime, and a prophet of God. Herod told them if it would not be considered a special mark of dishonor to them, he would not abide by his oath.

But though at first they were horror-stricken at the unnatural demand of the girl, they were so far intoxicated that they sat in silent stupor, without reason, reverence, or thought. Though they were invited to release the monarch from his oath, their tongues were dumb. No voice in all that company was raised to save the life of an innocent man, who had never done them harm. Herod, still under the delusion that, in order to maintain his reputation, he must keep an oath made under the influence of intoxication, unless formally released from it, waited in vain for a dissenting voice, but there was none. The life of God's prophet was in the hands of a company of drunken revelers. These men occupied high positions of trust in the nation, and grave responsibilities rested upon them, yet they had gorged themselves with dainty food, and added drunkenness to surfeiting, until their mental powers were enervated by the pleasure of sense, their brains turned with the giddy scene of music and dancing, and conscience lay dormant. By their silence they pronounced the sentence of death upon the anointed of the Lord, to gratify the horrible caprice of a wicked woman.

Too often in these days the most solemn responsibilities rest upon those who, from their intemperate habits, are not in a condition to exercise the calm judgment and keen perceptions of right and wrong with which their Creator endowed them. The guardians of the people, men in authority, upon whose decisions hang the lives of their fellow-creatures, should be subject to severe punishment if found guilty of intemperance. Those who enforce laws should be law-keepers. They should be men of self-government, in full harmony with the laws governing their physical, mental, and moral powers, that they may possess full vigor of intellect and a high sense of justice. In the martyrdom of John we have a result of intemperance among those invested with great authority. This eventful birthday feast should be a lesson of warning to the lovers of pleasure, and an exhortation to Christian temperance.

Herod waited in vain to be released from his oath, then reluctantly commanded the executioner to take the life of John. The head of the prophet was soon brought in before the king and his guests. Those lips were now forever sealed that had faithfully declared to Herod the reform he must make in his life, when that monarch inquired why he could not be the prophet's disciple. Never more would that voice be heard in trumpet notes calling sinners to repentance. The frivolities and dissipation of a single night had caused the sacrifice of one of the greatest prophets that ever bore a message from God to men.

Herodias received the gory head with fiendish satisfaction. She exulted in her revenge, and thought that Herod's conscience would be no more disturbed. But her calculations were greatly in error; no happiness resulted to her through her crime. Her name became notorious and abhorred because of her inhuman act, while the heart of Herod was more oppressed by remorse than it had been by the condemnation of John. And the very act which she imagined would rid the world of the prophet's influence, enshrined him as a holy martyr, not only in the hearts of his disciples, but of those who had not before ventured to stand boldy out as his followers. Many who had heard his message of warning, and had been secretly convinced by his teachings, now, spurred on by horror at his cold-blooded murder, publicly espoused his cause and declared themselves his disciples. Herodias utterly failed to silence the influence of John's teachings; they were to extend down through every generation to the close of time, while her corrupt life and Satanic revenge would reap a harvest of infamy.

After the feast of Herod had ended, and the effects of his intoxication had passed away, reason again resumed her throne, and the king was filled with remorse. His crime was ever before him, and he was constantly seeking to find relief from the stings of a guilty conscience. His

faith in John as an honored prophet of God,
was unshaken. As he reflected upon his life of
self-denial, his powerful discourses, his solemn,
earnest appeals, his sound judgment as a counselor, and then reflected that he had put him to
death, his conscience was fearfully troubled. Engaged in the affairs of the nation, receiving honors from men, he bore a smiling face and dignified mien, while he concealed an anxious, aching
heart, and was constantly terrified with fearful
forebodings that the curse of God was upon
him.

When Herod heard of the wonderful works of
Christ in healing the sick, casting out devils, and
raising the dead, he was exceedingly troubled
and perplexed. His convictions were that God,
whom John preached, was indeed present in
every place, and that he had witnessed the wild
mirth and wicked dissipation in the royal banqueting room, and that his ear had heard his
command to the executioner to behead John, that
his eye had seen the exultation of Herodias, and
the taunting and insult with which she had reproached the severed head of her enemy. And
many things which he had heard from the lips of
the prophet now spoke to his conscience in louder
tones than the preaching in the wilderness. He
had heard from John that nothing could be hidden from God, therefore he trembled lest some
terrible punishment should be visited upon him
for the sin he had committed.

When Herod heard of the words of Christ, he
thought that God had resurrected John, and sent
him forth with still greater power to condemn sin.
He was in constant fear that John would avenge
his death by passing condemnation upon him and

his house. "And king Herod heard of him [Christ] (for his name was spread abroad); and he said, That John the Baptist was risen from the dead, and therefore mighty works do show forth themselves in him. Others said, That it is Elias. And others said, That it is a prophet, or as one of the prophets. But when Herod heard thereof, he said, It is John, whom I beheaded; he is risen from the dead."

The Lord followed Herod as is described in Deuteronomy: "The Lord shall give thee there a trembling heart, and failing of eyes, and sorrow of mind. And thy life shall hang in doubt before thee; and thou shalt fear, day and night, and shalt have none assurance of thy life. In the morning thou shalt say, Would God it were even! and at even thou shalt say, Would God it were morning! for the fear of thine heart wherewith thou shalt fear, and for the sight of thine eyes which thou shalt see."

In these words is presented a vivid picture of the criminal's life. His own thoughts are his accusers, and there can be no torture keener than the stings of his own guilty conscience, which give him no rest night nor day.

The prophet John was the connecting link between the two dispensations. He was the lesser light which was to be followed by a greater. He was to shake the confidence of the people in their traditions, call their sins to their remembrance, and lead them to repentance; that they might be prepared to appreciate the work of Christ. God communicated to John by inspiration, illuminating the understanding of the prophet, that he might remove the superstition and darkness from the minds of the honest Jews, which had, through false teachings, been gathering upon them for generations.

But the least disciple who followed Christ, witnessing his miracles, and receiving his divine lessons of instruction and the comforting words that fell from his lips, was more privileged than John the Baptist. No light had ever shone or ever will shine so clearly upon the mind of fallen man, as that which emanated from the teachings and example of Jesus. Christ and his mission had been but dimly understood and typified in the shadowy sacrifice. Even John was for a time deceived, and thought he would become a temporal ruler over subjects who were just and holy, not then fully comprehending the future immortal life through the Saviour. "The light shone in the darkness, and the darkness comprehended it not."

Although not one of the prophets had a higher mission or greater work to perform than had John, yet he was not to see even the result of his own labors. He was not privileged to be with Christ and witness the divine power attending the greater light. It was not for him to see the blind restored to sight, the sick healed, and the dead raised to life. He did not behold the light which shone through every word of Christ, reflecting glory upon the promises in prophecy. The world was illuminated with the brightness of the Father's glory in the person of his Son; but the solitary prophet was denied the privilege of seeing and understanding the wisdom and mercy of God through a personal knowledge of the ministry of Christ.

In this sense, many who were favored by the

teachings of Christ and saw his miracles, were greater than John.

Those who were with Christ when he walked a man among men, and listened to his divine teachings under a variety of circumstances—while preaching in the temple walking in the streets, teaching the multitudes by the way, and by the sea-side, and while an invited guest at the table of his host, ever giving words of instruction to meet the cases of all who needed his help; healing, comforting, and reproving, as circumstances required—were more exalted than John the Baptist.

CHAPTER VI.

TEMPTATION OF CHRIST.

AFTER the baptism of Jesus, he was led by the Spirit into the wilderness to be tempted of the devil. When he came up out of Jordan, he bowed and plead with the great Eternal for strength to endure the conflict with the fallen foe. The opening heavens and the descent of the excellent glory attested his divine character; and the Father's voice declared the close relationship of Christ to his Infinite Majesty: "This is my beloved Son, in whom I am well pleased." The mission of Christ was now about to begin; but he must first withdraw from the busy scenes of life to a desolate wilderness for the express purpose of bearing a three-fold temptation in behalf of those whom he had come to redeem.

Let us pause in the history of Christ's earthly

life, and briefly notice the events prior to his advent in a world of sin. Satan, after compassing the fall of Adam and Eve, had boasted that he was monarch of the earth, and it was true that in all ages of the world he had found many followers. But he had failed to unite fallen man with him as he had hoped to do, and thus reign supreme over the whole earth. Though man in his fallen state was suffering the consequence of his disobedience, yet he was not without hope. He was unable, because of his guilt, to come directly before God with his supplications, but the plan of redemption, devised in Heaven, transferred the sentence of death from the obedient and faithful, to a substitute. There must be the shedding of blood, for death was the consequence of man's sin. In the slain victim, man was to see for the time being the fulfillment of God's word: "Ye shall surely die." The flowing blood also signified an atonement, and pointed forward to a Redeemer who would one day come to the world and die for the sins of man, thus fully vindicating his Father's law.

The hope of salvation through Christ led fallen man to be exceedingly faithful in the matter of sacrifices. Satan watched with intense interest every circumstance connected with these sacrificial ceremonies, and soon learned that they typified a future atonement for the human race. This caused him great uneasiness, as it threatened to frustrate his cherished plan of gaining dominion over the whole world and its inhabitants. But, instead of desponding under his discouragements, he redoubled his efforts to accomplish his purpose, and the ages were marked with his hellish triumphs. Indulgence of appetite and passion, war, intoxication, and crime spread over the earth as its inhabitants increased. God destroyed the people with the waters of a great flood, and rained fire and death upon the wicked cities; but the great adversary was still free to pursue his scheme of demoralization.

Satan is a diligent student of the Bible, and much better acquainted with the prophecies than many religious teachers. He has ever kept well-informed concerning the revealed purposes of God, that he might defeat the plans of the Infinite. It was plain to Satan that the sacrificial offerings were typical of a coming Redeemer who was to ransom man from the powers of darkness, and that this Redeemer was the Son of God. Therefore he laid deep plans to control the hearts of men from generation to generation, and to blind their understanding of the prophecies, that when Christ should come the people would refuse to accept him as their Saviour.

From the time when Christ was born in Bethlehem, Satan had never lost sight of him. He had set on foot various plans to destroy him, in all of which he was unsuccessful, as the Son of God was upheld by the strong arm of his Father. Well-aware of Christ's position in Heaven, Satan was filled with apprehension when this powerful Prince of light left the royal courts of his glory and became a simple man on earth. Satan now feared that, not only would he fail in his cherished purpose of reigning supreme over the whole earth, but that the power he already possessed would be wrested from him. Therefore when he went out into the wilderness to beset Christ with temptations, he brought every force and artifice

at his command to bear upon the Son of God that
he might allure him from his allegiance.

The great work of redemption could be carried
out only by the Redeemer taking the place of
fallen man.   Burdened with the sins of the
world, he must go over the ground where Adam
stumbled.   He must take up the work just
where Adam failed, and endure a test of the
same character, but infinitely more severe than
that which had vanquished him.   It is impossible for man to fully comprehend the strength of
Satan's temptations to our Saviour.   Every en-
ticement to evil, which men find so difficult to
resist, was brought to bear upon the Son of God
in as much greater degree as his character was
superior to that of fallen man.

When Adam was assailed by the tempter he
was without the taint of sin.   He stood before God
in the strength of perfect manhood, all the organs
and faculties of his being fully developed and
harmoniously balanced ; and he was surrounded
with things of beauty, and conversed daily with
the holy angels.   What a contrast to this perfect
being did the second Adam present, as he entered
the desolate wilderness to cope with Satan, sin-
gle-handed.   For four thousand years the race
had been decreasing in size and physical strength,
and deteriorating in moral worth ; and, in order to
elevate fallen man, Christ must reach him where
he stood.   He assumed human nature, bearing
the infirmities and degeneracy of the race.   He
humiliated himself to the lowest depths of human woe, that he might fully sympathize with
man and rescue him from the degradation into
which sin had plunged him.

" For it became Him, for whom are all things,

and by whom are all things, in bringing many sons unto glory, to make the Captain of their salvation perfect through sufferings." "And being made perfect, he became the author of eternal salvation unto all them that obey him." "Wherefore in all things it behooved him to be made like unto his brethren, that he might be a merciful and faithful high priest in things pertaining to God, to make reconciliation for the sins of the people. For in that he himself hath suffered, being tempted, he is able to succor them that are tempted." "For we have not an high priest which cannot be touched with the feeling of our infirmities; but was in all points tempted like as we are, yet without sin."

When Christ entered the wilderness his countenance was changed, its glory had departed, the weight of the sins of the world was pressing upon his soul, and his features expressed unutterable sorrow, a depth of anguish that fallen man had never realized. The indulgence of appetite had increased with every successive generation since Adam's transgression, until the race was so feeble in moral power that they could not overcome in their own strength. Christ in behalf of the race was to conquer appetite, by enduring the most powerful test on that point. He was to tread the path of temptation alone, with none to help or comfort him. Alone he was to wrestle with the powers of darkness, and exercise a self-control stronger than hunger or death. The length of this fast is the strongest evidence of the great sinfulness of debased appetite, and its power over the human family.

Through appetite, Satan had accomplished the

ruin of Adam and Eve, and through all succeeding generations, this had been his strongest weapon in corrupting the human race. As Christ had taken the form of man, and was subject to his infirmities, Satan hoped to conquer him through this powerful medium, and laid his plans accordingly. As soon as Christ's long fast commenced, he was at hand with his temptations. He came clothed in light, claiming to be an angel sent from the throne of God to sympathize with Christ and relieve him from his suffering condition. He represented to him that God did not desire him to pass through the pain and self-denial which he had anticipated. He claimed to bear the message from Heaven that God only designed to prove the willingness of Christ to endure his test.

Satan told him that he was to set his feet in the blood-stained path, but not to travel it, that, like Abraham, he was tried to show his perfect obedience. He claimed to be the angel who stayed the hand of Abraham, as the knife was raised to slay Isaac, and that he had now come to save the life of the Son of God, deliver him from a painful death by starvation, and assist him in the plan of salvation.

Satan is to-day deceiving many as he attempted to deceive Christ, claiming that he is Heaven-sent and doing a good work for humanity. And the masses of the people are so blinded by sophistry that they cannot discern his true character, and they honor him as a messenger of God, while he is working their eternal ruin.

But Christ turned from all these artful temptations, and remained steadfast in his purpose to carry out the divine plan. Foiled at one point,

Satan now tried another expedient. Believing that the angelic character he had assumed defied detection, he now feigned to doubt the divinity of Christ, because of his emaciated appearance and uncongenial surroundings.

In taking the nature of man, Christ was not equal in appearance with the angels of Heaven, but this was one of the necessary humiliations that he willingly accepted when he became man's Redeemer. Satan urged that if he was indeed the Son of God he should give him some evidence of his exalted character. He suggested that God would not leave his Son in so deplorable a condition. He declared that one of the heavenly angels had been exiled to earth, and his appearance indicated that instead of being the King of Heaven he was that fallen angel. He called attention to his own beautiful appearance, clothed with light and strength, and insultingly contrasted the wretchedness of Christ with his own glory.

He claimed direct authority from Heaven to demand proof of Christ that he was the Son of God. He taunted him with being a poor representative of the angels, much less their high Commander, the acknowledged King in the royal courts; and insinuated that his present appearance indicated that he was forsaken of God and man. He declared that if he were the Son of God he was equal with God and should evidence this by working a miracle to relieve his hunger. He then urged him to change the stone at his feet to bread, and agreed that if this were done he would at once yield his claims to superiority, and the contest between the two should be forever ended.

Satan thus hoped to shake the confidence of Christ in his Father, who had permitted him to be brought into this condition of extreme suffering in the desert, where the feet of man had never trodden. The arch-enemy hoped that under the force of despondency and extreme hunger, he could urge Christ to exert his miraculous power in his own behalf, and thus take himself out of the Father's hands.

The circumstances and surroundings of Christ were such as to make temptation upon this point peculiarly aggravating. The long fast had physically debilitated him, the pangs of hunger consumed his vitals, his fainting system clamored for food. He could have wrought a miracle in his own behalf, and satisfied his gnawing hunger; but this would not have been in accordance with the divine plan. It was no part of his mission to exercise divine power for his own benefit; this he never did in his earthly life; his miracles were all for the good of others.

Suffering humiliation, hunger, and contempt, Jesus repulsed Satan with the same scripture he had bidden Moses repeat to rebellious Israel: "Man shall not live by bread alone, but by every word that proceedeth out of the mouth of God." In this declaration, and also by his example, Christ showed that wanting temporal food was a much less calamity than meeting the disapprobation of God.

In becoming man's substitute, and conquering where man had been vanquished, Christ was not to manifest his divine power to relieve his own suffering, for fallen man could work no miracles in order to save himself from pain, and Christ, as his representative, was to bear his trials as a man, leaving an example of perfect faith and trust in his Heavenly Father.

Christ recognized Satan from the beginning, and it required strong self-control to listen to the propositions of this insulting deceiver, and not rebuke his bold assumption. But the Saviour of the world was neither provoked to give him evidence of his divine power, nor to enter into controversy with one who had been expelled from Heaven for leading a rebellion against the supreme Ruler of the universe, and whose very crime had been a refusal to recognize the dignity of the Son of God. Armed with faith in his Heavenly Father, bearing in his mind the precious memory of the words spoken from Heaven at his baptism, Jesus stood unmoved in the lonely wilderness, before the mighty enemy of souls.

It was not for the Son of God to descend from his lofty mission to prove his divinity to Satan, nor did he condescend to explain the reason of his present humiliation, and the manner in which he was to act as man's Redeemer. If the children of men would follow the example of their Saviour, and hold no converse with Satan, they would be spared many a defeat at his hands. Six thousand years has this arch-enemy been warring against the government of God, and continued practice has increased his skill to deceive and allure.

But Satan had too much at stake to lightly give up the battle. He knew that, if Christ came off victor, his influence would be lessened. So, in order to awe Christ with his superior strength, he carried him to Jerusalem and placed him on a pinnacle of the temple. He now demanded that, if he were indeed the Son of God, he should cast himself from that dizzy height, and thus indicate entire confidence in his Father's preserving care.

The sin of presumption lies close beside the virtue of perfect faith and confidence in God, and Satan endeavored to take advantage of Christ's humanity and urge him over the line of trust into presumption. He now admitted that Christ was right in the wilderness, when he placed such perfect confidence in the Father, and he now urged that one more proof should be given of his entire faith in God, by casting himself from the temple. He assured him that if he were indeed the Son of God he had nothing to fear, for the angels would uphold him. Satan was well aware that if Christ could be prevailed upon to fling himself from the temple, in order to prove his claim to the protection of his Heavenly Father, he would, by that very act, exhibit the weakness of human nature.

But Jesus came off victor from the second temptation, by spurning the sin of presumption. While manifesting perfect trust in his Father, he refused to voluntarily place himself in such peril that it would be necessary for the Father to display divine power in order to save his Son from death. This would have been forcing Providence to come to his rescue, and thus he would fail to give his people a perfect example of faith and trust in God.

Our Saviour showed entire confidence that his Heavenly Father would not suffer him to be tempted above what he should give him strength to endure. Christ had not willfully placed himself in danger, and he knew that if he preserved his integrity, an angel of God would be sent to deliver him from the tempter's power if it were necessary.

Finding that he prevailed nothing with Christ in the second great temptation, Satan began to be alarmed for the result of his efforts. The continued steadfastness of the Son of God filled him with apprehension, for he had not expected so strenuous an opposition. He now called all the resources of his Satanic nature to his aid in one last mighty effort to baffle and defeat the Saviour. In his first two temptations, he had concealed his true character and purpose, claiming to be an exalted messenger from the courts of Heaven. But he now throws off all disguise, avowing himself the Prince of Darkness, and claiming the earth for his dominion.

He took Jesus up into a high mountain and showed him the kingdoms of the world, spread out in a panoramic view before his eyes. The sunlight lay on templed cities, marble palaces, fruitful fields and vineyards, gilding the dark cedars of Lebanon and the blue waters of Galilee. The eyes of Jesus, so lately greeted by gloom and desolation, gazed upon a scene of unsurpassed loveliness and prosperity. Then the tempter's voice was heard: All this power will I give thee, and the glory of them; for that is delivered unto me, and to whomsoever I will, I give it. If thou therefore wilt worship me, all shall be thine.

Satan brought all his strength to bear upon this last inducement, for upon the result of this effort depended his destiny. He claimed the world as his dominion and himself to be the Prince of the power of the air. He promised to put Christ in possession of all the kingdoms without suffering or peril, if he would make one con-

cession, and that was to acknowledge Satan his
superior, and pay him homage. This last temptation was designed to be the most alluring of
all. Christ's life was one of sorrow, hardship,
and conflict. Poverty and privation attended
him; even the beasts and the birds had their
homes, but the Son of Man had not where to lay
his head. Homeless and friendless as he was,
there was offered him the mighty kingdoms of
the world and the glory of them for a single consideration.

The eyes of Jesus rested for a moment upon
the scene before him; he then turned resolutely
from it, refusing to dally with the tempter by
even looking upon the enchanting prospect he
had presented to him; but when Satan solicited
his homage, Christ's divine indignation was
aroused, and he could no longer tolerate his blas-
phemous assumption, or even permit him to remain in his presence. He exercised his divine
authority, and commanded Satan to desist, saying,
"Get thee hence, Satan; for it is written, Thou
shalt worship the Lord thy God, and him only
shalt thou serve."

Satan had asked Christ to give him evidence
that he was the Son of God, and he had, in this
instance, the proof he asked. He had no power
to withstand his peremptory dismissal, and was
compelled to obey the divine command. Writhing with baffled hate and rage, the rebel chief retired from the presence of the world's Redeemer.
The contest was ended. Christ's victory was as
complete as had been the failure of Adam.

But the conflict had been protracted and trying, and Christ was exhausted and fell fainting
to the ground, with the pallor of death upon his

countenance. Then the heavenly angels, who
had bowed before him in the royal courts, and
who had watched his conflict with painful interest, ministered unto him, strengthening him with
food, as he lay like one dying. They had beheld
with awe and amazement their heavenly Commander passing through inexpressible suffering
to achieve the salvation of man. He had endured a more severe test than man would ever be
called to bear. But, as he lay emaciated and
suffering, the angels brought messages of love
and comfort from the Father, and an assurance
that all Heaven triumphed in the victory he had
gained for man. Thus the great heart of Christ
warmed to life again, and became strengthened
for his coming work.

The cost of the redemption of the race can
never be fully realized by men until the redeemed
shall stand with the Redeemer by the throne of
God. Then, as the glorious value of the eternal
reward opens upon their enraptured senses, and
their eyes behold the wondrous glories of immortal life, they will swell the song of victory, " Worthy is the Lamb that was slain to receive power,
and riches, and wisdom, and strength, and honor,
and glory, and blessing !" " And every creature,"
says John, " which is in Heaven, and on the
earth, and under the earth, and such as are in the
sea, and all that are in them, heard I saying,
Blessing, and honor, and glory, and power, be
unto Him that sitteth upon the throne, and unto
the Lamb forever and ever !"

Although Satan had failed in his most powerful temptations, yet he had not given up all hope
that he might, at some future time, be successful
in his efforts. He looked forward to the period

of Christ's ministry, when he should have opportunities to try his artifices against him.   Baffled and defeated, he had no sooner retired from the scene of conflict than he began to lay plans for blinding the understanding of the Jews, God's chosen people, that they might not discern in Christ the world's Redeemer.   He determined to fill their hearts with envy, jealousy, and hatred against the Son of God, so that they would not receive him, but would make his life upon earth as bitter as possible.

Satan held a counsel with his angels, as to the course they should pursue to prevent the people from having faith in Christ as the Messiah whom the Jews had so long been anxiously expecting. He was·disappointed and enraged that he had prevailed nothing against Jesus by his manifold temptations.   But he now thought if he could inspire in the hearts of Christ's own people, unbelief as to his being the Promised One, he might discourage the Saviour in his mission and secure the Jews as his agents to carry out his own diabolical purposes.   So he went to work in his subtle manner, endeavoring to accomplish by strategy what he had failed to do by direct, personal effort.

CHAPTER VII.

THE MARRIAGE AT CANA.

AFTER this, Jesus returned to Jordan, as has been previously stated, and was declared by John to be the " Lamb of God that taketh away the

sin of the world." At this time, also, he chose
John, Andrew, Simon, Philip, and Nathanael, for
his disciples, all of which has been recounted in
connection with the history of John the Baptist.
Jesus now entered upon the great work of his
life.

There was to be a marriage in Cana of Galilee.
The parties were relatives of Joseph and Mary.
Christ knew of this family gathering, and that
many influential persons would be brought together there, so, in company with his newly-
made disciples, he made his way to Cana. As
soon as it was known that Jesus had come to the
place, a special invitation was sent to him and
his friends. This was what he had purposed,
and so he graced the feast with his presence.

He had been separated from his mother for
quite a length of time. During this period he
had been baptized by John and had endured the
temptations in the wilderness. Rumors had
reached Mary concerning her son and his sufferings. John, one of the new disciples, had searched
for Christ and had found him in his humiliation,
emaciated, and bearing the marks of great physical and mental distress. Jesus, unwilling that
John should witness his humiliation, had gently
yet firmly dismissed him from his presence. He
wished to be alone; no human eye must behold
his agony, no human heart be called out in sympathy with his distress.

The disciple had sought Mary in her home and
related to her the incidents of this meeting
with Jesus, as well as the event of his baptism, when the voice of God was heard in acknowledgment of his Son, and the prophet
John had pointed to Christ, saying, "Behold the

Lamb of God which taketh away the sin of the world." For thirty years this woman had been treasuring up evidences that Jesus was the Son of God, the promised Saviour of the world. Joseph was dead, and she had no one in whom to confide the cherished thoughts of her heart. She had fluctuated between hope and perplexing doubts, but always feeling more or less of an assurance that her son was indeed the Promised One.

She had been very sorrowful for the past two months, for she had been separated from her son, who had ever been faithful and obedient to her wishes. The widowed mother had mourned over the sufferings that Jesus had endured in his loneliness. His Messiahship had caused her deep sorrow as well as joy. Yet strangely, as it appears to her, she meets him at the marriage feast, the same tender, dutiful son, yet not the same, for his countenance is changed; she sees the marks of his fierce conflict in the wilderness of temptation, and the evidence of his high mission in his holy expression and the gentle dignity of his presence. She sees that he is accompanied by a number of young men who address him with reverence, calling him Master. These companions tell Mary of the wonderful things they have witnessed, not only at the baptism, but upon numerous other occasions, and they conclude by saying, "We have found Him of whom Moses in the law, and the prophets, did write, Jesus of Nazareth, who is the long-looked-for Messiah."

The heart of Mary was made glad by this assurance that the cherished hope of long years of anxious waiting was indeed true. It would have been strange enough if, mingled with this deep and holy joy, there had not been a trace of the fond mother's natural pride. But the guests assembled and time passed on. At length an incident occurred that caused much perplexity and regret. It was discovered that from some cause the wine had failed. The wine used was the pure juice of the grape, and it was impossible to provide it at that late hour. It was unusual to dispense with it on these occasions; so the mother of Christ, who, in her capacity of relative had a prominent part to perform at the feast, spoke to her son, saying, "They have no wine." In this communication was a hidden request, or rather, suggestion, that He to whom all things were possible would relieve their wants. But Jesus answered, "Woman, what have I to do with thee? mine hour is not yet come."

His manner was respectful, yet firm; he designed to teach Mary that the time for her to control him as a mother, was ended. His mighty work now lay before him, and no one must direct concerning the exercise of his divine power. There was danger that Mary would presume upon her relationship to Christ, and feel that she had special claims upon him and special rights. As Son of the Most High, and Saviour of the world, no earthly ties must hold him from his divine mission, nor influence the course he must pursue. It was needful that he should stand free from every personal consideration, ready to do the will of his Father in Heaven.

Jesus loved his mother tenderly; for thirty years he had been subject to parental control; but the time had now come when he was to go about his Father's business. In rebuking his

mother, Jesus also rebukes a large class who have
an idolatrous love for their family, and allow the
ties of relationship to draw them from the service of God. Human love is a sacred attribute;
but should not be allowed to mar our religious
experience, or draw our hearts from God.

The future life of Christ was mapped out before him. His divine power had been hidden,
and he had waited in obscurity and humiliation
for thirty years, and was in no haste to act until
the proper time should arrive. But Mary, in the
pride of her heart, longed to see him prove to the
company that he was really the honored of God.
It seemed to her a favorable opportunity to convince the people present of his divine power, by
working a miracle before their eyes, that would
place him in the position he should occupy before
the Jews. But he answered that his hour had
not yet come. His time to be honored and glorified as King was not yet come; it was his lot
to be a Man of sorrows and acquainted with
grief.

The earthly relation of Christ to his mother
was ended. He who had been her submissive
son was now her divine Lord. Her only hope,
in common with the rest of mankind, was to believe him to be the Redeemer of the world, and
yield him implicit obedience. The fearful delusion of the Roman church exalts the mother of
Christ equal with the Son of the Infinite God;
but he, the Saviour, places the matter in a vastly different light, and in a pointed manner indi-
cates that the tie of relationship between them
in no way raises her to his level, or insures her
future. Human sympathies must no longer affect the One whose mission is to the world.

The mother of Christ understood the character of her Son, and bowed in submission to his will. She knew that he would comply with her request if it was best to do so. Her manner evidenced her perfect faith in his wisdom and power, and it was this faith to which Jesus responded in the miracle that followed. Mary believed that Jesus was able to do that which she had desired of him, and she was exceedingly anxious that everything in regard to the feast should be properly ordered, and pass off with due honor. She said to those serving at table, "Whatsoever he sayeth unto you, do it." Thus she did what she could to prepare the way.

At the entrance of the dwelling there stood six stone water-pots. Jesus directed the servants to fill these pots with water. They readily obeyed this singular order. The wine was wanted for immediate use, and Jesus commanded, " Draw out now, and bear unto the governor of the feast." The servants beheld with astonishment, that instead of the crystal water with which they had just filled those vessels, there flowed forth wine. Neither the ruler of the feast nor the guests generally were aware that the supply of wine had failed; so, upon testing it, the ruler was astonished, for it was superior to any wine he had ever before drank, and vastly different from that which had been served at the commencement of the feast.

He addressed the bridegroom, saying, "Every man at the beginning doth set forth good wine; and when men have well drunk, then that which is worse; but thou hast kept the good wine until now." In this miracle, Jesus illustrates the truth that while the world presents its best gifts

first, to fascinate the senses and please the eye,
he gives good gifts, ever fresh and new unto the
end.   They never pall upon the taste, the heart
never sickens and tires of them.   The pleasures of
the world are unsatisfying, its wine turns to bitterness, its gayety to gloom.   That which was begun
with songs and mirth ends in weariness and disgust.   But Jesus provides a feast of the soul that
never fails to give satisfaction and joy.   Each
new gift increases the capacity of the receiver to
appreciate and enjoy the blessings of his Lord.
He gives, not with stinted measure, but above
what is asked or expected.

This donation of Christ to the marriage supper
was a symbol of the means of salvation.   The
water represented baptism into his death, the
wine, the shedding of his blood for the purifying
of the sins of the world.   The provision made
for the wedding-guests was ample, and not less
abundant is the provision for blotting out the
iniquities of men.

Jesus had just come from his long fast in the
wilderness, where he had suffered in order to
break the power of appetite over man, which,
among other evils, had led to the free use of intoxicating liquor.   Christ did not provide for
the wedding guests wine that from fermentation
or adulteration was of an intoxicating character,
but the pure juice of the grape, clarified and refined.   Its effect was to bring the taste into harmony with a healthful appetite.

The guests remarked upon the quality of the
wine, and presently inquiries were made that
drew from the servants an account of the wonderful work that the youthful Galilean had performed.   The company listened with unbounded

amazement, and exchanged words of doubt and surprise. At length they looked for Jesus, that they might pay him due respect and learn how he had accomplished this miraculous conversion of water into wine; but he was not to be found. He had, with dignified simplicity, performed the miracle, and had then quietly withdrawn.

When it was ascertained that Jesus had really departed, the attention of the company was directed to his disciples who had remained behind. For the first time they had the opportunity of acknowledging themselves to be believers in Jesus of Nazareth as Saviour of the world. John related what he had heard and seen of his teachings. He told of the wonderful manifestations at the time of the baptism of Jesus, by the prophet John, in the river Jordan; how the light and glory from Heaven had descended upon him in the form of a dove, while a voice from the cloudless heavens proclaimed him to be the Son of the Infinite Father. John narrated these facts with convincing clearness and accuracy. The curiosity of all present was aroused, and many anxious ones who were looking and longing for the Messiah, thought it was indeed possible that this might be the Promised One of Israel.

The news of this miracle wrought by Jesus spread through all that region and even reached Jerusalem. The priests and elders heard with wonder. They searched with new interest the prophecies pointing to the coming of Christ. There was the most intense anxiety to know the aim and mission of this new Teacher, who came among the people in so unassuming a manner, yet did that which no other man had ever done.

Unlike the Pharisees and other dignitaries who preserved an austere seclusion, he had joined the mixed assembly of a festal gathering, and, while no shadow of worldly levity marred his conduct, he had sanctioned the social gathering with his presence.

Here is a lesson for the disciples of Christ through all time, not to exclude themselves from society, renouncing all social communion and seeking a strict seclusion from their fellow-beings. In order to reach all classes, we must meet them where they are; for they will seldom seek us of their own accord. Not alone from the pulpit are the hearts of men and women touched by divine truth. Christ awakened their interest by going among them as one who desired their good. He sought them at their daily avocations, and manifested an unfeigned interest in their temporal affairs. He carried his instruction into the households of the people, bringing whole families in their own homes under the influence of his divine presence. His strong personal sympathies helped to win hearts to his cause.

This example of the great Master should be closely followed by his servants. However instructive and profitable may be their public discourses, they should remember there is another field of action, humbler it may be, but full as promising of abundant harvests. It is found in the lowly walks of life, as well as the more pretentious mansions of the great, at the board of hospitality and gatherings for innocent social enjoyment.

The course of Jesus in this respect was in direct contrast to that of the exclusive leaders of the Jews. They shut themselves up from sympathy with the people, and sought neither to benefit them nor win their friendship. But Christ linked himself with the interests of humanity, and so should those who preach his word. This should not be, however, from a desire to gratify the inclinations for personal enjoyment, or love of change and pleasure; but for the purpose of embracing every opportunity to do good, and shed the light of truth upon the hearts of men, keeping the life pure and uncorrupted by the follies and vanities of society.

The special object of Jesus in attending this marriage feast was to commence the work of breaking down the exclusiveness which existed with the Jewish people, and to open the way for their freer mingling with the people. He had come not only as the Messiah of the Jews, but the Redeemer of the world. The Pharisees and elders refrained from associating with any class but their own. They held themselves aloof, not only from the Gentiles, but from the majority of their own people; and their teaching led all classes to separate themselves from the rest of the world, in a manner calculated to render them self-righteous, egotistical, and intolerant. This rigorous seclusion and bigotry of the Pharisees had narrowed their influence and created a prejudice which Christ would have removed, that the influence of his mission might be felt upon all classes.

Those who think to preserve their religion by hiding it within stone walls to escape the contamination of the world, lose golden opportunities to enlighten and benefit humanity. The Saviour sought men in the public streets, in private houses, on the boats, in the synagogue, by the shores of lakes, and at the marriage feasts. He spent much time in the mountains, engaged in earnest prayer, in order to come forth braced for the conflict, strengthened for his active toil among men in real life, enlightening and relieving the poor, the sick, the ignorant, and those bound by the chains of Satan, as well as teaching the rich and honorable.

The ministry of Christ was in marked contrast with that of the Jewish elders. They held themselves aloof from sympathy with men; considering that they were the favored ones of God, they assumed an undue appearance of righteousness and dignity. The Jews had so far fallen from the ancient teachings of Jehovah that they held that they would be righteous in the sight of God, and receive the fulfillment of his promises, if they strictly kept the letter of the law given them by Moses.

The zeal with which they followed the teachings of the elders gave them an air of great piety. Not content with performing those services which God had specified to them through Moses, they were continually reaching for more rigid and difficult duties. They measured their holiness by the multitude of their ceremonies, while their hearts were filled with hypocrisy, pride, and avarice. The curse of God was upon them for their iniquities, while they professed to be the only righteous nation upon earth.

They had received unsanctified and confused interpretations of the law, they had added tradition to tradition, they had restricted freedom of thought and action, till the commandments, ordinances, and service of God, were lost in a ceaseless round of meaningless rites and ceremonies. Their religion was a yoke of bondage. They had become so fettered that it was impossible for them to attend to the essential duties of life, without employing the Gentiles to do many necessary things which were forbidden the Jews to do for fear of contamination. They were in continual dread that they should become defiled. Dwelling constantly upon these matters had dwarfed their minds and narrowed the orbit of their lives.

Jesus commenced the work of reformation by bringing himself into close sympathy with humanity. He was a Jew, and he designed to leave a perfect pattern of one who was a Jew inwardly. While he rebuked the Pharisees for their pretentious piety, endeavoring to free the people from the senseless exactions that bound them, he showed the greatest veneration for the law of God, and taught obedience of its precepts.

Jesus rebuked intemperance, self-indulgence, and folly; yet he was social in his nature. He accepted invitations to dine with the learned and noble, as well as the poor and afflicted. On these occasions, his conversation was elevating and instructive, holding his hearers entranced. He gave no license to scenes of dissipation and revelry, yet innocent happiness was pleasing to him. A Jewish marriage was a solemn and impressive occasion, the pleasure and joy of which were not displeasing to the Son of Man. This miracle pointed directly toward breaking down the prejudices of the Jews. The disciples of Jesus learned a lesson of sympathy and humanity from it. His relatives were drawn to him with warm affection, and when he left for Capernaum, they accompanied him.

By attending this feast, Jesus sanctioned marriage as a divine institution, and through all his subsequent ministry, he paid the marriage covenant a marked respect in illustrating many important truths by it.

Jesus next proceeded to introduce himself to his own people in his true character. He went to Nazareth, where he was known as an unpretending mechanic, and entered a synagogue upon the Sabbath. As was customary, the elder read from the prophets, and exhorted the people to continue to hope for the Coming One, who would bring in a glorious reign, and subdue all oppression. He sought to animate the faith and courage of the Jews, by rehearsing the evidences of Messiah's soon coming, dwelling especially upon the kingly power and glorious majesty that would attend his advent. He kept before his hearers the idea that the reign of Christ would be upon an earthly throne in Jerusalem, and his kingdom would be a temporal one. He taught them that Messiah would appear at the head of armies, to conquer the heathen and deliver Israel from the oppression of their enemies.

At the close of the service, Jesus rose with calm dignity, and requested them to bring him the book of the prophet Esaias. "And when he had opened the book, he found the place where it was written, The Spirit of the Lord is upon me, because he hath anointed me to preach the gospel to the poor; he hath sent me to heal the broken-hearted, to preach deliverance to the captives, and recovering of sight to the blind, to set at liberty them that are bruised, to preach the acceptable year of the Lord. And he closed the book, and he gave it again to the minister, and

sat down. And the eyes of all them that were in the synagogue were fastened on him. And he began to say unto them, This day is this scripture fulfilled in your ears. And all bare him witness, and wondered at the gracious words
· which proceeded out of his mouth."

The scripture which Jesus read was understood by all to refer to the coming Messiah and his work. And when the Saviour explained the words he had read, and pointed out the sacred office of the Messiah,—a reliever of the oppressed, a liberator of the captives, a healer of the afflicted, restoring sight to the blind, and revealing to the world the light of truth,—the people were thrilled with the wisdom and power of his words and responded to them with fervent amens and praises to the Lord. Jesus had not been educated in the school of the prophets, yet the most learned Rabbis could not speak with more confidence and authority than did this young Galilean.

His impressive manner, the mighty import of his words, and the divine light that emanated from his countenance, thrilled the people with a power they had never experienced before, as Jesus stood before them, a living expositor of the prophet's words concerning himself. But when he announced: "This day is this scripture fulfilled in your ears," the minds of his hearers were brought back to consider what were this man's claims to the Messiahship—the highest position that man could occupy.

The interest of the congregation had been thoroughly awakened, and their hearts had been stirred with joy; but Satan was at hand to suggest doubts and unbelief, and they remem-

bered who it was that addressed them as the
blind, and the captives in bondage who needed
special aid. Many of those present were acquainted with the humble life of Jesus, as the
son of a carpenter, working at his trade with his
father Joseph. He had made no claims to distinction or greatness, and his home was among
the poor and lowly.

In marked contrast with this humble man
was the expected Messiah of the Jews. They
believed that he would come with honor and
glory, and set up, by power of arms, the throne
of David. And they murmured: This cannot be
the One who is to redeem Israel. Is not this
Jesus, the son of Joseph, whose father and mother
we know? And they refused to believe him unless he gave them some marked sign. They
opened their hearts to unbelief, and prejudice
took possession of them, and blinded their judgment, so that they made no account of the evidence already given when their hearts had
thrilled with the knowledge that it was their
Redeemer who addressed them.

But Jesus now showed them a sign of his divine character by revealing the secrets of their
minds. "And he said unto them, Ye will surely
say unto me this proverb, Physician, heal thyself; whatsoever we have heard done in Capernaum, do also here in thy country. And he
said, Verily I say unto you, No prophet is accepted in his own country. But I tell you of
a truth, many widows were in Israel in the days
of Elias, when the heaven was shut up three
years and six months, when great famine was
throughout all the land ; but unto none of them
was Elias sent, save unto Sarepta, a city of Sidon,

unto a woman that was a widow. And many lepers were in Israel in the time of Eliseus the prophet; and none of them was cleansed, saving Naaman the Syrian."

Jesus read the inmost thoughts of those who were before him, and met their questioning with this relation of events in the lives of the prophets. Those men whom God had chosen for a special and important work were not allowed to labor for a hard-hearted and unbelieving people. But those who had hearts to feel, and faith to believe, were specially favored with evidences of God's power displayed through his prophets.

By the apostasy of Israel in Elijah's day, Jesus illustrated the true state of the people whom he was addressing. The unbelief and self-exaltation of the ancient Jewish nation caused God to pass over the many widows in Israel, and the poor and afflicted there, to find an asylum for his servant among a heathen people, and to place him in the care of a heathen woman; but she who was thus especially favored had lived in strict accordance with the light she possessed. God also passed over the many lepers of Israel, because their unbelief and abuse of precious privileges placed them in a position where he could not manifest his power in their behalf. On the other hand, a heathen nobleman, who had lived faithful to his convictions of right, and fully up to his highest privileges, but who felt his great need of help, and whose heart opened to receive the lessons of Christ, was, in the sight of God, more worthy of his special favors, and was cleansed from his leprosy, as well as enlightened in regard to divine truth.

Here Jesus taught an important lesson that

should be received by all who profess his name to the end of time. It was this: That even the heathen, who live according to the best light they have, doing right so far as they are able to distinguish right from wrong, are regarded with greater favor by God than those who, having great light, make high pretensions to godliness, but whose daily lives contradict their profession. Thus Jesus stood before the Jews, calmly revealing their secret thoughts, and pressing home upon them the bitter truth of their unrighteousness. Every word cut like a knife as their corrupt lives and wicked unbelief were laid before them. They now scorned the faith and reverence with which Jesus had at first inspired them, and they refused to acknowledge that this man, who had sprung from poverty and lowliness, was other than a common man. They would own no king who came unattended by riches and honor, and who stood not at the head of imposing legions.

Their unbelief bred malice. Satan controlled their minds, and they cried out against the Saviour with wrath and hatred. The assembly broke up, and the wicked people laid hands upon Jesus, thrusting him from the synagogue, and out of their city, and would have killed him if they had been able to do so. All seemed eager for his destruction. They hurried him to the brow of a steep precipice, intending to cast him headlong from it. Shouts and maledictions filled the air. Some were casting stones and dirt at him; but suddenly he disappeared out of their midst, they knew not how, or when. Angels of God attended Jesus in the midst of that infuriated mob, and preserved his life. The heavenly messengers were by his side in the synagogue, while he was speaking; and they accompanied him when pressed and urged on by the unbelieving, infuriated Jews. These angels blinded the eyes of that maddened throng, and conducted Jesus to a place of safety.

CHAPTER VIII.

CLEANSING THE TEMPLE.

AT the time of the passover, when Jerusalem was crowded with people who had come from a distance to celebrate this great annual festival, Jesus with his disciples mingled with the gathering throng. It was early in the morning, yet large crowds were already repairing to the temple. As Jesus entered, he was indignant to find the court of the temple arranged as a cattle market and a place of general traffic. There were not only stalls for the beasts, but there were tables where the priests themselves acted as money-brokers and exchangers. It was customary for each person who attended the passover to bring a piece of money, which was paid to the priests upon entering the temple.

From the changing of foreign coins and different denominations of money to accommodate strangers, this matter of receiving these offerings had grown into a disgraceful traffic, and a source of great profit to the priests. Many came from a great distance and could not bring their sacrificial offerings. Under the plea of accommodating such persons, in the outer court were cattle, sheep, doves, and sparrows for sale at exorbitant prices. The consequent confusion indicated a noisy cattle market, rather than the sacred temple of God. There could be heard sharp bargaining, buying and selling, the lowing of cattle, the bleating of sheep, and cooing of doves, mingled with the chinking of coin, and angry disputation. A great number of beasts were annually sacrificed at the passover, which made the sales at the temple immense. The dealers realized a large profit, which was shared with the avaricious priesthood and men of authority among the Jews. These hypocritical speculators, under cover of their holy profession, practiced all manner of extortion, and made their sacred office a source of personal revenue.

The babel of voices, the noises of animals, and the shouts of their drivers created such a confusion just without the sacred precincts that the worshipers within were disturbed, and the words addressed to the Most High were drowned in the uproar that invaded the temple erected to his glory. Yet the Jews were exceedingly proud of their piety, and tenacious of outward observances and forms. They rejoiced over their temple, and regarded a word spoken in its disfavor as blasphemy. They were rigorous in the performance of ceremonies connected with it, yet allowed the love of money and power to overrule their scruples, till they were scarcely aware of the distance they had wandered from the original purity of the sacrificial ceremony instituted by God himself.

When the Lord came down upon Mount Sinai, the place was consecrated by his presence. A divine command was given Moses to put bounds around the mount and sanctify it, and the word of God was heard in warning: "Take heed to yourselves, that ye go not up into the mount, or touch the border of it. Whosoever toucheth the mount shall be surely put to death. There shall not a hand touch it, but he shall surely be stoned, or shot through; whether it be beast or man, it shall not live." All the people were cleansed and sanctified for the presence of the Lord. In direct contrast to this example, the sacred temple, dedicated to the Almighty, was made a market-place and a house of merchandise.

As the youthful Galilean entered the enclosure, he stooped and picked up a whip of small cords that had been used in driving some of the animals. Jesus ascended the steps of the temple and surveyed the scene with a calm and dignified look. He saw and heard the traffic and bartering. His expression became stern and terrible. The eyes of many turned instinctively to look at this stranger; their gaze became riveted upon him. Others followed their example till the whole multitude were regarding him with a look of mingled fear and amazement.

They felt instinctively that this man read their inmost thoughts and their hidden motives of action. Some attempted to conceal their faces as if their evil deeds were written upon their countenances to be scanned by those searching eyes.

The confusion was hushed. The sound of traffic and bargaining ceased. The silence became painful. A sense of awe overpowered the entire assembly. It was as if they were arraigned before the tribunal of God to answer for their deeds. The Majesty of Heaven stood as the Judge will stand at the last day, and every one of that vast crowd for the time acknowledged him their Master. His eye swept over the multitude, taking in every individual. His form seemed to tower above them in commanding dignity, and a divine light illuminated his countenance. He spoke, and his clear, ringing voice, echoing through the arches of the temple, was like the voice that shook Mount Sinai, of old : " My house shall be called the house of prayer; but ye have made it a den of thieves."

He slowly descended the steps, and, raising the whip, which in his hand seemed changed to a kingly scepter, bade the bargaining company to quit the sacred limits of the temple, and take hence their merchandise. With a lofty zeal, and a severity he had never before manifested, he overthrew the tables of the money-changers, and the coin fell, ringing sharply upon the marble floor. The most hardened and defiant did not presume to question his authority, but, with prompt obedience, the dignitaries of the temple, the speculating priests, the cattle traders and brokers, rushed from his presence. The most avaricious did not stop to gather up their idolized money, but fled without a thought of their ill-gotten gains.

The beasts and birds were all hurried beyond the sacred portals. A panic of fear swept over the multitude who felt the over-shadowing of Christ's divinity. Cries of terror escaped from hundreds of blanched lips as the crowd rushed headlong from the place. Jesus smote them not with the whip of cords, but, to their guilty eyes, that simple instrument seemed like gleaming, angry swords, circling in every direction, and threatening to cut them down. Even the disciples quaked with fear, and were awe-struck by the words and manner of Jesus, so unlike the usual demeanor of the meek and lowly man of Galilee. But they remembered that it was written of him, "The zeal of thine house hath eaten me up." Soon the multitude, with their cattle, their sheep, doves, and sparrows, were far removed from the temple of the Lord. The courts were free from unholy commerce, and a deep silence and solemnity settled upon the late scene of confusion. If the presence of the Lord sanctified the mount, his presence made equally sacred the temple reared to his honor.

How easily could that vast throng have resisted the authority of one man; but the power of His divinity overwhelmed them with confusion and a sense of their guilt. They had no strength to resist the divine authority of the Saviour of the world. The desecrators of God's holy place were driven from its portals by the Majesty of Heaven.

After the temple was cleansed, the demeanor of Jesus changed; the terrible majesty of his countenance gave place to an expression of tenderest sympathy. He looked after the flying crowd with eyes full of sorrow and compassion. There were some who remained, held by the irresistible attraction of his presence. They were unterrified by his awful dignity, their hearts were drawn toward him with love and hope. These people were not the great and powerful, who expected to impress him with a sense of their grandeur; they were the poor, the sick, and the afflicted.

After the buyers and sellers, and the promiscuous crowd with their merchandise, were driven out, Jesus healed the stricken ones who flocked unto him. The sick were relieved, the blind received their sight, the dumb praised God with loosened tongues, the lame leaped for joy, and demons were cast out from those they had long tormented. Mothers, pale with anxiety and watching, brought their dying infants to receive his blessing. He folded them tenderly to his bosom, and returned them to their mothers' arms well and strong.

This was a scene worthy of the temple of the Lord. He who, a short time before, had stood upon the steps like an avenging angel, had now become a messenger of mercy, soothing the sorrows of the oppressed, encouraging the despairing, relieving the suffering. Hundreds returned to their homes from the passover sound in body and enlightened in mind, who had come there feeble and desponding.

During this time the people were slowly drifting back. They had partially recovered from the panic that had seized them, but their faces expressed an irresolution and timidity that could not be concealed. They looked with amazement upon the works of Jesus, beholding more wonderful cures than had ever been accomplished before. The Jews knew that the act of Jesus in purging the temple of its sacrilegious speculators, was not the exhibition of human power. The divine authority that inspired Jesus, and lifted him above humanity, was felt and realized by them, and should have been sufficient to bring them as worshipers at his feet. But they were determined to disbelieve him. They feared that this humble Galilean would take from them their power over the people, by his greater works and super-human authority. Their haughty spirits had looked for a king who would come with great pomp and heraldry, subduing the nations of the earth, and raising them to a much loftier station than they now occupied. This Man, who came teaching humility and love, aroused their hatred and scorn.

When he arose in the majesty of his sacred mission, they were stricken with sudden fear and condemnation. But, after the spell was broken, in the hardness of their hearts, they wondered why they had been so terror-stricken and fled so precipitately from the presence of a single man. What right had this youthful Galilean to interfere with the dignitaries of the temple? After a time they returned, but did not dare at once to resume their former occupation.

The crowd were comparatively innocent, for it was by the arrangement of the chief authorities of the temple that the outer court was turned into a market-place. The great sin of desecration lay upon the priesthood, who had perverted and disgraced their sacred office. The chief priests and elders counseled among themselves as to what course should be pursued toward Jesus, and what his conduct could mean, assuming an authority greater than their own, and rebuking them openly.

They went to Jesus with a deference born of the fear that still hung over them; for they concluded that he must be a prophet sent of God to restore the sanctity of the temple. They asked him, " What sign showest thou unto us, seeing that thou doest these things?" Jesus had already given them the strongest proof of his divine commission. He knew that no evidence he could present to them would convince them that he was the Messiah if his act of cleansing the temple had failed to do so. Therefore he answered their challenge with these words, "Destroy this temple, and in three days I will raise it up." They supposed he referred to the temple at Jerusalem, and were astounded at his apparent presumption. Their unbelieving minds were unable to discern that he referred to his own body, the earthly temple of the Son of God. With indignation they answered, "Forty and six years was this temple in building, and wilt thou rear it up in three days?"

Jesus did not design that the skeptical Jews should discover the hidden meaning of his words, nor even his disciples at that time. After his resurrection they called to mind these words he had uttered, and they then understood them correctly. They remembered that he had also said that he had power to lay down his life and to take it again. Jesus was acquainted with the path his feet had entered upon, even unto the end. His words possessed a double meaning, referring to the temple at Jerusalem as well as his own material body.

Christ was the foundation and life of that temple. His crucifixion would virtually destroy it, because its services were typical of the future sacrifice of the Son of God. They pointed to the great antitype, which was Christ himself. When the Jews should accomplish their wicked purpose, and do unto him what they listed, from that day forth sacrificial offerings, and the services connected with them, would be valueless in the sight of God, for type would have met anti-type in the perfect offering of the Son of God.

The whole priesthood was established to represent the mediatorial character and work of Christ; and the entire plan of sacrificial worship was a foreshadowing of the death of the Saviour to redeem the world from sin. There would be no more need of burnt-offerings and the blood of beasts when the great event toward which they had pointed for ages was consummated. The temple was Christ's; its services and ceremonies referred directly to him. What then must have been his feelings when he found it polluted by the spirit of avarice and extortion, a place of merchandise and traffic!

When Christ was crucified, the inner vail of the temple was rent in twain from top to bottom, which event signified that the ceremonial system of the sacrificial offerings was at an end forever, that the one great and final sacrifice was made in the Lamb of God, slain for the sins of the world.

In the defilement and cleansing of the temple we have a lesson for this time. The same spirit that existed among the Jews, leading them to substitute gain for godliness, and outward pomp for inward purity, curses the Christian world to-day. It spreads like a defiling leprousy among the professed worshipers of God. Sacred things are brought down to a level with the vain matters of the world. Vice is mistaken for virtue, and righteousness for crime. Temporal business is mingled with the worship of God. Extortion and wicked speculation are practiced by those who profess to be servants of the Most High. Said the inspired apostle, " Know ye not that ye are the temple of God, and that the Spirit of God dwelleth in you ? If any man defile the temple of God, him shall God destroy ; for the temple of God is holy, which temple ye are." It is neces- sary that Jesus should occupy his temple in the human heart every day, and cleanse it from the defilement of sin.

CHAPTER IX.

NICODEMUS COMES TO CHRIST.

THE great authority Jesus had assumed in the temple, in condemning the practices of the Jewish dignitaries, was freely commented upon by Phar- isees, priests, and elders. His appearance, and the tones of his voice, together with the irresistible power he had exercised over the multitude, were such as to lead many of them to believe that he was indeed the Messiah whom they had so long expected and desired to see.

A portion of the Jews had ever been fearful of opposing one who seemed to possess any re- markable power or seemed to be influenced by God's Spirit. Many messages had been given to Israel by the mouths of prophets. Yet some of these holy men had been slain through the in- stigation of the leaders in Israel, because they had denounced the sins of those in authority. The captivity of the Jews to a heathen nation, was their punishment for refusing to be reproved of their iniquities, slighting the warnings of God, and folding their sins still closer to their hearts.

The Jews, in the days of Christ, lamented

their humiliation to the Romans, and condemned the acts of their fathers in stoning the prophets who were sent to correct them. Yet their priests and elders cherished the spirit in their hearts which would lead them to commit the same crimes.

The dignitaries of the temple consulted to-gether in regard to the conduct of Jesus, and what course was best for them to pursue. One of their number, Nicodemus, advised moderation both in their feelings and acts. He argued that, if Jesus was really invested with authority from God, it would be perilous to reject his warnings, and the manifestations of his power. He could not look upon him as an impostor, nor join the rest of the Pharisees in their derision of him. He himself had seen and heard Jesus, and his mind was much disturbed in consequence. He anxiously perused the scrolls containing the prophecies relating to the coming of the Messiah. He sought earnestly for clear light upon the subject, and the more he searched the stronger was his conviction that this man was the one described by the prophets. If he was indeed the Christ, then this was an eventful epoch in the history of the world and especially of the Jewish nation.

During the entire day after Christ had cleansed the desecrated courts of the temple, he was healing the sick and relieving the afflicted. Nicodemus had seen with what pitying compassion he had received and ministered unto the poor and the oppressed. With the demeanor of a loving father toward his suffering children, he had wrought cures and removed sorrow. No suppliant was sent unrelieved from his presence. Moth-

ers were made glad by the restoration of their
babes to health, and voices of thanksgiving had
taken the place of weeping and moans of pain.
All day, Jesus had instructed the restless, curious
people, reasoning with the scribes, and silencing
the caviling of the haughty rulers by the wisdom of his words.   Nicodemus, after seeing and
hearing these wonderful things, and after searching the prophecies that pointed to Jesus as the
looked-for Messiah, dared not disbelieve that he
was sent of God.

When night came on, Jesus, pale with the
weariness of his long-continued labors, sought
for retirement and repose in the Mount of Olives.
Here Nicodemus found him and desired a conference.   This man was rich and honored of the
Jews.   He was famous throughout Jerusalem
for his wealth, his learning and benevolence, and
especially for his liberal offerings to the temple
to carry out its sacred services.   He was also one
of the prominent members of the national council.   Yet when he came into the presence of Jesus,
a strange agitation and timidity assailed him,
which he essayed to conceal beneath an air of
composure and dignity.

He endeavored to appear as if it were an act
of condescension on the part of a learned ruler, to
seek, uninvited, an audience with a young stranger at that unseasonable hour of night.   He began
with a conciliating address, "Rabbi, we know
that thou art a teacher come from God; for no
man can do these miracles that thou doest, except
God be with him."   But instead of acknowledging
this complimentary salutation, Jesus bent his
calm and searching eye upon the speaker, as if
reading his very soul; then, with a sweet and

solemn voice, he spoke and revealed the true condition of Nicodemus. "Verily, verily I say unto you, Except a man be born again, he cannot see the kingdom of God."

The Pharisee was surprised out of his self-possession by these words, the meaning of which he partially comprehended; for he had heard John the Baptist preach repentance and baptism, and also the coming of One who should baptize with the Holy Ghost. Nicodemus had long felt that there was a want of spirituality among the Jews; that bigotry, pride, and worldly ambition guided their actions in a great measure. He had hoped for a better state of things when the Messiah should come. But he was looking for a Saviour who would set up a temporal throne in Jerusalem, and who would gather the Jewish nation under his standard, bringing the Roman power into subjection by force of arms.

This learned dignitary was a strict Pharisee. He had prided himself upon his own good works and exalted piety. He considered his daily life perfect in the sight of God, and was startled to hear Jesus speak of a kingdom too pure for him to see in his present state. His mind misgave him, yet he felt irritated by the close application of the words to his own case, and he answered as if he had understood them in the most literal sense, "How can a man be born when he is old?"

Jesus, with solemn emphasis, repeated, "Verily, verily I say unto thee, Except a man be born of the water and of the Spirit, he cannot enter into the kingdom of God." The words of Jesus could no longer be misunderstood. His listener well knew that he referred to water baptism and the

grace of God.   The power of the Holy Spirit
transforms the entire man.   This change consti-
tutes the new birth.

Many of the Jews had acknowledged John as
a prophet sent of God, and had received baptism
at his hands unto repentance; meanwhile he had
plainly taught them that his work and mission
was to prepare the way for Christ, who was the
greater light, and would complete the work which
he had begun.   Nicodemus had meditated upon
these things, and he now felt convinced that he
was in the presence of that One foretold by John.

Said Jesus, "That which is born of the flesh
is flesh; and that which is born of the Spirit is
spirit.   Marvel not that I said unto thee, Ye
must be born again.   The wind bloweth where
it listeth, and thou hearest the sound thereof, but canst not tell whence it cometh, and
whither it goeth; so is every one that is born
of the Spirit."   Jesus here seeks to impress
upon Nicodemus the positive necessity of the
influence of the Spirit of God upon the human
heart to purify it preparatory to the development of a righteous and symmetrical character.
"Out of the heart proceed evil thoughts, mur-
ders, adulteries, fornications, thefts, false witness,
blasphemies."   This fountain of the heart being
purified, the stream thereof becomes pure.

This new birth looks mysterious to Nicodemus.
He asks, "How can these things be?"   Jesus, bidding him marvel not, uses the wind as an illustration of his meaning.   It is heard among the
branches of the trees, and rustling the leaves
and flowers, yet it is invisible to the eye, and
from whence it comes and whither it goeth, no
man knoweth.   So is the experience of every one

who is born of the Spirit. The mind is an invisible agent of God to produce tangible results. Its influence is powerful, and governs the actions of men. If purified from all evil, it is the motive power of good. The regenerating Spirit of God, taking possession of the mind, transforms the life; wicked thoughts are put away, evil deeds are renounced, love, peace, and humility take the place of anger, envy, and strife. That power which no human eye can see, has created a new being in the image of God.

The necessity of the new birth was not so strongly impressed upon Nicodemus as the manner of its accomplishment. Jesus reproves him, asking if he, a master and teacher in Israel, an expounder of the prophecies, can be ignorant of these things. Has he read those sacred writings in vain, that he has failed to understand from them that the heart must be cleansed from its natural defilement by the Spirit of God before it can be fit for the kingdom of Heaven? Christ made no reference here to the resurrection of the body from the grave, when a nation shall be born in a day, but he was speaking in regard to the inward work of grace upon the unregenerate heart.

He had just been engaged in cleansing the temple, by driving from its sacred courts those who had degraded it to a place of traffic and extortion. Not one who had fled that day from the presence of Jesus was fitted by the grace of God to be connected with the sacred services of the temple. True, there were some honorable men among the Pharisees, who deeply regretted the evils that were corrupting the Jewish nation and desecrating its religious rites. They also saw that traditions and useless forms had taken

the place of true holiness, but they were powerless to prevent these growing evils.

Jesus had commenced his work by striking
directly at the selfish, avaricious spirit of the
Jews, showing that while professing to be the
children of Abraham they refused to follow his
example. They were zealous for an external appearance of righteousness while they neglected
internal holiness. They were sticklers for the
letter of the law, while they grossly transgressed
its spirit every day. The law forbade hatred
and theft, yet Christ declared that the Jews had
made his Father's house a den of thieves. The
great necessity of the people was a new moral
birth, a removal of the sins that polluted them,
a renewal of true knowledge and genuine holiness.

This purifying of the temple illustrates the
work that must be accomplished in every one who
would secure eternal life. Patiently Jesus unfolded the plan of salvation to Nicodemus, showing him how the Holy Spirit brings light and
transforming power to every soul that is born of
the Spirit. Like the wind, which is invisible—
yet the effects of which are plainly seen and
felt—is the baptism of the Spirit of God upon
the heart, revealing itself in every action of him
who experiences its saving power.

He explained how Christ, the burden-bearer,
lifts the burden from the oppressed soul, and bids
it rejoice in deliverance from bondage. Joy takes
the place of sadness, and the countenance reflects
the light of Heaven. Yet no one sees the hand
that lifts the burden, nor beholds the light descend from the courts of God. The blessing
comes when the soul, by faith, surrenders itself to

the Lord. This mystery exceeds human knowledge, yet he who thus passes from death to life
realizes that it is a divine truth.

The conversion of the soul through faith in
Christ was but dimly comprehended by Nicodemus, who had been accustomed to consider cold
formality and rigid services as true religion. The
great Teacher explained that his mission upon
earth was not to set up a temporal kingdom, emu-
lating the pomp and display of the world, but to
establish the reign of peace and love, to bring
men to the Father through the mediatorial agency of his Son.

Nicodemus was bewildered. Said Jesus, "If I
have told you earthly things and ye believe not,
how shall ye believe if I tell you of heavenly
things?" If Nicodemus could not receive his
teachings illustrating the work of grace upon the
human heart, as represented by the figure of the
wind, how could he comprehend the character of
his glorious heavenly kingdom should he explain
it to him? Not discerning the nature of Christ's
work on earth, he could not understand his work
in Heaven. Jesus referred Nicodemus to the
prophecies of David and Ezekiel:—

"And I will give them one heart, and I will
put a new spirit within you; and I will take the
stony heart out of their flesh, and will give them
an heart of flesh; that they may walk in my statutes, and keep mine ordinances, and do them;
and they shall be my people, and I will be their
God." "And they shall come thither, and they
shall take away all the detestable things thereof
and all the abominations thereof from thence."
"Therefore, I will judge you, O house of Israel,
every one according to his ways, saith the Lord

God. Repent, and turn yourselves from all your transgressions; so iniquity shall not be your ruin. Cast away from you all your transgressions, whereby ye have transgressed; and make you a new heart and a new spirit." "Create in me a clean heart, O God; and renew a right spirit within me. Cast me not away from thy presence; and take not thy holy spirit from me. Restore unto me the joy of thy salvation; and uphold me with thy free spirit. Then will I teach transgressors thy ways; and sinners shall be converted unto thee." "A new heart also will I give you, and a new spirit will I put within you; and I will take away the stony heart out of your flesh, and I will give you an heart of flesh."

The learned Nicodemus had read these pointed prophecies with a clouded mind, but now he began to comprehend their true meaning, and to understand that even a man as just and honorable as himself must experience a new birth through Jesus Christ, as the only condition upon which he could be saved, and secure an entrance into the kingdom of God. Jesus spoke positively that unless a man is born again he cannot discern the kingdom which Christ came upon earth to set up. Rigid precision in obeying the law would entitle no man to enter the kingdom of Heaven.

There must be a new birth, a new mind through the operation of the Spirit of God, which purifies the life and ennobles the character. This connection with God fits man for the glorious kingdom of Heaven. No human invention can ever find a remedy for the sinning soul. Only by repentance and humiliation, a submission to the divine requirements, can the work of grace be performed. Iniquity is so offensive in the sight of God, whom the sinner has so long insulted and wronged, that a repentance commensurate with the character of the sins committed often produces an agony of spirit hard to bear.

Nothing less than a practical acceptance and application of divine truth opens the kingdom of God to man. Only a pure and lowly heart, obedient and loving, firm in the faith and service of the Most High, can enter there. Jesus also declares that as " Moses lifted up the serpent in the wilderness, even so must the Son of Man be lifted up, that whosoever believeth in him should not perish, but have eternal life." The serpent in the wilderness was lifted upon a pole before the people, that all who had been stung unto death by the fiery serpent might look upon this brazen serpent, a symbol of Christ, and be instantly healed. But they must look in faith, or it would be of no avail. Just so must men look upon the Son of Man as their Saviour unto eternal life. Man had separated himself from God by sin. Christ brought his divinity to earth, veiled by humanity, in order to rescue man from his lost condition. Human nature is vile, and man's character must be changed before it can harmonize with the pure and holy in God's immortal kingdom. This transformation is the new birth.

If man by faith takes hold of the divine love of God, he becomes a new creature through Christ Jesus. The world is overcome, human nature is subdued, and Satan is vanquished. In this important sermon to Nicodemus, Jesus unfolded before this noble Pharisee the whole plan of salvation, and his mission to the world. In none of his subsequent discourses did the Saviour explain so thoroughly, step by step, the work necessary to be done in the human heart, if it would inherit the kingdom of Heaven. He traced man's salvation directly to the love of the Father, which led him to give his Son unto death that man might be saved.

Jesus was acquainted with the soil into which he cast the seeds of truth. For three years there was little apparent fruit. Nicodemus was never an enemy to Jesus, but he did not publicly acknowledge him. He was weighing matters with an exactitude that accorded with his nature. He watched the life-work of Jesus with intense interest. He pondered over his teachings and beheld his mighty works. The raising of Lazarus from the dead was an evidence of his Messiahship that could not be disputed in the mind of the learned Jew.

Once, when the Sanhedrim council was planning the most effectual way of bringing about the condemnation and death of Jesus, his authoritative voice was heard in protest, "Doth our law judge any man, before it hear him, and know what he doeth?" This brought a sharp rebuff from the chief priest, "Art thou also of Galilee? Search and look, for out of Galilee ariseth no prophet." Yet the council dispersed, for they could not obtain a unanimous assent to the condemnation of Jesus.

The Jews suspected both Joseph and Nicodemus of being in sympathy with the Teacher of Galilee, and these men were not summoned when the council met that decided the fate of Jesus.

The words spoken at night to a single man in the
lonely mountain were not lost. When Nicodemus saw Jesus upon the cross, hanging like a
malefactor between heaven and earth, yet praying for his murderers; when he witnessed the
commotion of nature, in that awful hour when
the sun was hidden and the earth reeled in space,
when the rocks were split in sunder and the vail
of the temple rent in twain; then he remembered
the solemn teaching in the mountain: "As Moses
lifted up the serpent in the wilderness, even so
must the Son of Man be lifted up."

The scales fell from his eyes, and faith took the
place of doubt and uncertainty. Beams of light
streamed from the secret interview in the mountain and illuminated the cross of the Saviour. In
that time of discouragement and danger, when
the hearts of the disciples were failing them
through doubt and fear, Joseph of Arimathea, a
secret disciple of Jesus, came forward and obtained the Lord's body from Pilate, and Nicodemus, who at the first came to Jesus by night,
brought a hundred pounds' weight of myrrh and
aloes. These two men with their own hands
performed the last sacred rites, and laid the body
of the Saviour in a new sepulchre where never
man lay before. These lofty rulers of the Jews
mingled their tears together over the sacred form
of the dead.

Now, when the disciples were scattered and
discouraged, Nicodemus came boldly to the front.
He was rich, and he employed his wealth to sustain the infant church of Christ, that the Jews
thought would be blotted out with the death of
Jesus. He who had been so cautious and questioning, now, in the time of peril, was firm as the

granite rock, encouraging the flagging faith of
the followers of Christ, and furnishing means to
carry on the cause. He was defrauded, persecuted, and stigmatized by those who had paid
him reverence in other days. He became poor in
this world's goods, yet he faltered not in the faith
that had its beginning in that secret night conference with the young Galilean.

Nicodemus related to John the story of that
interview, and his inspired pen recorded it for
the instruction of millions. The vital truths there
taught are as important to-day as they were that
solemn night in the shadowy mountain, when the
mighty Jewish ruler came to learn the way of
life from the lowly carpenter of Nazareth.

"When therefore the Lord knew how the
Pharisees had heard that Jesus made and baptized more disciples than John (though Jesus
himself baptized not, but his disciples), he left
Judea, and departed again into Galilee."

The prejudice of the Jews was aroused because
the disciples of Jesus did not use the exact words
of John in the rite of baptism. John baptized
unto repentance, but the disciples of Jesus, on
profession of the faith, baptized in the name of
the Father, Son, and Holy Spirit. The teachings
of John were in perfect harmony with those of
Jesus, yet his disciples became jealous for fear his
influence was diminishing. A dispute arose between them and the disciples of Jesus in regard
to the form of words proper to use at baptism,
and finally as to the right of the latter to baptize at all.

John's disciples came to him with their griev-
ances, saying, "Rabbi, he that was with thee beyond Jordan, to whom thou barest witness, be-

hold, the same baptizeth, and all men come to him." John possessed the common infirmities of human nature. In this matter he was subjected to a severe trial. His influence as the prophet of God had been greater than any other man's, until the ministry of Christ commenced; but the fame of this new teacher was drawing the attention of all people, and in consequence, the popularity of John was waning. His disciples brought to him the true statement of the case, Jesus baptizeth, and all men come to him.

John stood in a dangerous position; had he justified the jealousy of his disciples by a word of sympathy or encouragement in their murmurings, a serious division would have been created. But the noble and unselfish spirit of the prophet shone forth in the answer he gave to his followers:—

"A man can receive nothing, except it be given him from Heaven. Ye yourselves bear me witness, that I said, I am not the Christ, but that I am sent before him. He that hath the bride is the bridegroom; but the friend of the bridegroom, which standeth and heareth him, rejoiceth greatly because of the bridegroom's voice; this my joy therefore is fulfilled. He must increase, but I must decrease."

Had John manifested disappointment or grief at being superseded by Jesus; had he allowed his sympathies to be aroused in his own favor, when he perceived that his power over the people was waning; had he for a moment lost sight of his mission in this hour of temptation, the result would have been disastrous to the establishment of the Christian church. The seeds of dis-

sension would have been sown, anarchy would
have sprung up, and the cause of God would
have languished for want of proper workers.

But John, irrespective of personal interest,
stood up in defense of Jesus, testifying to his superiority as the Promised One of Israel, whose
way he had come to prepare. He identified
himself fully with the cause of Christ, and declared that his greatest joy was in its success.
Then, rising above all worldly considerations, he
gave this remarkable testimony—almost the coun-
terpart of that which Jesus had given to Nicodemus in their secret interview :—

"He that cometh from above is above all; he
that is of the earth is earthly, and speaketh of
the earth; he that cometh from Heaven is above
all. And what he hath seen and heard, that he
testifieth; and no man receiveth his testimony.
He that hath received his testimony hath set to
his seal that God is true. For he whom God
hath sent speaketh the words of God; for God
giveth not the Spirit by measure unto him. The
Father loveth the Son, and hath given all things
into his hand. He that believeth on the Son
hath everlasting life; and he that believeth not
the Son shall not see life; but the wrath of God
abideth on him."

What a sermon was this to the Pharisees,
clearing the way for the ministry of Christ.
The same spirit that actuated Jesus, controlled
the mind of John the Baptist. Their testimony
corresponded; their lives were given to the same
reformatory work. The prophet points to the
Saviour as the Sun of Righteousness rising with
splendor, and soon to eclipse his own light, then

growing pale and dim in the glory of a greater light. John, by his unselfish joy in the successful ministry of Jesus, presents to the world the truest type of nobility ever exhibited by mortal man. It carries a lesson of submission and self-sacrifice to those whom God has placed in responsible positions. It teaches them never to appropriate to themselves undue honor, nor let the spirit of rivalry disgrace the cause of God. The true Christian should vindicate the right at the expense of all personal considerations.

The news that had been carried to John concerning the success of Jesus, was also borne to Jerusalem, and there created against him jealousy, envy, and hatred. Jesus knew the hard hearts and darkened minds of the Pharisees, and that they would spare no pains to create a division between his own disciples and those of John that would greatly injure the work, so he quietly ceased to baptize and withdrew to Galilee. He knew that the storm was gathering which was soon to sweep away the noblest prophet God had ever given to the world. He wished to avoid all division of feeling in the great work before him, and, for the time, removed from that region for the purpose of allaying all excitement detrimental to the cause of God.

Here is a lesson to the followers of Christ, that they should take every proper precaution to avoid disagreement; for in every division of interest, resulting in disputation and unhappy differences in the church, souls are lost that might have been saved in the kingdom of Heaven. In the occurrence of a religious crisis, leading men who profess to be God's instruments should follow the example of the great Master and that of thĕ noble prophet John. They should stand firm and united in defense of the truth, while they carefully labor to avoid all injurious dissensions.

CHAPTER X.

THE WOMAN OF SAMARIA.

As Jesus pursued his way to Galilee, his course lay through Samaria. He embraced every opportunity to teach as he traveled on foot from place to place. The Saviour was weary, and he sat on Jacob's well to rest, while his disciples went in search of food with which to refresh themselves and their Master. As he sat there alone, a woman of Samaria drew near as if unconscious of his presence; but his eye was upon her, and after she had drawn the water he asked her to give him a drink.

The Samaritan woman was surprised at this request from a Jew, and answered, "How is it that thou, being a Jew, askest drink of me, which am a woman of Samaria? for the Jews have no dealings with the Samaritans." Jesus answered, "If thou knewest the gift of God, and who it is that saith to thee, Give me to drink, thou wouldst have asked of him, and he would have given thee living water." He here referred to the divine grace which he alone could bestow, and which is as living water, purifying, refreshing, and invigorating the soul.

But the woman's understanding did not comprehend the meaning of Christ; she supposed that he was speaking of the well before them, and answered, "Sir, thou hast nothing to draw with, and the well is deep ; from whence then hast thou that living water ? Art thou greater than our father Jacob, which gave us the well, and drank thereof himself ?" She saw before her only a weary, thirsty traveler, wayworn and dusty; and her mind instinctively compared this humble stranger with the great and worthy Jacob.

Jesus did not immediately satisfy the woman in regard to himself, but with solemn earnestness said, "Whosoever drinketh of this water shall thirst again; but whosoever drinketh of the water that I shall give him shall never thirst; but the water that I shall give him shall be in him a well of water springing up into everlasting life."

The woman looked upon him with wondering attention; he had succeeded in arousing her interest and inspiring respect for himself. She now perceived that it was not the water of Jacob's well to which Jesus alluded, for of this she used continually, drinking, and thirsting again. With remarkable faith she asked him to give her the water of which he spoke, that she might not thirst nor come to draw from the well.

Jesus did not intend to convey the idea that simply one draught of the water of life would satisfy the receiver, but that whoever is united with Christ, has within his soul a living fountain from which to draw strength and grace sufficient for all emergencies. Words and deeds of righteousness flow from it and refresh the hearts of others, as well as the soul from which it springs. Jesus Christ, the never-failing source of this fountain, cheers the life and brightens the path of

all who come to him for aid. Love to God, the
satisfying hope of Heaven, springs up in good
works unto eternal life.

Jesus now abruptly changed the subject of
conversation, and bade her call her husband.
The woman answered frankly that she had no
husband. Jesus had now approached the desired
point where he could convince her that he had
the power to read her life history, although previously unacquainted with her. He addressed
her thus : " Thou hast well said, I have no husband ; for thou hast had five husbands ; and he '
whom thou now hast is not thy husband ; in that
saidst thou truly."

Jesus had a double object in view ; he wished
to arouse her conscience as to the sin of her manner of life, as well as to prove to her that a sight
wiser than human eyes had read the secrets of
her life. But the woman, although not fully realizing the guilt of her manner of living, was
greatly astonished that this stranger should possess such knowledge. With profound reverence
she said, " Sir, I perceive that thou art a prophet."
Her personal feelings were now lost in anxiety
concerning religious matters. She proceeded,
" Our fathers worshiped in this mountain ; and
ye say, that in Jerusalem is the place where men
ought to worship."

Just in sight was Mount Gerizim, its temple
demolished, and only the altar remaining. The
place of worship had been a subject of contention between the Jews and Samaritans. The
latter people had once belonged to Israel, but
had become divided from them because of their
transgressions in neglecting to obey the statutes
of God. The Lord suffered them to be overcome

by an idolatrous nation, whose religion had gradually contaminated their own. Still preserving their reverence for the true God, they represented him by images of wood and stone, before which they bowed in worship.

When the temple was rebuilt at Jerusalem, the Samaritans wished to join the Jews in its erection. This privilege was refused them, and, in consequence, a bitter animosity sprang up between the two people, which resulted in the Samaritans building a rival temple on Mount Gerizim, where they worshiped according to the ceremonies that God gave unto Moses, but mingled with their worship the taint of idolatry. But disasters attended the Samaritans, their temple was destroyed by the enemy, and they seemed to be under a curse.

They were forced to believe that God was punishing them for their apostasy. They determined to reform, and solicited teachers from the Jews to instruct them in the true religion. Through this teaching, their views of God and his requirements became clearer, and their religious service resembled more nearly that of the Jews. But to a certain degree they still clung to their idolatry, and there was a lack of harmony between them and the Jews. The Samaritans would not respect the temple of worship at Jerusalem, and refused to admit that it was the true place of worship.

Jesus answered the woman by saying that the time was at hand when they should neither worship the Father in that mountain nor in Jerusalem. Said he, " Ye worship ye know not what; we know what we worship; for salvation is of the Jews. But the hour cometh, and

now is, when the true worshipers shall worship
the Father in spirit and in truth; for the Father
seeketh such to worship him. God is a Spirit;
and they that worship him must worship him in
spirit and in truth."

This was a plain statement that the Jews
were more nearly correct in the principles of
their religion than any other nation. Jesus also
alluded to the faith of the Samaritans being amal-
gamated with the worship of graven images.
True, they held that these idols were only to remind them of the living God, the Ruler of the
universe; but, nevertheless, the people were led
to reverence these inanimate figures.

Jesus, who was the foundation of the old dispensation, identified himself with the Jews, sanc-
tioning their views of God and his government.
He opened great and important truths before this
woman. He declared to her that the time had
arrived when the true worshipers need not seek
a holy mountain nor sacred temple, but were to
worship the Father in spirit and in truth. Religion was not to be confined to external forms
and ceremonies, but was to be throned in the
heart, purifying the life and actuating to good
works.

The words of truth that fell from the lips of
the divine Teacher stirred the heart of his listener. Never had she heard such sentiments, either
from the priests of her own people or the Jews.
The impressive teachings of this stranger carried
her mind back to the prophecies concerning the
promised Christ; for the Samaritans as well as
the Jews looked for his coming. "I know that
Messias cometh," said she; "when he is come,

he will tell us all things." Jesus answered, " I
that speak unto thee am he."

Blessed woman of Samaria ! She had felt during the conference as if in the presence of divinity; now she gladly acknowledged her Lord.
She required of him no miracle, as did the
Jews, to prove his divine character. She accepted his assertion, feeling perfect confidence in his
words, and not questioning the holy influence
that emanated from him.

The disciples, returning from their errand, were
surprised to find their Master conversing with a
Samaritan woman; yet they did not inquire her
errand, nor ask Jesus why he talked with her.
The woman left her water-pot, forgetting her errand to the well, and went her way into the city,
saying to all whom she met, and the men of the
city, "Come, see a man who told me all things
that ever I did. Is not this the Christ ?"

This woman, though so sinful, was still in a
more favorable condition to become an heir of
Christ's kingdom than those of the Jews who
made exalted professions of piety, yet trusted
their salvation to the observance of outward
forms and ceremonies. They felt that they
needed no Saviour and no teacher. But this
poor woman hungered and thirsted after righteousness. She was eager for instruction, waiting
for the consolation of Israel, and ready to accept
the Saviour when he was revealed. Jesus, who
explained not his character to the proud and
skeptical Pharisees and rulers, declared himself
to this humble person who was ready to believe
on him.

As yet he had not taken the refreshing draught
that he desired, nor tasted the food that his

disciples had brought him. The salvation of perishing souls so absorbed his attention that his physical wants were forgotten. But his followers anxiously entreated him to eat. Still contemplating the great object of his mission, he answered them, "I have meat to eat that ye know not of." His disciples were surprised, and began to wonder among themselves who could have brought him food in their absence. But Jesus explained, "My meat is to do the will of Him that sent me, and to finish his work."

It was not temporal food alone that sustained him in his arduous life; but the accomplishment of the work which he left the royal courts of Heaven to perform, strengthened him for his labors, and lifted him above the necessities of humanity. To minister to a soul hungering and thirsting for the truth was more satisfying to the Son of Man than eating or drinking. He pitied sinners; his heart went out in sympathy for the poor Samaritans, who felt their ignorance and wretchedness, and were eagerly looking for the advent of Messiah, who would enlighten them and teach them the true religion.

The Jews felt secure in their self-righteousness, they desired no enlightenment; but they looked for a Saviour who would release them from the bondage of the Roman yoke, and exalt them above their oppressors. They could not receive one who reproved their sins and condemned their selfish, hypocritical lives. They looked for a Messiah who would reign with worldly power and glory, confound and defeat the Romans, and exalt the Jews to a nation of princes.

Jesus saw a field of labor among the Samaritans. Before him lay the fields of grain, their tender green lit by the golden sunlight. Viewing the beautiful scene, he employed it as a symbol, " Say not ye there are yet four months, and then cometh harvest ? Behold, I say unto you, Lift up your eyes, and look on the fields; for they are white already to harvest." He here referred to the gospel field, to the work of Christianity among the poor, despised Samaritans. His hand reached out to gather them into the garner; they were ready for the harvest.

The Saviour was above all prejudice of nation or people; he was willing to extend the blessings and privileges of the Jews to all who would accept the light which he came to the world to bring. It caused him great joy to behold even one soul reaching out to him from the night of spiritual blindness. That which Jesus had withheld from the Jews and enjoined upon his disciples to keep secret, was distinctly opened before the inquiring woman of Samaria; for He who knew all things perceived that she would make a right use of her knowledge and be the means of leading others to the true faith.

It was not merely the fact that Jesus told her concerning the secrets of her life which inspired the confidence of this woman in him, but it was also his look and his solemn words that reached her soul and convinced her that he was a superior being. At the same time she felt that he was her friend, pitying and loving her. This is the character of the world's Redeemer; while he condemned her life of sin, he directed her to his divine grace as the sure and perfect remedy. The pitying love of the Saviour is not confined to sect or party.

As the woman of Samaria hastened back to

her friends, publishing as she went the wonderful news, many left the highway and the town to go and ascertain if she indeed spoke the truth. Numbers of the citizens left their employments and hastened to Jacob's well to see and hear this remarkable man. They surrounded Jesus and listened attentively to his instruction. They plied him with questions, and eagerly received his explanation of matters that had perplexed their understandings. They were like a people in great darkness tracing up a sudden ray that had pierced their gloom and which they were eager to follow to its source, that they might bask in the light and warmth of day.

The Samaritans were attracted and interested by the teachings of Jesus. But they were not satisfied with this short conference; they were anxious to hear more and to have their fellow-citizens also listen to this wonderful teacher. They begged him to tarry with them and instruct them. For two days he remained in Samaria teaching the people. Many believed on him and accepted his words. Jesus was a Jew, yet he mingled freely with these Samaritans, setting at naught the custom and bigotry of his nation. He had already commenced to break down the partition wall between Jew and Gentile, and preach salvation to the world.

These Samaritan listeners were in darkness and superstition; but they were not contented with their condition, and the words of Jesus relieved them of many doubts and uncertainties that had harassed their minds. Many who had come from curiosity to see and hear this remarkable person were convicted of the truth of his teachings, and acknowledged him as their Saviour. Eagerly they listened to the words he spoke in reference to the kingdom of God. In their new joy they said unto the woman, "Now we believe, not because of thy saying; for we have heard him ourselves, and know that this is indeed the Christ, the Saviour of the world."

Christ, at the very beginning of his ministry, openly rebuked the superficial morality and ostentatious piety of the Jews. He did not conform his life and his work to their customs and regulations. He was not influenced by their unreasonable prejudices against the Gentiles. He, on the contrary, sternly rebuked their conceit and selfish seclusion. The Pharisees rejected Christ. They ignored his miracles and the truthful simplicity of his character. They refused to recognize his pure and elevated spirituality and all evidences of his divinity. They scornfully demanded of him a sign that they might know that he was indeed the Son of God.

But the Samaritans asked no sign, and Jesus performed no miracles among them; yet they received his teachings, were convicted of their great need of a Saviour, and accepted him as their Redeemer. They were therefore in a much more favorable position before God than the Jewish nation, with its pride and vanity, blind bigotry, narrow prejudice, and bitter hatred of every other people on the earth. Jesus, in face of all these prejudices, accepted the hospitality of this despised people, slept under their roofs, ate with them at their tables—partaking of the food prepared and served by their hands—taught in their streets, and treated them with the greatest kindness and courtesy.

In the temple at Jerusalem there was a partition wall separating the outer court from the inner one. Gentiles were permitted to enter the outer court, but it was only lawful for the Jews to penetrate to the inner inclosure. Had a Samaritan passed this sacred boundary, the temple would have been desecrated, and his life would have paid the penalty of its pollution. But Jesus, who was virtually the foundation and originator of the temple—the services and ceremonies of which were but a type of his great sacrifice, pointing to him as the Son of God—encircled the Gentiles with his human arm of sympathy and association, while, with his divine arm of grace and power, he brought to them the salvation which the Jews refused to accept.

Jesus had spent several months in Judea, giving the rulers of Israel a fair opportunity of proving his character as the Saviour of the world. He had performed many mighty works in their midst; but he was still treated by them with suspicion and jealousy. In passing through Samaria on his way to Galilee, his reception among the Samaritans, and the eagerness with which they listened to his teachings, were in marked contrast with the incredulity of the Jews, who had misinterpreted the prophecies of Daniel, Zechariah, and Ezekiel, confusing the first advent of Christ with his second majestic and glorious appearing.

Their blindness was in consequence of their lofty pride and arrogance, looking only for worldly station and emolument. They urged their interpretation of the prophecies upon the Samaritans, who believed that Messiah was to come not only as a Redeemer of the Jews, but of the world. This caused great bitterness toward them from

the Jews, who contended that Christ would come
to exalt Israel and to bring into subjection all
other nations.   This perversion of the prophecies
led the Samaritans to discard all the sacred writings but those of Moses.   But their minds were
open to enlightenment, and they received the
Saviour's instruction joyfully and accepted him
as the promised Messiah.

CHAPTER XI.

THE CENTURION'S SON.

AFTER laboring two days with the Samaritans,
Jesus left them to continue his journey to Galilee.   He made no tarry at Nazareth, where he
had spent his youth and early manhood.   His
reception in the synagogue there, when he announced himself as the Anointed One, was so
unfavorable that he decided to seek more fruitful fields, to preach to ears that would listen, and
to hearts that would receive his message.   He
declared to his disciples that a prophet hath no
honor in his own country.   This saying sets forth
that natural reluctance which many people have
to acknowledge any wonderfully admirable development in one who has unostentatiously lived
in their midst, and whom they have intimately
known from childhood.   At the same time, these
same persons might become wildly excited over
the pretensions of a stranger and an adventurer.
   The miracle that Jesus had performed in Cana
prepared the way for his cordial reception.   The
'people who had returned from the passover had

brought back the report of his marvelous cleansing of the desecrated temple, followed by his miracles of healing the sick and restoring sight to the blind and hearing to the deaf. The judgment passed upon his acts by the dignitaries of the temple, opened his way at Galilee; for many of the people lamented the abuse of the temple and the lofty arrogance of the priests, and hoped that this man, who had the power to put these rulers to flight, might indeed be the looked-for Deliverer.

The news that Jesus had returned from Judea to Cana soon spread throughout Galilee and the region round about. It reached the ears of a nobleman in Capernaum, who was a Jew of some honor. He was much interested in what he had heard of the power of Jesus to heal the sick, for he had a son suffering with disease. The father had consulted the most learned physicians among the Jews, and they had pronounced the case incurable, and told him that his son must soon die.

But when he heard that Jesus was in Galilee his heart was encouraged; for he believed that one who could miraculously change water into wine, and drive out the desecrators of the temple, could raise his son to health even from the brink of the grave. Capernaum was quite a distance from Cana, and the centurion feared that, if he left his home to seek Jesus and present his plea to him, the child, who was very low, might die in his absence. Yet he dared not trust this errand to a servant; for he hoped that the prayers of a fond parent might touch the heart of the great Physician with pity, and induce him to accompany the father to the bedside of his dying son.

He went to Cana, hastening for fear of being too late. Forcing a passage through the crowd that surrounded Jesus, he at length stood before him. But his faith faltered when he saw only a plainly dressed man, dusty and worn with travel. He doubted that this person could do what he had come to ask of him; yet he determined to make a trial. He secured a hearing from Jesus, told him his errand, and besought the Saviour to accompany him to his home for the purpose of healing his son. But Jesus already knew of his sorrow. Even before the centurion had left his home, the pitying Redeemer had read the father's grief, and his great heart of love had gone out in sympathy for the suffering child.

But he was also aware that the father had made conditions in his mind concerning his belief in the Saviour. Unless his petition should be granted he would not have faith in him as the Messiah. While the father waited in an agony of suspense, Jesus addressed him, "Except ye see signs and wonders, ye will not believe." He here revealed the superficial faith of the centurion, that would lead him to accept or reject Christ according as he did or did not perform the work required of him.

Jesus designed, not only to heal the child, but to illuminate the darkened mind of the father. He saw unbelief struggling with his faith. He knew that this man had sought his help as a last and only hope. In this centurion he saw represented the condition of many of his nation. They were interested in Jesus from selfish motives; they desired some special benefit that they hoped to receive through his power, but they were ignorant as to their spiritual disease, and saw not their terrible need of divine grace, but staked their faith on the granting of some temporal favor. Jesus met this case as illustrating the position of many of the Jewish people. He contrasted this questioning unbelief with the faith of the Samaritans, who were ready to receive him as a teacher sent by God, and to accept him as the promised Messiah without a sign or miracle to establish his divinity.

The father's soul was stirred to its depths with the thought that his doubts might cost him the life of his son. The words of Jesus had the desired effect; the centurion saw that his motives in seeking the Saviour were purely selfish; his vacillating faith appeared before him in its true light; he realized that he was indeed in the presence of One who could read the hearts of men, and to whom all things were possible. This thought brings his suffering child to his mind with new vividness, and he cries out in an agony of supplication, "Sir, come down ere my child die!"

He fears that while he has been doubting and questioning, death may have closed the scene. This was enough. The father in his need seizes the merits of Jesus as his Saviour. In demanding him to come down ere his child dies, he clings alone to the strength of Jesus as his only hope. His faith is as imperative as was that of Jacob, when, wrestling with the mighty angel, he cried, "I will not let thee go, except thou bless me!"

Jesus responds to the demands of the centurion by commanding him, "Go thy way; thy son liveth." These brief and simple words thrill through the heart of the father; he feels the holy power of the speaker in every tone. In-

stead of going to Capernaum, Jesus, by a flash of
divine telegraphy, sends the message of healing
to the bedside of the suffering son. He dismisses
the suppliant, who, with unspeakable gratitude,
and perfect faith in the words of the Saviour,
turns his steps homeward with a peace and joy
he has never felt before.

At the same hour the watchers stood around
the dying child, in the distant home of the centurion. The form that had been so strong and
symmetrical in its youthful grace, was now worn
and emaciated. The hollow cheeks burned with
a hectic fire. Suddenly the fever leaves him, intelligence beams from his eyes, his mind becomes
clear, and health and strength return to his body.
The fever has left him in the very heat of the day.
The attendants behold the change with amazement; the family is summoned, and great is the
rejoicing. No signs of his malady linger about
the child, his burning flesh has become soft and
moist, and he sinks into the peaceful slumber of
childhood.

Meanwhile the father hastens on his way with
a hopeful heart. He went to Jesus with grief
and trembling. He leaves him in joy and confidence. He feels the solemn assurance that he
has talked with One whose power is unlimited.
No doubt crosses his mind that Jesus has really
healed his son at Capernaum. While still some
distance from home, his servants meet him with
the glad tidings that his son has recovered.
With a light heart he hurries on, and, as he ap-
proaches his house, is met by the child, bounding
out to receive him, radiant in health and beauty.
He clasps him to his heart as one restored from

the dead, and thanks God again and again for this miraculous restoration.

The centurion and all his household become disciples of Jesus. Thus their affliction was sanctified to the conversion of the entire family. They published this miracle through all Capernaum, and thus opened the way for Christ's further labors there. Many of his most wonderful works were done at that place.

This case of the centurion should be a lesson to all the followers of Christ. He would have them place implicit faith in him as their Redeemer, ready and willing to save all who come unto him. But he sometimes delays bestowing his precious gifts, in order to impress our hearts with a sense of our deep need of that true piety which entitles us to ask of him what we will. We are to lay by the selfishness that is frequently the sole cause of seeking him, and, confessing our helplessness and bitter need, trust in his promises. He invites all to come unto him who are weary and heavy-laden, and he will give them rest.

CHAPTER XII.

JESUS AT BETHESDA.

"AFTER this there was a feast of the Jews; and Jesus went up to Jerusalem. Now there is at Jerusalem by the sheep market a pool, which is called in the Hebrew tongue Bethesda, having five porches. In these lay a great multitude of impotent folk, of blind, halt, withered, waiting for

the moving of the water. For an angel went
down at a certain season into the pool, and
troubled the water; whosoever then first after
the troubling of the water stepped in was made
whole of whatsoever disease he had."

Jesus did not hold himself aloof from the poor,
the suffering, and sinful. His great heart of love
went out in yearning tenderness for wretched
objects who needed his help. He was acquainted
with the sufferers who had learned to look forward to the period when it was thought that .the
waters were agitated by a supernatural power.
Many suffering from different maladies visited
the pool; but so great was the crowd at the appointed time, that they rushed forward, tramp-
ling under foot men, women, and children weaker
than themselves.

Hundreds were pressed back and could not
get near the water. Many disappointed sufferers, who had, by great pains and effort, succeeded
in reaching the pool, died upon its brink without
being able to make the first plunge into its
depths. Shelters had been erected about the
place that the sick might be protected from the
scorching rays of the sun and the chilliness of the
night. Some wretched sufferers spent their
nights in the porches, and would drag their diseased bodies to the favored spot day after day in
the vain hope of obtaining relief.

One man had been afflicted by an incurable disease for thirty-eight years, and he had repeatedly
visited the pool. Those who pitied his helplessness would bear him to and fro at the time when
the waters were supposed to be troubled. But
those stronger than himself would rush in before
him and seize the opportunity that he coveted.

Thus the poor, palsied sufferer waited by the pool day and night, hoping that the favored moment would at length come when he could plunge into the water and be healed. His persistent efforts toward this object, and the doubt and anxiety of his mind, were fast wearing away the poor remnant of his strength.

Jesus visited this retreat of misery, and his eye rested upon this helpless invalid. The poor creature was weak and despairing, but as the looked-for moment arrived, he gathered his feeble energies in a last effort to reach the water, but, just as he had almost gained his object, another stepped in before him. He crept back to his pallet to die. But a pitying face bends over him, saying, "Wilt thou be made whole?" The desponding man looked up, thinking it might be some one who had come to assist him into the pool; but the faint glow of encouragement faded out of his heart when he remembered that it was too late, his opportunity for that time was gone, and, in his state of sickness and exposure, he could scarcely hope that he might live to see another.

He turned away wearily, saying, "Sir, I have no man, when the water is troubled, to put me into the pool; but while I am coming, another steppeth down before me." Poor man! how could he hope to contend successfully with the selfish, scrambling crowd! Jesus did not ask this wretched sufferer to exercise faith in him; but with a voice of command said, "Rise, take up thy bed, and walk." A sudden vigor was communicated to the paralyzed cripple. His whole being was stirred with a healing power, new blood and strength leaped into every limb and member. He bounded to his feet in obedience to the

Saviour's command, and stooped to take up his
bed, which was only a simple rug and blanket.
As he straightened himself again, with a sense
of delight at standing upon his feet after so many
years of helpless infirmity, he looked around for
his deliverer, but he was nowhere to be seen.
Jesus was lost in the crowd, and the restored paralytic feared that he would not know him again
if he should see him. He was disappointed, for
he longed to pour forth his gratitude to the stranger. As he hurried on toward Jerusalem, with
firm, free step, praising God as he went, and rejoicing in his new-found strength, he met the
Pharisees, and immediately related to them the
wonderful cure he had experienced. He was
surprised at the coolness with which they listened
to his story.

Presently they interrupted him by asking why
he was carrying that bed on the Sabbath day.
They sternly reminded him that it was not lawful for him to bear burdens upon the Lord's day.
In his joy the man had forgotten that it was the
Sabbath; yet he felt no condemnation for obeying the command of one who had power from
God to perform so wonderful a miracle. He answered boldly, "He that made me whole, the
same said unto me, Take up thy bed, and walk."
The Pharisees were not delighted at the cure
which had been effected upon this poor invalid of
thirty-eight years. They overlooked the object
of the wondrous miracle, and, with their charac-
teristic bigotry, seized upon the act as a violation
of the Sabbath law.

They excused the restored man from blame,
but appeared shocked at the guilt of him who
had assumed the responsibility of ordering a man

to take up his bed upon the Sabbath day. They
asked him who it was that had done this thing,
but he could not enlighten them on that subject.
These rulers knew very well that only one person had shown himself able to do this deed; but
they wished to get direct proof that it was Jesus,
for they then hoped to be able to condemn him
as a Sabbath-breaker. They considered that he
had not only broken the law in healing the sick
man on the Sabbath, but had committed an act of
sacrilege in bidding him take up his bed and
bear it away.

Jesus did not come into the world to lessen
the dignity of the law, but to exalt it. The Jews
had perverted it by their traditions and miscon-
ceptions. They had made it a yoke of bondage.
Their meaningless exactions and requirements
had become a by-word among all other nations.
Especially was the Sabbath hedged in by all
manner of senseless restrictions which made that
holy day almost unendurable. A Jew was not
allowed to kindle a fire upon the Sabbath, nor
even to light a candle on that day. The views of
the people were so narrow that they had become
slaves to their own useless regulations. As a consequence, they were dependent upon the Gentiles
to do many services which their rules forbade
them to do for themselves.

They did not reflect that if these necessary duties of life were sins they were full as guilty in
employing others to perform them as in doing
them themselves. They thought salvation was
restricted to the Jews, and the condition of all
others, being entirely hopeless, could neither be
improved nor made worse. But a just God has
given no commandment which cannot be con-

sistently kept by all. His laws sanction no meaningless usages nor clumsy restrictions.

Soon after, Jesus met the man he had healed in the temple. He had come to bring a trespass-offering, a sin-offering, and a thank-offering for the great mercy he had received. Jesus, finding him among the worshipers, made himself known to him. The great Physician addressed him with a timely warning, "Behold, thou art made whole; sin no more, lest a worse thing come unto thee." He who had suffered for thirty-eight years, as the result, in part, of his own dissipation, was thus plainly warned to avoid the sins that had caused him such suffering.

The healed man was overjoyed to behold his deliverer, and, ignorant of the malice which the Jews held against Jesus, informed the Pharisees, who had before questioned him, that this was he who had wrought the wondrous cure. The Jewish dignitaries had only waited for proof that it was Jesus; from the first they had been confident that it could be no other. Now, a great uproar ensued in the court of the temple; for they sought to slay Jesus, but were prevented by the people, many of whom recognized in him a friend who had healed them from their infirmities and relieved their sorrows.

A controversy now took place in regard to the true claims of the Sabbath law. Jesus had purposely chosen the Sabbath day upon which to perform the miracle at the pool. He could have healed the sick man as well on any other day of the week; also he might have simply cured him, and avoided arousing the indignation of the Jews, by bidding him take up his bed and depart. But a wise purpose underlay every act of Christ's

life on earth; everything he did was important
in itself and its teaching. He came to vindicate
his Father's law and make it honorable. The
Sabbath, instead of being the blessing it was designed to be, had become a curse through the
added requirements of the Jews. Jesus wished
to rid it of these incumbrances and leave it standing upon its own holy dignity.

Therefore he chose the Sabbath for this special
work. He selected the worst case among the afflicted ones at the pool of Bethesda upon whom
to exercise his miraculous healing power, and
bade him carry his bed through the city in order
to publish the great work that had been wrought
upon him, to call the attention of the people to
his case, to the circumstances attending his cure,
and to Him by whom it had been accomplished.
This would raise the question of what it was
lawful to do on the Sabbath day, and would
give him an opportunity to denounce the narrow prejudice and restrictions of the Jews in regard to the Lord's day, and declare their bigotry
and traditions void.

Jesus stated to them that the work of relieving the sufferings of the afflicted was in harmony with the Sabbath law, whether it was relative
to the salvation of souls or the removal of physical pain. Such work was in harmony with that
of God's angels, who were ever descending and
ascending between Heaven and earth to minister to suffering humanity. Jesus answered their
accusations by declaring, "My Father worketh
hitherto, and I work." All days are God's, in
which to carry out his great plans for the human race. If the Jews' interpretation of the
law was correct, then Jehovah was at fault,

whose work had upheld and quickened creation since first he laid the foundations of the earth, when the morning stars sang together, and all the sons of God shouted for joy. He who pronounced his work good, and established the institution of the Sabbath to commemorate its completion, must put a period to his labor, and stop the never-ending routine of the universe.

Should God forbid the sun to do its office upon the Sabbath, cut off its genial rays from warming the earth and nourishing vegetation? Must the system of worlds stand still through that holy day? Should he command the babbling brooks to stay their course from watering the fields and forests, and bid the advancing and receding waves to still their ceaseless ebbing and flowing? Must the wheat and corn stop growing, and the ripening cluster defer its purple bloom for a single day? Must the waving trees and the delicate flowers put forth no bud nor blossom on the Sabbath?

Surely in such a case man would miss the fruit of the earth and the blessings that make life desirable. Nature must continue her unvarying course; God must not stay his hand a single moment, or man would faint and die. And, in a like proportion, man has a labor to perform on this day. The necessities of life must be attended to, the sick must be cared for, the wants of the needy must be met. God does not hold him guiltless who stays his hand from relieving the suffering on the Sabbath day. The holy Sabbath was made for man, and acts of mercy and benevolence are always in order upon that day. God does not desire his creatures to suffer an hour's pain that may be relieved upon the Sabbath or any other day.

Jesus sought to impress upon the narrow minds of the Jews a sense of the folly of their view of the Sabbath. He showed them that God's work never ceases. It is even greater upon the Sabbath than upon ordinary occasions, for at that time his people leave their usual employments and spend the time in prayerful meditation and worship. They ask more favors of him upon the Sabbath than upon other days, they demand his special attention, they crave his choicest blessings, they offer importunate prayers for special favors. God does not wait for the Sabbath to pass before he grants those requests, but he deals to the petitioners, with judicious wisdom, whatever is best for them to have.

Heaven's work never ceases for a moment, and men should never rest from doing good. The Sabbath law forbids labor on the sanctified rest-day of the Lord. The toil that gains a livelihood must cease; no labor for worldly pleasure or profit is lawful upon the Lord's day; but the work of Christ in healing the sick did honor to the holy Sabbath. Jesus claimed equal rights with God in doing a work equally sacred and of the same character with that which engaged his Father in Heaven. But the Pharisees were still more incensed, because he had not only broken the law, according to their understanding, but added to this offense the heinous sin of declaring himself equal with God. Nothing but the interference of the people prevented the Jewish authorities from slaying him on the spot. "Then answered Jesus and said unto them, Verily, verily, I say unto you, The Son can do nothing of

himself, but what he seeth the Father do; for
what things soever he doeth, these also doeth
the Son likewise. For the Father loveth the
Son, and sheweth him all things that himself
doeth; and he will show him greater works than
these, that ye may marvel. For as the Father
raiseth up the dead, and quickeneth them; even
so the Son quickeneth whom he will."

Here Jesus elevated himself to his true station
before the Jews, and declared himself to be the
the Son of God. He then, in mild and dignified
language, instructed them regarding the Sabbath.
He told them that the rest-day which Jehovah
had sanctified and set apart for a special purpose,
after he had completed the work of creation, was
not intended to be a period of useless inactivity.
As God ceased his labor of creating, and rested
upon that day and blessed it, so man was to leave
the occupation of his daily life, and devote those
sacred hours to healthful rest, to worship, and to
holy deeds.

The rulers of the people could not answer these
elevated truths that were brought home to their
consciences. They had no arguments with which
to meet them; they could only cite their customs
and traditions, and these seemed weak and vapid
compared with the strong arguments that Jesus
had drawn from the work of God and the un-
ceasing round of nature. Had they felt any desire to receive light, their hearts would have
been convinced that Jesus spoke the truth. But
they evaded the points he made concerning the
Sabbath, and sought to stir up anger against him
because he had made himself equal with God.
The fury of the rulers knew no bounds, and it

was with difficulty that they were prevented from seizing upon Jesus to put him to death.

But the people were not excited to violence, and put the rulers to shame by the candor with which they listened to the words of Jesus. They justified him in healing the poor sufferer who had been afflicted for thirty-eight years. So the priests and elders were obliged to restrain their hatred for the time, and wait for a more favorable opportunity to carry out their evil designs.

Jesus declared that he could do nothing of himself " but what he seeth the Father do." His relationship with God forbade him from working independent of him, and he could do nothing against his will. What a rebuke were these words to men, and especially to those who were calling the Son of God to task for the very work that he was sent upon earth to do. They had separated themselves from God by wicked acts, and, in their pride and vanity, were moving independent of him, feeling sufficient in themselves for all things, and realizing no need of a higher wisdom than their own, to aid them in the direction of their acts.

Few realize the full force of Christ's words in regard to his connection with the Father. They teach man that he should consider himself inseperably bound to his Heavenly Parent, that, whatever position he may occupy, he is responsible to God, who holds all destinies in his hands. He has appointed man to do his work, he has endowed him with faculties and means for that purpose, and so long as man is faithful to his high stewardship, he may feel warranted in claiming the blessings and promises of his Master. But if, when raised to a position of sacred trust, he becomes exalted in his own estimation,—depending upon his own wisdom and power, taking affairs into his own hands, and separating himself from Him whom he professes to serve,—God will call him to an account for his unauthorized acts; he has not worked in unison with his Commander.

Jesus now stood before the Jews in his true character. He declared that whatsoever things the Father did, those did also the Son in like manner, by the exercise of a like power, and with like results. He also promised those who heard him that they should witness greater acts than he had yet performed in healing the sick, the lame, and the blind. The Sadducees were in opposition to the Pharisees regarding the resurrection of the dead. The former claimed that there would be no resurrection of the body. But Jesus tells them that one of the greatest works of his Father is raising up the dead, and even so the Son of God has power in himself to raise from the dead. "Marvel not," said he, "at this; for the hour is coming, in the which all that are in the graves shall hear his voice, and shall come forth; they that have done good, unto the resurrection of life; and they that have done evil, unto the resurrection of damnation."

The humble Nazarene asserts his real nobility. He rises above humanity, throws off the guise of sin and shame, and stands revealed, the Honored of the angels, the Son of God, equal with the Creator of the universe. The rulers of the Jews, and the listening multitude are spell-bound before his mighty truths, and the lofty dignity of his bearing. No man had ever spoken words like these, nor borne himself with such a kingly majesty. His utterances were clear and plain, fully declaring his mission and the duty of the world. "For the Father judgeth no man, but hath committed all judgment unto the Son, that all men should honor the Son, even as they honor the Father. He that honoreth not the Son honoreth not the Father who hath sent him. Verily, verily, I say unto you, He that heareth my word, and believeth on Him that sent me, hath everlasting life, and shall not come into condemnation; but is passed from death unto life. Verily, verily, I say unto you, The hour is coming, and now is, when the dead shall hear the voice of the Son of God, and they that hear shall live. For as the Father hath life in himself, so hath he given to the Son to have life in himself; and hath given him authority to execute judgment also, because he is the Son of man."

Here Jesus throws back upon the rulers their accusations against him, and their attempts to prescribe his work, and to judge, by their narrow bigotry, his acts of mercy and benevolence. He declared himself their Judge, and the Judge of all the world. When he came to earth as the Redeemer, it was given into his hands, and all men are responsible unto him. He took the burden of humanity that he might save men from the consequences of their sins. He is in one their Advocate and Judge. Having tasted the very dregs of human affliction and temptation, he is qualified to understand the frailties and sins of men, and to pronounce judgment upon them. Therefore, the Father has given this work into the hands of his Son, knowing that He who victoriously withstood the temptations of Satan, in behalf of man, will be all-wise, just, and gracious in his dealing with him.

The words of Jesus were more impressive because the controversy had risen very high. He was virtually summoned before the dignitaries of the Jews to be tried for his life. He, the Lord of the Sabbath, was arraigned before an earthly tribunal, to answer to the charge of breaking the Sabbath law. When he so boldly made known his mission and work, his judges looked upon him with mingled astonishment and rage, but his words were unanswerable and they could not condemn him.

He denied the right of the Pharisees to question him or to interfere with his business. The Jewish system invested them with no such authority; their claims were based upon their own pride and arrogance. He refused to plead guilty to any wrong or submit to being catechised by them.

After presenting before them these grand truths concerning his work in connection with the Father, he binds his assertions with the testimonies that have been borne of him: "I can of mine own self do nothing; as I hear, I judge; and my judgment is just; because I seek not mine own will, but the will of the Father which hath sent me. If I bear witness of myself, my witness is not true. There is another that beareth witness of me; and I know that the witness which he witnesseth of me is true. Ye sent unto John, and he bare witness unto the truth. But I receive not testimony from man; but these things I say, that ye might be saved. He was a burning and a shining light; and ye were willing for a season to rejoice in his light." From his sublime height he reads the secrets of their hearts and reminds them that for a time they had accepted John as a prophet of God and rejoiced in the message that he brought them. He affirms that the mission of John was solely to prepare the way of himself, whom the prophet testified was the Christ, the Redeemer of the world.

But no man could witness concerning the mysterious connection of Jesus with the Father; human knowledge cannot reach the courts of Heaven. Jesus assures them that he does not refer to the testimony of John in order to sustain his claims, but only that his persecutors may be convinced of their blindness and inconsistency in defiantly opposing him whom John had stated was the Son of God. They were not in ignorance regarding the evidence of John, for they had sent a deputy to him who had brought back his statement of the baptism of Jesus and the wonderful manifestations of God at that time.

Jesus speaks of John that they may see how, in rejecting himself, they also reject the prophet whom they had received with joy. He further declares : "But I have greater witness than that of John; for the works which the Father hath given me to finish, the same works that I do, bear witness of me, that the Father hath sent me." Had not the heavens opened and light from the throne of God encircled him with glory, while the voice of Jehovah proclaimed, "This is my beloved Son, in whom I am well pleased"? Besides all this, his own works declared his divinity. He who had been arraigned as a Sabbath-breaker stood before his accusers clothed with divine grace, and uttering words that pierced them like arrows of truth. Instead of apologizing for the act of which they complained, or explaining his purpose in doing it, he turns upon the rulers, and the accused becomes the accuser.

He rebukes them for the hardness of their hearts, for the blind ignorance with which they read the Scriptures, while they boasted of their superiority over every other people. They who assume to be teachers of the Scriptures and expounders of the law are themselves basely ignorant of its claims. He denounces their worldliness, their love of praise and power, their avarice and want of compassion. He charges them with disbelieving the Scriptures which they profess to revere, carrying out its forms and ceremonies while ignoring the great principles of truth that are the foundation of the law. He declares that they have rejected the word of God, inasmuch as they have rejected him whom God has sent. He commands them to "search the Scriptures; for in them ye think ye have eternal life; and they are they which testify of me."

The truth spoken by Jesus collided with their prejudices and customs, and they cast it from them, hardening their hearts against it. They refused to listen to the teachings of Christ, because those teachings directly condemned their cherished sins. Had the Son of Man come flattering their pride and justifying their iniquity, they would have hastened to do him honor. Said Jesus, "I am come in my Father's name, and ye receive me not; if another shall come in his own name, him ye will receive." Pretenders, who could present no evidence of divine authority, might arise, who by prophesying smooth things, and gratifying the vanity of the rich and unsanctified, might secure their firm allegiance. These false prophets would lead their followers to eternal ruin.

Jesus declared that there was no necessity for him to accuse them to the Father, for Moses, whom they professed to believe, had already accused them. "For," said he, "had ye believed Moses, ye would have believed me; for he wrote of me. But if ye believe not his writings, how shall ye believe my words?" Jesus knew that the Jews were determined to take his life, yet in this discourse he fully explained to them his Sonship, the relation he bore to the Father and his equality with him. This left them without an excuse for their blind opposition and insane rage against the Saviour. But, though baffled in their designs, and overawed by his divine eloquence and truth, the murderous hatred of the priests and elders was not quenched. Fear seized them, for they could not close their understanding to the convincing power which attended the ministry of Christ. But they were so bound by the chains of pride and arrogance that they rejected the evidence of his divine power, resisted his appeals, and locked themselves in darkness.

They had signally failed to subvert the authority of Jesus, or to turn from him the respect and attention of the people, many of whom were powerfully affected, and deeply convicted, by his impressive discourse. His mighty works had first arrested their notice and aroused their wonder, and when his searching words disclosed his true character, they were ready to acknowledge his divine authority. On the other hand, his words had thrilled the hearts of the rulers with condemnation for their course. He had pressed their guilt home upon their consciences, yet this only made them more bitter against him, and they were fully determined to take his life. They sent messengers all over the country to warn the people against Jesus, whom they denounced as an impostor. Spies were sent to watch him and report what he said and did. The precious Saviour was now most surely standing under the shadow of the cross.

CHAPTER XIII.

JESUS AT CAPERNAUM.

AFTER the work of healing that Jesus had performed upon the Sabbath at the Pool of Bethesda, the malice of the leading Jews was so kindled against him that they plotted against his life, and it was no longer safe for him to remain in Jerusalem. Therefore he repaired to Galilee, making Capernaum the scene of his labors. At this place he taught; and upon the Sabbaths, multitudes gathered to listen to his doctrine. Here his way seemed to be unobstructed, although spies were upon his track, watching for something whereof they might accuse him.

The hearts of the common people were open to receive his divine instruction. His heart was overflowing with sympathy for suffering humanity, and it was with joy that he saw men respond to his teachings of love and benevolence. His hearers were charmed with the eloquent simplicity with which he preached the truth. His illustrations were drawn from scenes transpiring in their every-day lives. He adapted his language to all classes and conditions of men.

Jesus did not go to Capernaum to avoid society nor to find rest from his labors. Capernaum was a great thoroughfare of travel; people from many countries passed through the city, or tarried there for rest in their journeyings to and fro. Here the great Teacher could meet all nations and all ranks. He could give lessons that would not only be received by those present, but would be carried to other countries and into many households. Investigations of the prophecies would thus be excited, notice would be directed to the Saviour, and his work and mission would be brought before the world.

Here he had a better opportunity than elsewhere of meeting the representatives of all classes, as they mingled together, every one intent upon his own errand. The rich who were courted for their wealth could here be reached by his ministrations, as well as the poor and needy. Christ presented himself to the people as the Saviour of the world. As soon as it was known that he was in Capernaum, multitudes crowded to hear his words of heavenly wisdom. Jesus had taken his disciples up into a mountain for a little season of retirement, but when he saw the people flocking to him he had not the heart to turn them away.

The feast of the Jews was near, and many had come in from the region about Jerusalem, seeking Jesus, of whose wonderful miracles they had heard. The sick and the afflicted were brought to him, and he healed their maladies. As he witnessed the joy of those whom he had relieved, his own heart of love rejoiced with those who had received his blessing. He made many families happy by restoring their suffering ones to health. He caused light to dawn upon households that had been plunged into the shadows of affliction. The sorrowing were comforted, the ignorant instructed, and hope was wakened in the hearts of the despairing.

The people received the message that he brought them, and believed his words. None were more willing to accept the truth than the poor and humble, who were not separated from their Saviour by vanity and pride, the treasures of this world, or the praise of men. They found in him a consolation for all their toil and privations. He turned none away. He was touched with tender pity for the distress of those who sought his aid, and they left his presence, bearing evidence in their own persons of his healing and life-giving power. The hearts of the people went out in reverential love for their Benefactor, and he was a partaker of their joy. His labors while in Capernaum resulted in great good, and many were led to believe on him. His acts of matchless mercy won the hearts of the multitudes.

The scribes and Pharisees were confounded; their purposes in regard to Jesus were defeated. They had listened to his teachings in order to catch him in his words, and turn the minds of the people from him to themselves. They knew that since the ministry of Jesus had commenced, their own influence over the people had greatly decreased. The sympathetic hearts of the multitude accepted lessons of love and kindly benevolence in preference to the cold forms and rigid ceremonies exacted by the priests.

Although the Pharisees were astonished by the miracles that Jesus wrought, they were all the more anxious to remove one, who, by his great power, was most dangerous to their claims and pretensions.

Bodily diseases, however aggravated and apparently hopeless, were met and baffled by his divine power; but the disease of the soul, fastened in unbelief and blind prejudice, took firmer hold upon those who closed their eyes against the light. The most powerful evidence that could be produced only strengthened their opposition. Leprosy and palsy were not so terrible as bigotry and unbelief. Jesus turned from the teachers of Israel, and their chains of darkness and skepticism tightened about them.

The inhabitants of Capernaum had been greatly astonished by the sudden and effectual cure of the ruler's son at a word from Jesus, when he was more than twenty miles distant from the sufferer. They were rejoiced to learn that he who possessed such miraculous power was in their own city. On the Sabbath day, the synagogue where he spoke was packed with people, and yet many who desired to enter were unable to do so. As usual, a great number came through curiosity, but there were many who earnestly desired to learn regarding the gospel of the kingdom of God.

All who heard him were astonished, "for he taught them as one having authority, and not as the scribes." His words were a demonstration of the Spirit of God, and they struck home to the souls of men with divine power. The teaching of the scribes and elders was cold and formal, like a lesson learned by rote. They explained the law as a matter of custom, but no authority from God sanctified their utterances, no holy inspiration stirred their own hearts and those of their hearers.

Jesus had nothing to do with the various subjects of dissension among the Jews. His words were so simple that a child could understand them, yet lofty enough in their grand simplicity to charm the highest mind with their noble truths. He spoke of a new kingdom which he came to set up among them, in opposition to the kingdom of this world, and of his power to wrest from Satan his dominion, and deliver the captives bound by his power.

There was a man in the synagogue who was possessed of the spirit of Satan. He broke in upon the discourse of Jesus with a piercing shriek, that chilled the blood of the hearers with a nameless terror. "Let us alone!" he cried. "What have we to do with thee, thou Jesus of Nazareth? Art thou come to destroy us? I know thee, who thou art, the Holy One of God!"

Devils even believed and trembled, but the Israel of God had closed their eyes and ears to divine evidences, and knew not the time of their visitation. Satan's object in leading his wretched victim to the synagogue, was to distract the attention of the people from Jesus to the paroxysms of the poor sufferer and prevent the words of truth from reaching the hearts of the people. But the darkened understanding of the man comprehended that the teachings of Jesus were from Heaven. The power of divinity aroused the terror of the demon which controlled his mind, and a conflict ensued between it and his remnant of reason.

As the victim realized that the Healer was near to release him, his heart was aroused to long for freedom from Satan's power. The demon resisted this power and held control over the poor wretch who was wrestling against him. The sufferer tried to appeal to Jesus for help, but when he opened his lips, the demon put words in his mouth so that he shrieked out in an agony of fear, "Let us alone! what have we to do with thee, thou Jesus of Nazareth?" The darkened reason of the poor man partially comprehended that he was in the presence of one who could free him from the bondage that had so long enslaved him; but when he sought to come within reach of that mighty hand, another's will held him back, another's words found utterance through him.

By his own sinful course, this man had placed himself on the enemy's ground, and Satan had taken possession of all his faculties, so that when the gloom of his understanding was pierced by feeble rays of light from the Saviour's presence, the conflict between his desire for freedom and the devil's power threw him into terrible contortions, and drew from him unearthly cries. The demon exerted all his hellish power to retain the control of his victim. To lose ground here would be to give Jesus a victory. He who had, in his own person, conquered the prince of the power of darkness in the wilderness of temptation, was now again brought face to face with his enemy.

It seemed that the tortured man must lose his life in the terrible struggle with the demon that had been the ruin of his manhood. Only one power could break this cruel tyranny. Jesus spoke with a voice of authority and set the captive free. The demoniac spirit made a last effort to rend the life from his victim before he was forced to depart. Then the man who had been possessed stood before the wondering people happy in the freedom of self-possession. In the synagogue on the Sabbath day, before the assembled congregation, the prince of darkness was again met and conquered. And even the demon had testified to the divine power of the Saviour, crying, "Thou Jesus of Nazareth! Art thou come to destroy us? I know thee, who thou art, the Holy One of God!"

The man whose reason was thus suddenly restored praised God for his deliverance. The eye that had so lately glared with the fire of insanity, now beamed with intelligence and overflowed with grateful tears. The people were dumb with amazement. As soon as they recovered speech they marveled one with another, saying, "What a word is this! for with authority and power he commandeth the unclean spirits, and they come out!"

It was not according to the will of God that this man should be visited with so terrible an affliction as to be delivered wholly into the hands of Satan. The secret source of his calamity, which had made him a fearful spectacle to his friends and a burden to himself, was in his own life. The pleasures of sin had fascinated him, the path of dissipation had looked bright and tempting, he had thought to make life a grand carnival. He did not dream of becoming a disgust and terror to the world and the reproach of his family. He thought his time could be spent in innocent folly; but once on the downward path, his feet rapidly descended till he had broken the laws of health and morality.

Intemperance and frivolity chained his senses, the fine qualities of his mind were perverted, and Satan stepped in and took absolute control of him.

Remorse came too late, and though he would then have sacrificed wealth and pleasure to regain his lost manhood, he had become helpless in the hands of the evil one. Satan had allured that young man with many charming presentations; he had cloaked vice with a flowery mantle that the victim might clasp it to his breast; but when his object was once accomplished and the wretched man was in his power, the fiend had become relentless in his cruelty, and terrible in his fierce and angry visitations. So it is ever with those who succumb to evil; the fascinating pleasure of their early career ends in the darkness of despair, or the madness of a lost and ruined soul.

But he who conquered the arch-enemy in the wilderness, wrested this writhing captive from the grasp of Satan. Jesus well knew that although assuming another form, this demon was the same evil spirit that had tempted him in the wilderness. Satan seeks by various devices to gain his object. The same spirit that saw and recognized the Saviour, and cried out to him, "Let us alone! What have we to do with thee?" possessed the wicked Jews who rejected Christ and scorned his teachings. But with them he assumed an air of piety and learning, seeking to deceive them as to their real motives in refusing the Saviour.

Jesus then retired from the synagogue while the people were still spell-bound with wonder and admiration. This miracle was then followed by another quite as wonderful. Jesus sought the house of Peter for a little rest; but there was no rest for the Son of Man. He was told that the mother of Peter's wife was sick with a fever. His sympathetic heart was at once called out to relieve the suffering woman. He rebuked the disease, and it was at once removed from her. She rose from the bed, filled with joy and gratitude, and ministered with willing hands to the wants of the Master and his disciples.

These miracles and works of healing were spread abroad throughout the city. Yet these acts of mercy only made the bitterness of the Pharisees more intense. They closely watched all the movements of Jesus, seeking for cause to accuse him. Their influence prevented many from applying to Jesus for relief from their infirmities upon the Sabbath day. They feared being stigmatized as transgressors of the law. But no sooner had the sun passed out of sight in the west than a great commotion ensued. The diseased flocked to Jesus from every quarter. Those who had sufficient strength came by themselves, but a much larger number were borne by their friends to the great Physician.

They were in every condition of helplessness and approaching death. Some were burning with fevers, others were paralyzed, stricken with dropsy, blind, deaf, and lame. And in the distance was heard the pitiful cry of the leper, Unclean! Unclean! as he stretched his decaying hands toward the Healer. The work of Jesus commenced when the first afflicted one was brought before him. The supplicants were healed by a word from his lips or a touch of his hand. With gratitude and rejoicing they re-

turned to gladden with their enlightened minds
and healthy bodies the homes that they had so
recently left as helpless invalids.

Those who had carefully borne them from their
couches to the presence of Jesus returned with
them, weeping tears of joy, and shouting the
praises of the Saviour. Little children were not
overlooked, but the puny sufferers were handed
back to their happy mothers rosy with life and
health. These living evidences of the divine
power of Jesus created a great excitement in all
that region. Never before had Capernaum witnessed a day like this. The air was filled with
the voice of triumph and shouts of deliverance.

The heart of the blessed Saviour, who had
worked so great cures, was joyful in the joy he
had awakened in the hearts of suffering humanity. He had healed every one who had applied
to him for help. His great love for man was
stirred to its very depths as he witnessed the
suffering of those who had come to him, and he
rejoiced in his power to restore them to health
and happiness.

CHAPTER XIV.

CHOOSING THE DISCIPLES.

THE disciples had not yet fully joined themselves to Jesus to be co-laborers with him. They
had witnessed many of his miracles, and their
minds had been enlightened by the discourses
they had heard from his lips; but they had not
entirely left their employment as fishermen.

Their hearts were filled with grief by the death of John, and they were troubled with conflicting thoughts. If the life of John had been permitted to end so ingloriously, what would be the fate of their Master, when the scribes and Pharisees were so bitter against him? Amid their doubt and fear, it was a relief for them to return once more to their fishing, and, for a brief space, find in their old employment a diversion from their anxiety.

Jesus frequently dismissed them to visit their homes and rest; but he gently though firmly resisted all their entreaties that he should himself rest. At night he found the seasons of prayer for which he could not claim time during the day. While the world he had come to save was wrapped in slumber, the Redeemer, in the sanctuary of the mountains, would intercede for man with the Father. Often he spent entire nights in prayer and meditation, going back in the morning to his active work.

It was morning on the Lake of Galilee, and the fishermen were in their boats, weary with a long night of fruitless toil. But, with the dawn, Simon discovered the form of Jesus walking upon the beach. He directed the attention of his disciples to their beloved Teacher, and they all pulled for the shore. It seemed impossible for the Saviour to obtain any retirement. Already the crowd had gathered thickly about him as he walked on the shore. The sick and afflicted were brought for him to relieve. At length the people had pressed so closely about him that they scarcely left him comfortable standing-room. It was just at this time that the fishermen were nearing the shore. Jesus requested Peter to take him in his boat, and, immediately, upon entering it, directed the disciple to pull out a little from the land. Then, being removed a short distance from the people, he was in a better position to be seen and heard by them, and from the boat upon the lake he preached in regard to the mysteries of the kingdom of God. His language was simple and earnest, appealing to the minds of the people with convincing power.

The discourse ended, Jesus turned to Peter and bade him launch out into the deep, and let down his net for a draught. But Peter was thoroughly disheartened; not only was he sorrowful because of the death of John the Baptist, and his mind tortured with unbelief in consequence of that event, but he was discouraged in regard to his temporal prospects. He had been unsuccessful in his fishing, and the past night had been spent in unavailing labor. It was therefore in a desponding tone that he replied to the command of Jesus: "Master, we have toiled all night, and have taken nothing; nevertheless, at thy word I will let down the net."

He called his brother to his aid, and together they let down the net into the deep water, as Jesus had directed. When they came to draw in the net they were unable to do so because of the great quantity of fish it contained, and they were obliged to summon James and John to their aid before they could draw in the net and unload it. When this was done the boat was so heavily laden that there was danger of its sinking.

Peter had seen Jesus perform wonderful miracles, but none made so strong an impression upon his mind as this miraculous draught of fish, after a night of disappointment. The unbelief

and discouragement that had been oppressing
the disciples through the long, weary night, now
gave way to awe and amazement. Peter was
thrilled with a sense of the divine power of his
Master. He felt ashamed of his sinful unbelief.
He knew that he was in the presence of the Son
of God, and felt unworthy to be in such companionship. He impulsively flung himself at the
feet of Jesus, crying, "Depart from me; for I am
a sinful man, O Lord!" But even as he spoke,
he was clinging to the feet of Jesus, and would
not have been willing for the Saviour to take
him at his word, even if he had attempted to
do so.

But Jesus understood the conflicting emotions
of the impetuous disciple, and said to him, "Fear
not; from henceforth thou shalt catch men."
Similar words were afterward addressed to the
three other fishermen, when they were all upon
the shore. As they were busily employed in
mending their nets, which had been broken by
the great weight of the fish they had taken, Jesus said to them, "Follow me, and I will make
you fishers of men." Immediately after this they
left their nets and boats and followed the Saviour. These humble fishermen recognized the
divine authority of Jesus, and forthwith gave up
their regular occupation and left their worldly
possessions in obedience to the command of their
Lord.

These four disciples were more closely associated with Jesus in his earthly life than any of
the others. Christ, the light of the world, was
abundantly able to qualify these unlearned fishermen of Galilee for the high commission he had

chosen for them. The words spoken to these
lowly men were of mighty signification ; they
were to influence the world through all time.
It seemed a simple thing for Jesus to call those
poor, discouraged men to follow him ; but it was
an event productive of tremendous results ; it
was to shake the world. The quickening power
of God, enlightening the minds of those illiterate
fishermen, was to enable them to spread the doctrines of Christ far and wide, and others were to
take up the task, until it would reach all lands,
and be taught in all ages, winning many to salvation. Thus would the poor fishermen of Galilee be, indeed, "fishers of men."

Jesus did not oppose education. The highest
culture, if sanctified by the love and fear of God,
receives his approbation. An objection is sometimes brought against education because Jesus
chose ignorant fishermen for his disciples. But
these men were subject to his refining influence
for three years, and the Saviour was the most
perfect educator the world has ever known. The
Prince of Life did not choose the learned lawyers,
the scribes and elders, for his disciples, because
they would not follow him. Therefore he chose
the humble peasants for his helpers. The rich
and educated among the Jews were exalted by
their own worldly wisdom and self-righteousness,
and felt all-sufficient in themselves, realizing no
special need of a Redeemer. Their characters
were fixed, and they would not receive the
teachings of Christ. But the humble fishermen
were rejoiced to be connected with the Saviour,
and become co-laborers with him.

As Jesus passed on his way to Jerusalem, he
saw Matthew engaged in his business of tax-

gathering. He was a Jew, but when he became a publican his brethren despised him. The Jewish people were continually irritated on account of the Roman yoke. That a despised and heathen nation should collect tribute of them was a constant reminder that their power and glory as an independent nation had departed. Their indignation knew no bounds when one of their own people so far forgot the honor of his exalted race as to accept the office of tax-gatherer.

Those who thus assisted to sustain the Roman authority were considered apostate. The Jews regarded it as degrading to associate in any way with a publican. They considered the office identical with oppression and extortion. But the mind of Jesus was not molded after the prejudices of the Pharisees. He looked below the surface and read the heart. His divine eye saw in Matthew one whom he could use for the establishment of his church. This man had listened to the teachings of Christ, and had been attracted to him. His heart was full of reverence for the Saviour, but the thought had never entered the mind of Matthew that this great Teacher would condescend to notice him, much less choose him as a disciple. Therefore his astonishment was great when Jesus addressed him with the words, " Follow me."

Without a doubtful murmur, or question as to his consequent pecuniary loss, Matthew rose up and followed his Master, and united his interest with the few disciples of Jesus. The despised publican felt that the Saviour had bestowed upon him an honor which he did not deserve. He gave no thought to the lucrative business he had exchanged for poverty and fatigue. It was enough that he would be in the presence of Christ, that he could learn wisdom and goodness from his lips, behold his marvelous works, and be a co-laborer with him in his arduous toil.

Matthew was wealthy, but he was willing to sacrifice all for his Master. He had many friends and acquaintances whom he was anxious should become followers of Jesus, and he was desirous that they should have an opportunity to meet him. He felt certain that they would be charmed with his pure and simple doctrine, taught without ostentation or display.

He accordingly made a feast at his own house and called together his friends and relatives, among whom were a number of publicans. Jesus was invited as a guest, in whose honor the feast was prepared. He, with his disciples, accepted the courteous invitation, and graced the banquet with his presence. The envious scribes and Pharisees, who were ever watching and following the movements of Jesus, did not lose this opportunity of seeking to condemn the cause of Christ.

They were highly indignant that one who called himself a Jew should mingle with publicans. Though they refused to acknowledge him the Messiah, and would accept none of his teachings, yet they could not shut their eyes to the fact that he had great influence over the people; this being the case they were chagrined that he should, by his example, ignore their prejudices and traditions. When Jesus called Matthew to follow him their anger knew no bounds that he should thus honor a hated publican. They openly attacked the disciples on the subject, and accused them of eating with publicans and sinners.

"And it came to pass, as Jesus sat at meat in the house, behold, many publicans and sinners came and sat down with him and his disciples. And when the Pharisees saw it, they said unto his disciples, Why eateth your Master with publicans and sinners?" It was with bitter contempt that they asked this question. Jesus did not wait for his disciples to answer this scornful charge, but himself replied, "They that be whole need not a physician, but they that are sick. But go ye and learn what that meaneth, I will have mercy, and not sacrifice; for I am not come to call the righteous, but sinners to repentance." He here explained his course by taking the case of a physician, whose work is not among the well, but among those who are diseased. He who came to save the sin-sick soul must go among those who most need his forgiving mercy and pitying love.

Those poor publicans and sinners, although stained with guilt, felt their need of repentance and pardon. It was the mission of Heaven to relieve just such want as theirs. Although these persons apparently disregarded religious rites and observances, yet in heart and life they were better fitted to become sincere Christians than the Pharisees and priests who scorned them. Many of them were possessed of noble integrity, and would not wrong their conscience by rejecting a doctrine which their reason declared to be true.

Jesus had come to heal the wounds of sin among his own nation, but they refused his proffered aid; they trampled upon his teachings and made light of his mighty works. The Lord turned, therefore, to those who would hear his words. Matthew and his associates obeyed the summons

of the Master and followed him. The despised
publican became one of the most devoted evan-
gelists. His unselfish heart was drawn out for
souls that needed the light. He did not repulse
sinners by magnifying his own piety, and contrasting it with their sinfulness; but linked them
to himself through kindly sympathy, as he presented to them the precious gospel of Christ.
His labors were attended with marked success.
Many of those who sat at that feast, and listened
to the divine instruction of Jesus, became instruments of enlightenment to the people.

The pointed words addressed by Jesus to the
Pharisees on the occasion of this feast silenced
them, but did not remove their prejudice nor
soften their hearts. They went away and complained to the disciples of John concerning the
practices of Jesus and his followers. They di-
lated upon the dangerous influence that he exerted over the people, setting at naught their ancient traditions, and preaching a doctrine of mercy and love to the world. They sought to arouse
dissatisfaction in the minds of John's disciples by
contrasting their austere piety and rigorous fasting with the example of Jesus in feasting with
publicans and sinners.

The feelings of John's disciples were stirred,
and they complained to the disciples of Jesus concerning the course of their Master, which was so
contrary to the teachings of John. If John was
sent of God, and taught according to his Spirit,
how could the practices of Jesus be right? The
followers of the Saviour, being unable to answer
these questions, brought the matter to their Master. "And they said unto him, Why do the disciples of John fast often, and make prayers, and

likewise the disciples of the Pharisees; but thine eat and drink? And he said unto them, Can ye make the children of the bridechamber fast, while the bridegroom is with them? But the days will come, when the bridegroom shall be taken away from them, and then shall they fast in those days."

Jesus had come to the world, bringing the light of Heaven. He came as the Redeemer of mankind, to limit the power of Satan and set the captive free. At his birth the heavenly messengers had borne the glad tidings of great joy to the humble shepherds upon the plains of Bethlehem, "Glory to God in the highest, and on earth peace, good will toward men!"

The greatest gift of Heaven had been given to the world. Joy to the poor, for Christ has come to make them heirs of his kingdom! Joy to the rich, for he will teach them how to apply their earthly treasure that it may secure for them eternal riches in Heaven! Joy to the ignorant, for he has come to give them wisdom unto salvation! Joy to the learned, for he will open to their understanding deeper mysteries than they have ever before fathomed!

Said the Saviour, "Blessed are your eyes, for they see; and your ears, for they hear. For verily I say unto you, that many prophets and righteous men have desired to see these things which ye see, and have not seen them, and to hear these things which ye hear, and have not heard them." The mission of Christ opened to the minds of men truths that had been hidden from the foundation of the world.

Every human enterprise sinks into insignificance when compared with the advent of Christ upon the earth. What occasion for joy had the disciples who were permitted to walk and talk with the Majesty of Heaven! Happy were they who had the Prince of Peace in their very midst, bestowing upon them daily new mercies and blessings. Why should they mourn and fast? It was more fitting for them to mourn who rejected the Saviour and closed their eyes and ears to his divine teachings, who turned from the peace and joy of infinite love and truth. The treasure of Heaven was entrusted to them for a time, and they, heedless of the gift, chose bondage and darkness rather than freedom and light through Christ.

In the synagogue at Nazareth Jesus had announced himself the Redeemer of mankind. Said he, "The Spirit of the Lord is upon me, because he hath anointed me to preach the gospel to the poor; he hath sent me to heal the broken-hearted, to preach deliverance to the captives, and recovering of sight to the blind, to set at liberty them that are bruised; to preach the acceptable year of the Lord."

How could the children of the bridechamber fast when the bridegroom was yet with them? But when he should go back to Heaven, leaving his disciples to meet alone the unbelief and darkness of the world, then it would be fitting for the church to fast and mourn, until her absent Lord should return the second time.

The jealous Pharisees misinterpreted all the actions of our Lord. The very deeds that should have melted their hearts and won their admiration, only served as an excuse to charge him with immorality. These self-righteous men had so often been rebuked by Jesus for their iniquity, and exposed in their evil purposes and wicked natures, that they did not dare to bring their complaints to him, but carry them where they will be most likely to create prejudice and unbelief. Had the disciples of Jesus listened to these insinuations, they would have ceased from following their Master. But they heeded not the base charges of impiety and evil associations against him by those who were themselves filled with malice and hatred.

The Saviour ate with sinners, he spoke to them the words of life, and many accepted him as their Redeemer. The feast of Christ was holy; but the fasting Pharisees will have their portion with the hypocrites and unbelievers, when Christ shall come in his glory, and those whom they scorned will be gathered into his kingdom.

CHAPTER XV.

THE SABBATH.

NOTHING so distinguished the Jews from surrounding nations, and designated them as true worshipers of the Creator, as the institution of the Sabbath. Its observance was a continual visible token of their connection with God, and separation from other people. All ordinary labor for a livelihood or for worldly profit was forbidden upon the seventh day. According to the fourth commandment the Sabbath was dedicated to rest and religious worship. All secular employment was to be suspended; but works of

mercy and benevolence were in accordance with
the purpose of the Lord. They were not to be
limited by time nor place. To relieve the afflicted,
to comfort the sorrowing is a labor of love that
does honor to God's holy day.

The work of the priests in connection with the
sacrificial offerings was increased upon the Sabbath, yet in their holy work in the service of
God they did not violate the fourth commandment of the decalogue. As Israel separated
from God, the true object of the Sabbath institution became less distinct in their minds. They
grew careless of its observance, and unmindful of
its ordinances. The prophets testified to them
of God's displeasure in the violation of his Sabbath. Nehemiah says: "In those days saw I in
Judah some treading wine-presses on the Sabbath, and bringing in sheaves, and lading asses;
as also wine, grapes, and figs, and all manner of
burdens, which they brought into Jerusalem on
the Sabbath-day, and I testified against them in
the day wherein they sold victuals."

And Jeremiah commands them: "Take heed
to yourselves, and bear no burden on the Sabbath day, nor bring it in by the gates of Jerusalem; neither carry forth a burden out of your
houses on the Sabbath day, neither do ye any
work, but hallow ye the Sabbath day, as I commanded your fathers."

But they heeded not the admonitions of the
inspired prophets, and departed more and more
from the religion of their fathers. At length calamities, persecution, and bondage came upon
them in consequence of their disregard of God's
requirements.

Alarmed at these visitations of divine punishment, they returned to the strict observance of all the outward forms enjoined by the sacred law. Not satisfied with this, they made burdensome additions to those ceremonies. Their pride and bigotry led them to the narrowest interpretation of the requirements of God. As time passed they gradually hedged themselves in with the traditions and customs of their ancestors, till they regarded them with all the sanctity of the original law. This confidence in themselves and their own regulations, with its attendant prejudice against all other nations, caused them to resist the Spirit of God, and separated them still farther from his favor.

Their exactions and restrictions were so wearisome that Jesus declared: "They bind heavy burdens, and grievous to be borne, and lay them on men's shoulders." Their false standard of duty, their superficial tests of piety and godliness, obscured the real and positive requirements of God. Heart service was neglected in the rigid performance of outward ceremonies. The Jews had so perverted the divine commandments, by heaping tradition upon tradition, that, in the days of Christ, they were ready to accuse him of breaking the Sabbath, because of his acts of mercy upon that day.

The grain was ready for the sickle when Jesus and his disciples passed through the corn fields on the Sabbath. The disciples were hungry, for their Master had extended his work of teaching and healing to a late hour, and they had been without food for a long time. They accordingly began to pluck the ears of corn and to eat, rubbing them in their hands, in accordance with the law of Moses, which provides that: " When thou

comest into the standing corn of thy neighbor,
then thou mayest pluck the ears with thine
hand ; but thou shalt not move a sickle unto thy
neighbor's standing corn."

But spies were continually upon the track of
Jesus, watching for some occasion to accuse and
condemn him. When they saw this act of the
disciples, they immediately complained to him,
saying, "Behold thy disciples do that which is
not lawful to do upon the Sabbath day." In
this they expressed their own narrow views of
the law. But Jesus defended his followers thus:
"Have ye never read what David did, when he
had need, and was a hungered, he, and they that
were with him ? how he went into the house of
God in the days of Abiathar the high priest, and
did eat the shewbread, which is not lawful to eat
but for the priests, and gave also to them which
were with him ? And he said unto them, The
Sabbath was made for man and not man for the
Sabbath. Therefore the Son of Man is Lord also
of the Sabbath."

If excessive hunger excused David for violating even the holiness of the sanctuary, and made
his act guiltless, how much more excusable was
the simple act of the disciples in plucking the
grain and eating it upon the Sabbath day. Jesus would teach his disciples and his enemies
that the service of God was first of all; and, if
fatigue and hunger attended the work, it was
right to satisfy the wants of humanity, even upon the Sabbath day. That holy institution was
not given to interfere with the needs of our being, bringing pain, and discomfort, instead of
blessings. "The Sabbath was made for man," to
give him rest and peace, and remind him of the

work of his Creator, not to be a grievous burden.

The work done in the temple upon the Sabbath was in harmony with the law; yet the same labor, if employed in ordinary business, would be a violation of it. The act of plucking and eating the grain to sustain the bodily strength, to be used in the service of God, was right and lawful. Jesus then crowned his argument by declaring himself the "Lord of the Sabbath,"—One above all question and above all law. This Infinite Judge acquits the disciples from blame, appealing to the very statutes they are accused of violating.

But Jesus did not let the matter drop without administering a rebuke to his enemies. He declared that in their blindness they had mistaken the object of the Sabbath. Said he: "But if ye had known what this meaneth, I will have mercy, and not sacrifice, ye would not have condemned the guiltless." He then contrasted their many heartless rites with the truthful integrity, and tender love that should characterize the true worshipers of God: "For I desired mercy, and not sacrifice; and the knowledge of God more than burnt-offerings. But they like men have transgressed the covenant; there have they dealt treacherously against me."

Jesus was reared among this people, so marked with bigotry and prejudice; and he therefore knew that in healing upon the Sabbath day, he would be regarded as a transgressor of the law. He was aware that the Pharisees would seize upon such acts with great indignation, and thereby seek to influence the people against him. He knew that they would use these works of mercy as strong arguments to affect the minds of the masses, who had all their lives been bound by the Jewish restrictions and exactions.   Nevertheless he was not prevented by this knowledge from breaking down the senseless wall of superstition that barricaded the Sabbath, and teaching men that charity and benevolence were lawful upon all days.

He entered the synagogue, and saw there a man who had a withered hand.   The Pharisees watched him, eager to see what he would do with regard to this case—whether or not he would heal the man upon the Sabbath day. Their sole object was to find cause for accusation against him.   Jesus looked upon the man with the withered hand, and commanded him to stand forth.   He then asked, "Is it lawful to do good on the Sabbath days, or to do evil?   to save life, or to kill?   But they held their peace.   And when he had looked round about on them with anger, being grieved for the hardness of their hearts, he saith unto the man, Stretch forth thine hand.   And he stretched it out; and his hand was restored whole as the other."

He justified this work of healing the paralytic, as in perfect keeping with the principles of the fourth commandment.   But they questioned him: "Is it lawful to heal on the Sabbath days?"   Jesus made them the clear and forcible answer, "What man shall there be among you, that shall have one sheep, and if it fall into a pit on the Sabbath day, will he not lay hold on it, and lift it out?   How much then is a man better than a sheep?   Wherefore it is lawful to do well on the Sabbath days."

The spies upon our Saviour's words dared not, in the presence of the multitude answer this

question for fear of involving themselves in difficulties. They knew that while they would leave
men to suffer and die rather than to violate their
traditions by relieving them upon the Lord's day,
a brute which had fallen into danger would be
at once relieved, because of the loss that would
accrue to the owner if he was neglected. Thus
the dumb animal was exalted above man, made
in the image of God.

Jesus wished to correct the false teachings of
the Jews in regard to the Sabbath and also to
impress his disciples with the fact that deeds of
mercy were lawful on that day. In the matter
of healing the withered hand he broke down the
custom of the Jews, and left the fourth commandment standing as God had given it to the world.
By this act he exalted the Sabbath, sweeping
away the senseless restrictions that encumbered
it. His act of mercy did honor to the day, while
those who complained of him, were, by their
many useless rites and ceremonies, themselves
dishonoring the Sabbath.

There are ministers to-day who teach that the
Son of God broke the Sabbath and justified his
disciples in doing the same. They take the same
ground as did the caviling Jews, although osten-
sibly for another purpose, since they hold that
Christ abolished the Sabbath.

Jesus in turning upon the Pharisees with the
question whether it was lawful to do good upon
the Sabbath day or evil, to save life or to kill,
confronted them with their own wicked purposes.
They were following upon his track to find occasion for falsely accusing him ; they were hunting
his life with bitter hatred and malice, while he
was saving life and bringing happiness to many

hearts. Was it better to slay upon the Sabbath, as they were planning to do, than to heal the afflicted as he had done? Was it more right-eous to have murder in the heart upon God's holy day, than love to all men which finds ex-pression in deeds of charity and mercy?

CHAPTER XVI.

SERMON ON THE MOUNT.

THE Redeemer of the world sought to make his lessons so simple that all could understand who heard them. It was not his choice to teach within walls or temples. True, he often did so in order to reach a class whom he would not be likely to meet while speaking in the open air, but Jesus preferred the fields, the groves, and the lake-sides for his temples. There were also his favorite resorts for meditation and prayer.

He had special reasons for choosing these nat-ural sanctuaries in which to give instruction to the people. The landscape lay before him, rich in scenes and objects familiar alike to the lofty and the humble. From these he drew illustra-tions that simplified his teachings, and impressed them firmly upon the minds of his hearers. The birds caroling in the leafy branches, the glowing flowers of the valley, the spotless lily resting on the bosom of the lake, the lofty trees, the fruitful lands, the waving grain, the barren soil, the tree that bore no fruit, the mighty hills, the bubbling brooks, the setting sun that tinted and gilded the heavens, all served as means of instruction, or as emblems by which he taught the beauties of divine truth. He connected the visible works of the Creator with the words of life which he spoke, and thus led the mind from the contemplation of Nature unto Nature's God.

The malice of the Jews was so great in consequence of the miracle of Jesus in healing the man with the withered hand on the Sabbath day, that he with his disciples withdrew to a more favorable field of labor. They went to the seaside of Galilee, and great multitudes followed him, for this new miracle wrought upon the Sabbath day was noised abroad through all that region. As Jesus taught, many of the sick, and those possessed with demons, were brought to him, and he made them whole. His great heart of love was filled with divine pity for the poor sufferers, many of whom sought only to draw near enough to touch him, believing that in so doing they would be healed, and in this they were not disappointed, for the touch of faith brought healing power from the great Physician, and their distress and gloom were changed to joy and thanksgiving. He also cast out many demons, who, in leaving their victims, acknowledged Christ, saying, "Thou art the Son of God."

The people of Galilee were greatly aroused, and flocked to the presence of the Saviour. At length the crowd so increased that he scarcely had room to stand, and therefore entered a small ship, which was near the shore, and there preached to the crowd that thronged upon the beach. So he labored uninterruptedly in teaching the people and in healing the sick. But when the day was far spent he stole away and hid himself in the solitude of the mountain, to commune with his Father in secret. Jesus spent the entire night in prayer, while his disciples slept at the foot of the mountain. About dawn he came and wakened them. The disciples were now about to receive an office of sacred responsibility, second only to that of Christ himself. They were to be set apart for the gospel work. They were to be linked with Jesus, to be with him, to share his joys and trials, to receive his teachings, and be faithful witnesses of his mighty works, that they might be able to impart the instruction thus gained to the world. They were to be qualified so that Jesus could at times send them forth alone to teach and work even as he taught and worked. Jesus wished his disciples to gain an experience in the gospel labor while he was on earth to comfort and direct them, so that they would be able to successfully continue the work after his death, and lay the foundation of the Christian church.

While Jesus was preparing his disciples for their ordination, and instructing them as to the duties of the great work that lay before them, Judas urged his presence among them. This man made great professions of devotion to Jesus, and proposed to become one of his disciples. Said he, "Master, I will follow thee whithersoever thou goest." Jesus did not warmly receive him, neither did he repulse him, but addressed him with these words of mournful pathos, "The foxes have holes, and the birds of the air have nests; but the Son of Man hath not where to lay his head." Judas was selfish, and his main object in seeking a connection with Christ was to obtain temporal advantages through him; but Christ's reference to his own poverty, contrasting his con-

dition with that of the foxes and the birds, was
designed to cut off any hope Judas might cherish
of securing earthly gain by becoming a follower
of Christ. Judas was a man of acknowledged
executive ability, and possessed of no small influence. For these reasons the disciples were anxious that he should form one of their number.
They commended him in the highest terms to
Jesus, as one who would greatly assist him in his
work. They were therefore surprised that he
received him so coolly; but the Saviour read the
heart of Judas, and knew, even then, the part he
was to act in his future betrayal and execution.
Still, Jesus wished to connect this man with himself, that he might learn his divine mission, and
gain moral strength to overcome the defects in
his character, and experience an entire change of
heart that would ensure his salvation. This it
was possible for him to do, through the help of
Christ.

Had Jesus repulsed Judas, the disciples, who
regarded him with such favor, would have questioned, in their own minds, the wisdom of their
Master. In receiving him, Jesus avoided this, and
also placed the selfish and avaricious Judas in the
most favorable position to develop qualities of
mind and heart that would eventually gain for
him a place in the kingdom of Heaven. But
notwithstanding these precious opportunities
Judas chose a course that covered him with
everlasting infamy.

Gathering his disciples about him, Jesus bowed
in their midst, and, laying his hands upon their
heads, offered a prayer, dedicating them to his
sacred work. Thus were the Lord's disciples ordained to the gospel ministry. This being ac-

complished, Jesus with his companions returned
to the sea-side, where the multitudes were already
gathering to hear him.   Many of them were there
for the purpose of being relieved of various maladies.   Here he healed the sick and comforted
the sorrowing, until the crowd increased so that
there was not room for them upon the narrow
beach.   Jesus therefore moved up the mountain
to a level space where the people could be ac-
commodated.   Here Jesus called his disciples near
him, that the great truths he uttered might not
fail to be indelibly impressed upon their minds,
and that nothing might divert their attention
from his words.

Though the disciples were close about him,
and his words seemed specially addressed to
them, yet they were also designed to reach the
hearts and consciences of the mixed crowd there
assembled.   At every large gathering of this
kind, the people still expected that Jesus would
make some great display of power in regard to
the new kingdom of which he had spoken.   The
believing Jews looked for him to free them from
the yoke of bondage and reinstate them in their
ancient glory.   But in his sermon on the mount
Christ disappointed their hopes of earthly glory.
He opened his discourse by stating the principles
that should govern his kingdom of divine grace,
as contained in the several beatitudes.

"Blessed are the poor in spirit; for theirs is the
kingdom of Heaven."   The poor in spirit are
those who claim no personal merit, and boast of
no virtue in themselves.   Realizing their utter
helplessness, and deeply convicted of sin, they
put no faith in mere outward ceremonies, but
cast themselves upon Jesus who is all-righteous

and all-compassionate. The Christian can only rise through humility. The proud heart strives in vain to earn salvation by good works; for though one cannot be saved without good works, yet these alone will not suffice to win eternal life. After he has done all he can, Christ must impute to him his own righteousness.

In Christ, God has bestowed Heaven's best gift to redeem man, and, as the gift is full and infinite, so is saving grace boundless and all-sufficient. This saying of Christ struck at the very root of the self-righteousness of the Pharisees, who felt themselves already rich in spiritual knowledge, and did not realize their need to learn more. Such characters could have no part in the kingdom of Christ.

"Blessed are they that mourn; for they shall be comforted." In pronouncing a blessing upon those who mourn, Jesus did not design to teach that there is any virtue in living under a perpetual cloud, nor that selfish sorrow and repining has any merit of itself to remove a single stain of sin. The mourning spoken of by Christ is a godly sorrow for sin, that works repentance unto eternal life. Many grieve when their guilt is discovered, because the result of their evil course has brought them into disagreeable circumstances. It was thus that Esau mourned the sin of despising and selling his birth-right; but it was the unexpected consequences of that sin which caused his grief. So Pharaoh regretted his stubborn defiance of God, when he cried for the plagues to be removed from him; but his heart was unchanged, and he was ready to repeat his crime when tempted. Such mourning is not unto repentance.

He who is truly convicted of sin feels his whole life to have been one continued scene of ingratitude. He feels that he has robbed his best friend of the time and strength which was bought for him at an infinite price. His whole soul is filled with unutterable sorrow that he has slighted and grieved his compassionate Saviour. Such mourning is precious, for it will yield the peaceable fruits of righteousness. The worldling, from his stand-point, may pronounce this sorrow a weakness; but it is the strength which binds the penitent to the Infinite One with links that cannot be broken. It reveals that the angels of God are bringing back to his soul the graces which were lost through hardness of heart and transgression. To confess and deplore one's errors evinces an excellence of character capable of discerning and correcting them. The tears of the penitent are only the clouds and the rain-drops that precede the sunshine of holiness, the sorrow that heralds a joy that will be a living fountain in the soul. Men are sowing in God's great field with toil and tears, yet with patient expectation; and they will be blessed, for the heavens will open and the rain will fall, insuring a bountiful harvest. Then when the Reaper comes, he will return with joy bringing home his sheaves.

"Blessed are the meek; for they shall inherit the earth." The difficulties that the Christian encounters may be very much lessened by that meekness of character which hides itself in Christ. Jesus invites all the weary and heavy laden to come unto him who is meek and lowly in heart, that they may find rest. If the Christian possesses the humility of his Master, he will rise·

above the slights, the rebuffs, and annoyances to which he is daily exposed, and they will cease to cast a gloom over his spirit. That meekness which Jesus blessed, operates amid the scenes of domestic life; it makes the home happy, it provokes no quarrels, gives back no angry answers, but soothes the irritated temper, and diffuses a gentleness which is felt by all within its charmed circle. It calms the inflammable spirit of retaliation, and mirrors forth the character of Christ.

Far better would it be for Christians to suffer under false accusations than to inflict upon themselves the torture of retaliation against their enemies. Hatred and revenge are instigated by Satan, and bring only remorse to him who cherishes them. Lowliness of heart is the strength that gives victory to the Christian. His reward is an inheritance of glory.

"Blessed are they who do hunger and thirst after righteousness; for they shall be filled." As the body feels the necessity for temporal food to supply the waste of the system, and preserve the physical strength, so the soul should long for that spiritual nourishment that increases the moral strength, and satisfies the cravings of the mind and heart. As the body is continually receiving the nutriment that sustains life and vigor, so should the soul constantly receive the heavenly food which gives nerve and muscle to spirituality. As the weary traveler eagerly seeks the spring in the desert, and, finding it, quenches his burning thirst with its cool and sparkling water, so should the Christian thirst for and seek the pure water of life, of which Christ is the fountain. There the soul may be satisfied, there the fever born of worldly strife is allayed, and the spirit is forever refreshed. But a majority of those who listened to Jesus hungered only for worldly advantages and honor. Especially did the self-exaltation of the Pharisees prevent them from longing for any higher attainments than they had already reached, for in their own estimation they were at the very pinnacle of perfect righteousness. However, there were many who heard thankfully the lessons of Jesus, and from that time, shaped their lives according to his teachings.

"Blessed are the merciful; for they shall obtain mercy." Here Jesus struck a blow at the arrogance and cruel intolerance of the Jews. Both priests and people were, as a rule, overbearing, quarreling with all who opposed them, severely critical and resentful of any reflection cast upon their own acts. Jesus said of the Pharisees, "Ye tithe mint, and rue, and all manner of herbs, and pass over judgment and the love of God." The Saviour desired to teach his followers a lesson of mercy that they should not be wanting in that tender compassion which pities and aids the suffering and erring, and avoids magnifying the faults of others.

"Blessed are the pure in heart; for they shall see God." The Jews were so exacting in regard to ceremonial purity that their regulations were extremely burdensome. Their minds were so occupied with rules and restrictions, and the fear of outward defilement, that they lost sight of the necessity for purity of motive and nobility of action. They did not perceive the stain that selfishness, injustice, and malice, leave upon the soul.

Jesus declared that the pure in heart should

see God. They would recognize him in the person of his Son, who was sent to the world for the salvation of the human race. Their minds, being cleansed and occupied with pure thoughts, would more clearly discover the Creator in the works of his mighty hand, in the things of beauty and magnificence which comprise the universe. They would live as in the visible presence of the Almighty, in a world of his creation, during the time that he apportions them here. They would also see God in the future immortal state, as did Adam when he walked and talked with God in Eden. Even now the pure in heart see God " through a glass darkly, but then face to face."

" Blessed are the peace-makers ; for they shall be called the children of God." Our Heavenly Father is a God of peace. When he created man he placed him in an abode of peace and security. All was unity and happiness in the garden of Eden. Those who are partakers of the divine nature will love peace and contentment; they will cultivate the virtues that insure those results. They will seek to allay wrath, to quiet resentment and fault finding, and all the evil passions that foster quarrels and dissensions. The more men unite with the world, and fall into its ways, the less they have of the true elements of peace in their hearts, and the more they are leavened with the bitterness of worldly strife, jealousy, and evil thoughts toward each other, which only needs certain circumstances to develop them into active agents for evil. Those whose anger kindles at slight provocations, and those who watch the words and acts of others to secretly report them where they will stir up enmity, are the direct opposite of the peace-makers who are called the children of God.

The true Christian will in his intercourse with men suppress words that would tend to produce unnecessary anger and strife. All Heaven is at peace, and those who are closely connected with Christ will be in harmony with Heaven. Jesus declared: "In the world ye shall have tribulation; but in me ye shall have peace." Those who are in sympathy with the Saviour will not be restless and dissatisfied. They will partake of the nature of Christ, and their lives will emulate his example.

The multitudes were amazed at this doctrine, so at variance with the precepts and example of the scribes and Pharisees. The people had imbibed the idea from them that happiness consisted in the possession of the things of this world, and that fame and the honor of men were much to be coveted. It was very pleasing to be called "Rabbi," and to be extolled as very wise and religious, having their virtues paraded before the public. This was considered the crown of happiness. But Jesus, in the presence of that vast throng, declared that earthly gain and honor was all the reward such persons would ever receive. Jesus spoke with certainty, and a convincing power attended his words. The people were silenced, and a feeling of fear crept over them. They looked at each other doubtfully. Who of them would be saved if this man's teachings were true? Many were deeply convicted that this remarkable teacher was actuated by the Spirit of God, and that the sentiments he uttered were divine.

These lessons of instruction were particularly

calculated to benefit the disciples, whose lives
would be governed by the principles therein
taught. It was to be their work to impart the
divine knowledge they derived from Jesus, to
the world. It was their task to spread the gospel far and wide among the people of all lands,
and it was very important that all the lessons of
Jesus should be plain to their minds, stamped
upon their memories, and incorporated in their
lives. Every truth was to be stored away in
their minds and hearts for future use.

After Jesus had explained to the people what
constituted true happiness, and how it could be
obtained, he more definitely pointed out the duty
of his disciples, as teachers chosen of God to lead
others into the path of righteousness and eternal
life. He knew that they would often suffer from
disappointment and discouragement, that they
would meet with decided opposition, that they
would be insulted, and their testimony rejected.
His penetrating eye looked down the coming
years of their ministry, and saw the sorrow and
abuse that would attend their efforts to lead men
to salvation. Well he knew that the humble
men who listened so attentively to his words
were to bear, in the fulfillment of their mission,
calumny, torture, imprisonment and death, and
he continues :—

"Blessed are they which are persecuted for
righteousness' sake; for theirs is the kingdom of
Heaven. Blessed are ye when men shall revile
you, and persecute you, and shall say all manner
of evil against you falsely, for my sake. Rejoice, and be exceeding glad; for great is your
reward in Heaven; for so persecuted they the
prophets which were before you." Jesus here

shows them that at the very time when they are experiencing great suffering in his cause, they have reason to be glad, and recognize that their afflictions are profitable to them, having an influence to wean their affections from the world and concentrate them upon Heaven. He taught them that their losses and disappointments would result in actual gain, that the severe trials of their faith and patience should be cheerfully accepted, rather than dreaded and avoided. These afflictions were God's agents to refine and fit them for their peculiar work, and would add to the precious reward that awaited them in Heaven. He charged them, when persecuted by men, not to lose confidence, nor become depressed and mourn over their hard lot, but to remember that righteous men of the past had likewise suffered for their obedience. Anxious to fulfill their duty to the world, fixing their desire upon the approbation of God, they were calmly and faithfully to discharge every duty, irrespective of the fear or favor of man.

Those things which seem to the Christian most grievous to be borne often prove his greatest blessing. Reproach and falsehood have ever followed those who were faithful in the discharge of duty. A righteous character, though blackened in reputation by slander and falsehood, will preserve the purity of its virtue and excellence. Trampled in the mire, or exalted to heaven, the Christian's life should be the same, and the proud consciousness of innocence is its own reward. The persecution of enemies tests the foundation upon which the reputation really rests. Sooner or later it is revealed to the world whether or not the evil reports were true, or were the poi-

soned shafts of malice and revenge. Constancy
in serving God is the only safe manner of settl-
ing such questions. Jesus would have his people use great care to give the enemies of his
cause no ground to condemn their holy faith.
No wrong action should cast a stigma upon its
purity. When all arguments fail, the slanderers
frequently open their galling fire upon the besieged servants of God; but their lying tongues
eventually bring curses upon themselves. God
will finally vindicate the right, honor the guiltless, and hide them in the secret of his pavilion
from the strife of tongues.

God's servants have always suffered reproach;
but the great work moves on, amid persecution,
imprisonments, stripes, and death. The character
of the persecution changes with the times, but
the principle—the spirit that underlies it—is the
same that stoned and beat and slew the chosen
of the Lord centuries ago.

There was never one who walked a man among
men more cruelly slandered than the Son of God.
He was met at every point with bitter reproaches. They hated him without a cause. The Pharisees even hired men to repeat from city to city
the falsehoods which they themselves fabricated
to destroy the influence of Jesus. Yet he stood
calmly before them declaring that reproach was a
part of the Christian's legacy, counseling his
followers how to meet the arrows of malice, bidding them not to faint under persecutions, but,
"Rejoice, and be exceeding glad;" "for so persecuted they the prophets which were before you."
Jesus continued to impress upon the minds of his
disciples the responsibility of their relation to the
world. Said he:—

"Ye are the salt of the earth; but if the salt have lost its savor, wherewith shall it be salted? it is thenceforth good for nothing but to be cast out, and to be trodden under foot of men." The people could see the white salt, glistening in the pathway, where it had been cast out because it had lost its savor and was therefore useless. Jesus used salt as an illustration of the Christian's life and teachings upon the world. Were it not for the few righteous who inhabit the earth, the wrath of God would not be delayed a moment from punishing the wicked. But the prayers and good works of the people of God preserve the world; they are the savor of life. But if Christians are only so in name, if they have not virtuous characters and godly lives, they are like the salt that has lost its savor. Their influence upon the world is bad; they are worse than unbelievers.

Jesus took objects in the view of his listeners as emblems by which to teach his truth. The people had come together to hear him while it was yet early morning. The glorious sun, climbing higher and higher in the blue sky, was chasing away the shadows that lurked in the valleys and among the narrow defiles of the mountains. The glory of the eastern heavens had not yet faded out. The sunlight flooded the land with its splendor, the placid surface of the lake reflected the golden light, and mirrored the rosy clouds of morning. Every bud and flower and leafy spray glistened with dew-drops. Nature smiled under the benediction of a new day, and the birds sang sweetly among the spreading trees. The Saviour looked upon the company before him, and then upon the rising sun, and said to his disciples, "Ye are the

light of the world." The figure was peculiarly
striking. As the sun lit up the landscape with
his genial rays and scattered the shades of night,
so the disciples were to diffuse the light of truth,
and scatter the moral darkness that brooded over
the world. In the brilliant light of morning the
towns and villages situated upon the surrounding hills stood forth clearly and made an attract-
ive feature of the scene. Jesus, pointing to them
said, "A city that is set on a hill can not be hid.
Neither do men light a candle, and put it under
a bushel, but on a candlestick, and it giveth
light unto all that are in the house. Let your
light so shine before men that they may see your
good works, and glorify your Father which is in
Heaven." In these words Jesus taught his disciples that if they wished to direct others in the
path of righteousness, their own example should
be correct, and their acts reflect the light of
truth.

Moral disease abounds, and darkness covers the
earth; but the disciples of Christ are represented
as lights shining amid the gloom of night. Those
rays reveal the dangers that lie in the sinner's
path, and point the true way to righteousness
and safety. If those who profess to be Christ's
followers, and to have the light of truth, are not
careful to present that truth to others in a proper
manner, those who are in the darkness of error
will see no beauty in it. In carrying a lantern
on a dark night, to light the way for one who is
following, the bearer sometimes becomes careless,
and permits his person to interpose between the
light and the one whom he is guiding, and the
darkness of the way is rendered more intense to
him from the temporary light that has been shed

upon it. So with many who essay to present the truth of God to others; they hide the precious light with their own defective characters, which stand out darkly conspicuous in their deformity, and turn many from the truth. The characters of the professed followers of Christ should be so admirable, and their deeds so exemplary, that the world will be attracted toward a religion that bears such fruits of righteousness. They will thus be led to investigate and embrace its principles from the fact that the lives of its representatives shine forth with such holiness that they are the beacon lights of the world.

The Pharisees shut themselves away from the world, and thereby made it impossible for them to exert an influence over the people of the world; but Jesus names his disciples the "light the world." Their teachings and example are to scatter the clouds of error, and all nations and people are to feel their influence. The religion of the Bible is not to be confined between two covers nor within the walls of a church. It is not to be brought out only occasionally simply for our own benefit, and then carefully laid aside again, but it is to sanctify the daily life, to manifest itself in every business transaction and in all the social relations of life. Such a religion was in marked contrast with that of the Pharisees, which consisted only in the hollow observance of rules and ceremonies, and shed no ennobling influence over their lives.

Jesus was closely watched by spies, who were ready to seize any unguarded word that might drop from his lips. The Saviour was well aware of the prejudice existing in the minds of many of his hearers. He said nothing to unsettle the faith of the Jews in the religion and institutions of Moses. The same voice that declared the moral and ceremonial law, which was the foundation of the whole Jewish system, also uttered the words of instruction on the mount. It was because of his great reverence for the law and the prophets that Jesus sought to break through the wall of superstitious exactions that hemmed in the Jews. He wished them not only to observe the law, but to develop the principles of that law and the teachings of the prophets.

Jesus severely criticised the false interpretations which the Jews had given to the law, yet he sufficiently guarded his disciples against the danger of yielding up the vital truths given to the Hebrews. Jesus came not to destroy their confidence in the instruction which he himself had given them through Moses in the wilderness. But, while he taught them due reverence for that law, he desired to lead them on to higher truths and a greater knowledge, that they might advance into clearer light.

As Jesus explained the duty of his disciples in the works of righteousness, the Pharisees saw that the doctrines taught condemned their course, and, in order to prejudice the people against the great Teacher, whispered to one another that the lessons of Jesus were in opposition to the law of Moses, in that he made no mention of that law. In this way they designed to arouse the indignation of the people against Christ. But Jesus, perceiving their intent, in the presence of the vast multitude, and in a clear and distinct voice, declared, to the utter discomfiture of his enemies, these words :—

"Think not that I am come to destroy the
law, or the prophets; I am not come to destroy,
but to fulfill. For verily, I say unto you, Till
heaven and earth pass, one jot or one tittle shall
in no wise pass from the law, till all be fulfilled."
Here Jesus refutes the charge of the Pharisees.
His mission to the world is to vindicate the
claims of that sacred law which they charge him
with breaking. If the law of God could have
been changed or abolished, then Christ need not
have come to a fallen world to suffer the consequence of man's transgression. Jesus came to
explain the relation of the law of God to man,
and to illustrate its precepts by his own example of obedience. He further declares that,
"Whosoever therefore shall break one of these
least commandments, and shall teach men so, he
shall be called the least in the kingdom of
Heaven." Thus did the Saviour declare the validity of the moral law. Those who disobey the
commandments of God, and teach others to do
the same by their example and doctrine, are condemned by Christ. They are the children of the
wicked one, who was the first rebel against the
law of God. Having explicitly declared his reverence for his Father's law, Jesus in these words
condemns the practices of the Pharisees, who
were strict in their outward observance of that
law while their hearts and lives were corrupt:—

"For I say unto you, That except your righteousness shall exceed the righteousness of the
scribes and Pharisees, ye shall in no case enter
into the kingdom of Heaven." The righteousness
here taught was conformity of the heart and life
to the revealed will of God. Jesus taught that
the law of God should regulate the thoughts and

purposes of the mind. True godliness elevates the thoughts and actions; *then* the external forms of religion accord with the Christian's internal purity; then those ceremonies required in the service of God are not meaningless rites, like those of the hypocritical Pharisees.

Many religious teachers of to-day are themselves breaking the commandments of God, and teaching others to do so. In place of those holy commandments, they boldly teach the customs and traditions of men, regardless of the direct testimony of Christ that such ones should be "least in the kingdom of Heaven." Jesus declared to the multitude assembled to hear him, to the Pharisees, who sought to accuse him of lightly regarding the law, and to the people of all time, that the precepts of Jehovah were immutable and eternal.

The report had been brought of murder and robbery in the wild region near Capernaum, and there was a general expression of indignation and horror in consequence among those who were assembled to hear Jesus. The divine Teacher took advantage of this circumstance to point an important lesson. Said he:—

"Ye have heard that it was said by them of old time, Thou shalt not kill; and whosoever shall kill shall be in danger of the Judgment. But I say unto you, That whosoever is angry with his brother without a cause shall be in danger of the Judgment; and whosoever shall say to his brother, Raca, shall be in danger of the council; but whosoever shall say, Thou fool, shall be in danger of hell fire." Here Jesus describes murder as first existing in the mind. That malice and revenge which would delight in deeds of

violence is of itself murder. Jesus goes further
still, and says, "Whoever is angry with his brother
without a cause shall be in danger of the Judgment." There is an anger that is not of this criminal nature. A certain kind of indignation is justi-
fiable, under some circumstances, even in the followers of Christ. When they see God dishonored,
his name reviled, and the precious cause of truth
brought into disrepute by those who profess to
revere it, when they see the innocent oppressed
and persecuted, a righteous indignation stirs their
soul; such anger, born of sensitive morals, is not
a sin. Among the listeners are those who con-
gratulate themselves upon their righteousness
because they have committed no outward crime,
while they are cherishing in their hearts feelings
of the same nature as that which prompts the
assassin to do his fearful deed. Yet these men
make professions of piety, and conform to the
outward requirements of religion. To such Jesus addresses these words :—

"Therefore if thou bring thy gift to the altar,
and there rememberest that thy brother hath
aught against thee, leave there thy gift before
the altar, and go thy way; first be reconciled to
thy brother, and then come and offer thy gift."
He thus shows that crimes originate in the mind,
and those who permit hatred and revenge to
find a place in their hearts have already set their
feet in the path of the murderer, and their offerings are not acceptable to God. The only remedy is to root out all bitterness and animosity
from the heart. But the Saviour even goes further than this, and declares that if another has
aught against us, we should endeavor to relieve
his mind, and, if possible, remove those feelings

from it, before our offering can be acceptable with God. This lesson is of special importance to the church at this time. Many are zealous in religious services while unhappy differences exist between them and their brethren which it is in their power to remove, and which God requires them to remove before he will accept their services. Christ has so clearly pointed out the Christian's course in this matter that there should be no question in his mind as to his duty.

While Jesus is teaching, there are pleasure-boats upon the water, and it is evident to all that the idlers who occupy them are disreputable characters. The listening people expect Jesus to severely denounce this class, but are surprised when he declares: "Ye have heard that it was said by them of old time, Thou shalt not commit adultery. But I say unto you, That whosoever looketh on a woman to lust after her hath committed adultery with her already in his heart." Those who have looked upon the guilty characters who lead lives of sensual dissipation as sinners above all others, are astonished to hear Jesus assert that those who cherish lascivious thoughts are as guilty at heart as the shameless violators of the seventh commandment. Jesus condemned the custom then existing of a man putting away his wife for trivial offenses. This practice led to great wretchedness and crime. Jesus strikes at the primary cause of the laxness with which the marriage relation was held, when he condemns the unholy passions which find the marriage institution a barrier to the gratification of their lust. Christ would have the marriage relation hedged about with judicial. restrictions, so that there could be no legal separation between husband and wife, save for the cause of adultery.

Many who had regarded the commandments as prohibiting actual crime but reaching no farther, now perceive that the law of God should be obeyed in spirit as well as in letter. In this manner Jesus takes up the commandments separately and explains the depth and breadth of their requirements, exposing the fatal mistake of the Jews in their merely outward obedience. Jesus gives a lesson upon oath-taking, saying, "Let your communication be Yea, yea; Nay, nay; for whatsoever is more than these cometh of evil." The third commandment condemns the profane swearer, but the spirit of the precept reaches farther still, and forbids that the name of God be introduced into the conversation in a careless or irreverent manner. Many, even of the professed followers of Christ, are in the habit of using lightly the name of God, and, even in their prayers and exhortations, do not use the Supreme name with a proper solemnity.

A detachment of the Roman troops was encamped near by, on the sea-shore, and Jesus is now interrupted by the loud blast of the trumpet which is the signal for the soldiers to assemble on the plain below. They form in the regular order, bowing in homage to the Roman standard which is uplifted before them. With bitterness the Jews look upon this scene which reminds them of their own degradation as a nation. Presently messengers are dispatched from the army, with orders to various distant posts. As they toil up the abrupt bank that borders the shore, they are brought near to the listening crowd that surrounds Jesus, and they force some of the Jewish peasants to carry their burdens for them up the steep ascent. The peasants resist this act of oppression, and address their persecutors with violent language; but they are finally compelled to obey the soldiers, and perform the menial task required of them. This exhibition of Roman authority stirs the people with indignation, and they turn eagerly to hear what the great Teacher will say of this cruel act of oppression. With sadness, because of the sins which had brought the Jews into such bondage, Jesus looks upon the shameful scene. He also notes the hatred and revenge stamped upon the faces of the Jews, and knows how bitterly they long for power to crush their oppressors. Mournfully he says:—

"Ye have heard that it hath been said, An eye for an eye, and a tooth for a tooth. But I say unto you, That ye resist not evil; but whosoever shall smite thee on thy right cheek, turn to him the other also. And if any man will sue thee at the law, and take away thy coat, let him have thy cloak also. And whosoever shall compel thee to go a mile, go with him twain. Give to him that asketh thee, and from him that would borrow of thee turn not thou away."

The example of Jesus was a practical illustration of the lesson here taught; contumely and persecution never caused him to retaliate upon his enemies. But this was a hard saying for the revengeful Jews, and they murmured against it among themselves. Jesus now makes a still stronger declaration :—

"Ye have heard that it hath been said, Thou shalt love thy neighbor, and hate thine enemy. But I say unto you, Love your enemies, bless them that curse you, do good to them that hate you, and pray for them which despitefully use you, and persecute you; that ye may be the children of your Father which is in Heaven; for he maketh his sun to rise on the evil and on the good, and sendeth rain on the just and on the unjust. For if ye love them that love you, what reward have ye? do not even the publicans the same? And if ye salute your brethren only, what do ye more than others? do not even the publicans so?"

The manifestation of hatred never breaks down the malice of our enemies. But love and kindness beget love and kindness in return. Although God faithfully rewards virtue and punishes guilt, yet he does not withhold his blessings from the wicked, although they daily dishonor his name. He allows the sunshine and the showers to fall upon the just and the unjust, bringing alike worldly prosperity to both. If a holy God exercises such forbearance and benevolence toward the rebellious and the idolatrous, how necessary it is that erring man should manifest a like spirit toward his fellow-men. Instead of cursing those who injure him, it is his duty to seek to win them from their evil ways by a kindness similar to that with which Christ treated them who persecuted him. Jesus taught his followers that they should exercise a Christian courtesy toward all who came within their influence, that they should not be forgetful in deeds of mercy, and that when solicited for favors, they should show a benevolence superior to that of the worldling. The children of God should represent the spirit that rules in Heaven. Their principles of action should not be of the same character with the narrow, selfish spirit of the

world. Perfection alone can meet the standard
of Heaven. As God himself is perfect in his
exalted sphere, so should his children be perfect
in the humble sphere they occupy. Thus only
can they be fit for the companionship of sinless
beings in the kingdom of Heaven. Christ addresses to his followers these words that establish the standard of Christian character : " Be ye
therefore perfect, even as your Father which is
in Heaven is perfect."

CHAPTER XVII.

THE LEPER HEALED.

JESUS was frequently obliged to hide himself
from the people; for the crowds collected so
densely about him to witness his miracles, and
the enthusiasm ran so high, that it became necessary to take precautions, lest the priests and
rulers should take advantage of the great assem-
blies to arouse the Roman authorities to fear an
insurrection.

Never had there been such a period as this for
the world. Heaven was brought down to men.
All who came to Jesus for the purpose of instruction realized indeed that the Lord was gracious
and full of wisdom. They received precious lessons of divine knowledge from the great source
of intelligence. Many hungering and thirsting
souls that had waited long for the redemption of
Israel now feasted upon the bounteous grace
of a merciful Saviour. The expected Teacher
had come, and a favored people were living un-

der the full splendor of his light, yet many comprehended it not, and turned from the divine radiance with indifference or unbelief.

Jesus healed many and various cases of bodily disease, while he was preaching and ministering to sin-sick souls. Many hearts were liberated from the cruel bondage of sin. Unbelief, discouragement, and despair, gave place to faith, hope, and happiness. But when the sick and wretched applied to the Saviour for help, he first relieved the poor, suffering body before he attempted to minister to the darkened mind. When the present misery of the supplicant was removed, his thoughts could better be directed into the channel of light and truth.

Leprosy was the most fearful and loathsome disease of the East. It was looked upon with great dread by all classes on account of its contagious character and its horrible effect upon its victim. Great precautions were taken to prevent the disease from spreading among the people. With the Hebrews the leper was pronounced unclean. He was isolated from his family, restricted from the privileges of society, and cut off from the congregation of Israel. He was doomed to associate only with those who were similarly afflicted with himself.

Away from his friends and kindred he must bear the curse of his terrible malady. No affectionate hands could soothe his pain. He was obliged to publish his own calamity, to rend his garment, and sound the alarm, warning all to flee from his polluted and decaying body. The cry, Unclean! Unclean! coming with mournful tone from the lonely exile, was a signal heard with fear and abhorrence.

There were many of these loathsome subjects in the region of Christ's ministry. The news of the great Healer had reached even them in their isolation, and a gleam of hope sprang up in their hearts that if they could come into the presence of Jesus he might relieve them. But as they were debarred from entering any city or village, it seemed impossible for them to reach the great Physician, whose chief work lay among the populace.

There was one leper who had been a man of high distinction. It was with the greatest grief that he and his family had become convinced that he was a victim to the fatal disease. Physicians of note had been consulted, and they had examined his case thoroughly, and anxiously searched their books to obtain further knowledge; but they were reluctantly compelled to acknowledge that their skill was baffled, the disease was incurable. It was then the duty of the priest to make an examination; this resulted in a decision that his was the worst form of leprosy. This verdict sentenced him to a living death separated from his friends and the society in which he had held so lofty a position. But now those who had courted his favor and accepted his hospitality fled from his presence with horror. He went out an exile from his home.

Jesus was teaching by the lake outside the city limits, and many were gathered to hear his words. The leper, who in his seclusion had heard of some of his mighty works, came out to see him, and drew as near as he dared. Since his exile, the disease had made fearful inroads upon his system. He was now a loathsome spectacle, his decaying body was horrible to look upon. Standing afar off, he heard some of the words of Jesus, and saw him laying hands upon the sick to heal them. He beheld, with amazement, the lame, the blind, the paralytic, and those dying of various maladies, rise up at a word from the Saviour, restored to health and praising God for their salvation. He looked upon his own wretched body and wondered if this great Physician could not cure even him. The more he heard, and saw, and considered the matter, the more he was convinced that this was really the promised Saviour of the world, to whom all things were possible. None could perform such miracles but Him who was authorized of God, and the leper longed to come into his presence and be healed.

He had not intended to approach near enough to endanger the people; but now his mind was so powerfully wrought upon that he forgot the restrictions that had been placed upon him, the safety of the people, and the horror with which they regarded him. He thought only of his blessed hope that the power of Jesus could set him free from his infirmity. His faith laid hold of the Saviour, and he pressed forward, heedless of the frightened multitude that fell back as he approached and crowded over and upon each other to avoid him.

Some thought to prevent him from approaching Jesus, but their efforts were in vain. He neither saw nor heard them. The expressions of loathing and looks of horror that greeted his appearance were lost upon him. He saw only the Son of God, he heard only the voice that was giving health and happiness to the suffering and unfortunate. As he came before Jesus, his pent-up feelings found vent, he prostrated his foul, decaying body before him, crying out, "Lord, if thou wilt, thou canst make me clean." His words were few, but comprehended his great need. He believed that Christ was able to give him life and health.

Jesus did not shrink from his approach, but drew near him. The people fell back, and even the disciples were filled with terror, and would fain have prevented their Master from touching him; for by the law of Moses he who touched a leper was himself unclean. But Jesus, with calm fearlessness, laid his hand upon the supplicant and answered his petition with the magic words, "Be thou clean!"

No sooner were these life-giving words spoken than the dying body of corruption was changed to a being of healthy flesh, sensitive nerves, and firm muscle. The rough, scaly surface peculiar to leprosy was gone, and a soft glow, like that upon the skin of a healthy child, appeared in its place. The eager multitude now lose their terror, and crowd around to behold this new manifestation of divine power.

Jesus charged the cleansed leper not to make known the work he had wrought upon him, saying, "See thou say nothing to any man; but go thy way, shew thyself to the priest, and offer for thy cleansing those things which Moses commanded, for a testimony unto them." Accordingly the now happy man went to the same priests who had previously examined him, and whose decision had banished him from his family and friends.

Joyfully he presented his offering to the priests and magnified the name of Jesus who had restored him to health. This irrefutable testimony convinced the priests of the divine power of Jesus, although they still refused to acknowledge him as the Messiah. The Pharisees had asserted that his teachings were directly opposed to the law of Moses, and for the purpose of exalting himself; yet his special directions to the cleansed leper to make an offering to the priest according to the law of Moses, evidenced to the people that these accusations were false.

The priests were not allowed to accept an offering from the hands of one who had been afflicted with leprosy, unless they first thoroughly examined him and proclaimed to the people that he was entirely free from the infectious disease, was in sound health, and could again unite with his family and friends without endangering them. However unwilling the priest might have been to accredit this marvelous cure to Jesus, he could not evade an examination and decision of the case. The multitude were anxious to learn the result of the investigation, and when he was pronounced free from disease, and privileged to return to his family and friends, great was the excitement. Such a thing had never before been known.

But notwithstanding the caution of Jesus to the cleansed leper he published the matter abroad. Conceiving that it was only the retiring modesty of Jesus that laid these restrictions upon him, he went about proclaiming the mighty power of this great Healer. He did not understand that every new manifestation of divine power on the part of Jesus only made the chief priests and elders more determined to destroy him. The restored man felt the boon of health was very precious. The pure blood coursing through his veins quickened his entire being with a new and delightful animation. He rejoiced in the full vigor of manhood and in his restoration to his family and society. He felt it impossible to refrain from giving full glory to the Physician who had made him whole.

But the publicity of this affair created so great a commotion that Jesus was obliged to retire beyond the city. "And they came to him from every quarter." These miracles were not worked for display; the acts of Christ were in direct contrast to those of the Pharisees, whose greatest ambition was to secure the praise and honor of men. Jesus well knew that if the fact of his cleansing the leper was noised abroad, those in a similar condition would be urgent to obtain the same cure. This would raise the cry that the people would be contaminated by contact with the loathsome disease of leprosy. His enemies would seize such an opportunity to accuse and condemn him.

Jesus knew that many of the lepers who would seek him did not deserve the blessing of health, nor would they use it to the honor and glory of God should they obtain it. They had no real faith nor principle, but only a strong desire to be delivered from the certain doom that awaited them. The Saviour also knew that his enemies were ever seeking to limit his work and turn the people from him. If they could use the case of the cleansed leper for that purpose they would do so. But in directing the healed man to present his offering to the priest, as enjoined by the law of Moses, he would convince them that he was not opposed to the Jewish code, if their minds were open to conviction.

CHAPTER XVIII.

PARABLE OF THE SOWER.

JESUS had spent the entire night in prayer, and he came down to the beach in the early morning to look for his disciples who were fishing near the shore. He could not long remain undisturbed by the people. As soon as it was known that Christ was by the sea-side, the multitude flocked to him. Their numbers increased so that he was pressed upon all sides. As he stood teaching them, the crowd became so dense that he stepped into a boat, and pulling out a little from the shore, gave the people a better opportunity to see and hear him, as he continued his discourse.

He frequently adopted this plan to escape from the eager throng that crowded upon each other to get into his presence. In this way he could speak the things that he desired them to hear without interruption. The Saviour, seated in the rude boat of a fisherman, taught the words of life to the listening people upon the beach. He was patient with those who were laboring under temptation, tender and kind to the sorrowing and disheartened. His words found a response in many hearts, and light from his divine instruction poured in upon many darkened minds.

What a scene was this for angels to contemplate! Their glorious Commander, sitting in a fisherman's boat, swayed to and fro by the restless water, and preaching salvation to the listening crowd that are pressing down to the water's edge! He who was the honored of Heaven

teaches his grand doctrine of deliverance in the
open air to the common crowd. Yet he could
have no more magnificent scene for his labors.
The lake, the mountains, the spreading fields,
the sunlight flooding the earth, all furnish subjects by which his lessons can be impressed upon
the human mind.

In plain sight are the sowers and the reapers,
side by side, the one casting the seed, and the
other harvesting the early grain. The fruitful
valleys, and the hill-sides are clothed in beauty.
The barren rocks are seen upon the beach, and the
birds make the air vocal with their music. The
sea-fowls skim upon the surface of the water.
Jesus takes this opportunity to draw lessons from
nature that will sink into the minds of his listeners. He employs the scenery about him to
illustrate his doctrine, so that in the future, when-
ever these objects are presented to their eyes, their
thoughts will revert to the lessons of truth drawn
from them by Jesus. They will be daily reminders of the precious instruction which they had received from him.

Sitting thus, and looking upon the animated
scene before him, Jesus uttered the parable that
has been handed down to us through the ages, as
pure and beautiful to-day in its unadorned simplicity as when it was given that morning on
the Sea of Galilee more than eighteen hundred
years ago :—

"Hearken; behold, there went out a sower to
sow. And it came to pass, as he sowed, some fell
by the wayside, and the fowls of the air came and
devoured it up. And some fell on stony ground,
where it had not much earth; and immediately

it sprang up, because it had no depth of earth; but when the sun was up, it was scorched; and because it had no root, it withered away. And some fell among thorns, and the thorns grew up, and choked it, and it yielded no fruit. And other fell on good ground, and did yield fruit that sprang up and increased, and brought forth, some thirty, and some sixty, and some an hundred. And he said unto them,.He that hath ears to hear, let him hear."

This striking illustration of the spreading abroad of the gospel of the Son of God engaged the earnest attention of the people. The speaker carried with him the minds of his hearers. Their souls were stirred, and many a heart throbbed with the animation of a new purpose. They were charmed with a doctrine so ennobling in its principles, yet so easily understood. The high spiritual attainments which Jesus taught seemed then very desirable. But how soon the impressions there received were to pass from the minds of many, when they again mingled with the world. The sins that had seemed so heinous under the holy light of the Master's presence, would be clasped again to their erring hearts. Unfavorable surroundings, and worldly cares and temptations would cause them to relapse again into indifference.

But others who listened commenced from that moment a holier life, carrying out daily the principles of Christ's teachings. The subject matter of his discourse, illustrated by the scene before them, would never be effaced from their minds. The varied ground, some producing only thistles and noxious weeds, the ledges of rock covered with a surface of earth, the sowers with their seed, all being before their eyes, fastened his words in their minds as nothing else could have done.

The existing state of things led Jesus to give the parable of the sower. The people who followed Christ had been disappointed that he did not set up a new kingdom. Long had they looked for a Messiah who would exalt and glorify them as a nation, and now that their expectations were not realized, they refused to receive him as their Redeemer. Even his chosen disciples were becoming impatient that he did not assume temporal authority, and his relatives were disappointed in him and rejected him. They had addressed him in these words: "Depart hence, and go into Judea, that thy disciples may see the works that thou doest. For there is no man that doeth any thing in secret, and he himself seeketh to be known openly. If thou do these things, show thyself to the world."

His followers were mortified that the learned and wealthy were not the most willing to accept Jesus as their Saviour. They felt the stigma that attached to their Master, because it was the poor, the afflicted, and the humbler class generally, who became his disciples. Why, they asked themselves, did not the scribes and Pharisees, the teachers in the schools of the prophets, acknowledge that he was the long-looked-for Messiah? It was to meet this doubt and discontent that Jesus spoke this parable. When the multitude had departed, the twelve with the other believers gathered about him, and asked him to explain it to them. "And he said unto them, Unto you it is given to know the mystery of the kingdom of God; but unto them that are without, all these things are done in parables; that seeing they may see, and not perceive; and hearing they may hear, and not understand; lest at any time they should be converted, and their sins should be forgiven them. And he said unto them, Know ye not this parable? and how then will ye know all parables?" In these words he explained that his illustrations were to awaken thought in the minds of his hearers. If they desired a fuller explanation of his words they could ask it of him, as the disciples had done, and receive it.

The Pharisees understood the parable, but affected not to perceive its meaning. They closed their eyes lest they should see and their ears lest they should hear; therefore their hearts could not be reached. They were to suffer retribution for their willful ignorance and self-imposed blindness. One reason why he taught so much in parables was that the spies of the Jews were ever watching to find cause for complaint against him. Jesus designed to expose their hypocrisy and evil deeds without laying himself liable to the danger of being arrested and imprisoned by them, and thus cut off from the work which he came to do among the people.

He could speak cutting truths in parables, reveal the iniquity that it was necessary to expose, without any fear of their laws. They could make the application, for they could not fail to recognize his meaning, yet they were powerless to condemn him for using a simple illustration in his discourse.

The words of Jesus implied a reproof to his disciples, because of their dullness to comprehend his meaning; for in the parable of the sower, he had illustrated the doctrine he had come to the world to teach. If they could not discern things so easily to be understood, how could they fathom greater truths that he would declare to them in parables ? He also said that he would reveal greater mysteries concerning the kingdom of God unto them who followed him so closely and obeyed him than unto those who were outside of his companionship. They must open their minds to instruction and be ready to believe.

Those who had hardened their hearts to love pomp and ceremony did not wish to understand his teachings nor desire the work of God's grace within their hearts. This class would remain in ignorance of their own choosing. Those who connected with Heaven, and received Christ, who is the source of light and truth, would understand his words and gain practical knowledge concerning the kingdom of God. But those who, for any reason, neglected their present opportunities of acquaintance with the truth, and did not rightly use their powers of comprehension, but refused to be convinced by what their eyes saw and their ears heard, would be left in darkness ; seeing they would not perceive, and hearing, they would not understand. The truths of God involved too much self-denial and personal purity to attract their carnal minds, and they closed their hearts with bigotry and unbelief.

The great Teacher blessed his disciples because they both saw and heard with eyes and ears that believed. Said he, " Many prophets and righteous men have desired to see these things which ye see, and have not seen them ; and to hear the things which ye hear, and have not heard them." Jesus then explained to his disciples the differ-

U OF M

ent classes represented in the parable he had given them.

Christ, the Sower, scatters the seed. There are the worldly ones, whose hearts are like the hard-beaten highway, insensible to the teachings of divine wisdom. They love not the requirements of God, and follow their natural impulses. Many are convinced as they listen to the important lessons of Christ. They believe his words, and resolve to lead holy lives, but when Satan comes with his evil suggestions, they are overcome before the good seed has fairly sprung into life.

Had the soil of the heart been broken up by deep repentance for sin, they would have seen how wicked was their selfish love of the world, their pride and avarice, and would have put them away. The seeds of truth would have struck deep into the fallow ground prepared for them in the heart, and would have sprung up and borne fruit. But evil habits had so long held sway over their lives that their good resolutions had vanished before the voice of the tempter. " And these are they by the wayside, where the word is sown ; but when they have heard, Satan cometh immediately, and taketh away the word that was sown in their hearts."

There are those who receive the precious truth with joy ; they are exceedingly zealous, and express amazement that all cannot see the things that are so plain to them. They urge others to embrace the doctrine that they find so satisfying. They hastily condemn the hesitating and those who carefully weigh the evidences of the truth and consider it in all its bearings. They call such ones cold and unbelieving. But in the time of trial these enthusiastic persons falter and fail. They did not accept the cross as a part of their religious life, and they turn from it with dampened ardor, and refuse to take it up.

If life moves smoothly with this class, if their way is never crossed, if all things are in harmony with their inclinations, they appear to be consistent Christians. But they faint beneath the fiery test of temptation; they cannot endure reproach for the truth's sake. The good seed that had sprung into so flourishing a plant, withers and dies because it has no root to sustain it in the time of drought. The very thing which should have caused the fibers to strike down deeper and send up more vigorous growth, parches and kills the whole plant. Just so the hot summer sun, that strengthens and ripens the hardy grain, withers and destroys that which, though fresh and green, has no depth of root, because the tender fibers cannot pierce the hard and stony ground.

These persons could cultivate and enrich the soil of their hearts, if they would, so that the truth would take deeper hold; but this involves too much patience and self-denial. It costs them too much effort to make a radical change in their lives. They are easily offended by reproof, and ready to say with the disciples who left Jesus, "This is a hard saying; who can hear it?" "And these are they likewise which are sown on stony ground; who, when they have heard the word, immediately receive it with gladness; and have no root in themselves, and so endure but for a time; afterward, when affliction or persecution ariseth for the word's sake, immediately they are offended."

Jesus represents the seed as falling into neglected borders and patches covered with rank
weeds which choke the precious plants that
spring up among them; they grow sickly and
perish. Many hearts respond to the voice of
truth, but they do not properly receive and cherish it. They give it a place in the soil of the
natural heart, without preparing the ground and
rooting out the poisonous weeds that flourish
there, and watching every hour in order to destroy them should they again appear. The cares
of life, the fascination of riches, the longing for
forbidden things, crowd out the love of righteousness before the good seed can bear fruit. Pride,
passion, self-love, and love of the world, with envy and malice, are no companions for the truth of
God. As it is necessary thoroughly to cultivate
the soil that has once been overgrown with
weeds, so it is necessary for the Christian to be
diligent in exterminating the faults that threat-
en his eternal ruin. Patient, earnest effort in the
name and strength of Jesus, can alone remove the
evil tendencies of the natural heart. But those
who have allowed their faith to be overcome by
the growth of Satan's influences, fall into a worse
state than that which they occupied before they
heard the words of life. "And these are they
which are sown among thorns; such as hear the
word, and the cares of this world, and the deceit-
fulness of riches, and the lusts of other things
entering in, choke the word, and it becometh un-
fruitful."

Few hearts are like the good soil, well-cul-
tivated, and receive the seeds of truth and
bring forth abundant fruit to the glory of God.
But Jesus finds some earnest Christians, rich in

good works and sincere in their endeavors. "And these are they which are sown on good ground; such as hear the word, and receive it, and bring forth fruit, some thirty-fold, some sixty, and some an hundred."

Thus Christ represents the characters of those whom he came to teach, in a brief and comprehensive parable. The worldly-minded, the evil-disposed, the hard-hearted, are all exhibited to the minds of his hearers. He thus answers the question that we often hear to-day: Why was the work of Christ productive of such meager results, during his personal ministry upon earth? Miracles of goodness and mercy marked his life; but while he healed the afflicted, and cast out the demons that persecuted men, he left to themselves the work of correcting the evils of their natures. He instructed them how to unite their human efforts with his divine power, and triumph through his strength over the sins that beset them.

This experience was necessary in order to give moral power to the Christian character and fit it for the courts of Heaven. Jesus employed no miraculous agency to compel men to believe in him. They were left to choose or reject him, of their own free will. No direct power was to force them into obedience, and destroy the free moral agency that God has given to man. The parable of the sower plainly sets forth the tendencies of the human heart, and the different classes with which Christ had to deal, and also explains the reasons that his ministry was not more successful in its immediate effects.

The parables of Jesus were designed to arouse a spirit of inquiry which would result in a clearer

exposition of the truth.   As he was thus instructing his disciples in the meaning of his words,
the people again gathered about to listen, and
his teachings were received and cherished in the
minds of many who heard them.   These discourses of Jesus were not merely to a class of inferior minds; but there were intelligent and cul-
tivated persons present who were capable of the
closest criticism.   Scribes, Pharisees, doctors, rulers, lawyers, and the representatives of all nations, were there to hear; yet there were none to
gainsay his words in all that vast assembly.

CHAPTER XIX.

OTHER PARABLES.

THERE was much curiosity and questioning
among the people concerning this kingdom which
they could not see with their material eyes.   Jesus knew every perplexity that agitated the
minds of his hearers, and as the multitude again
thronged about him, he continued to teach them
in parables.   " And he said unto them, Is a candle brought to be put under a bushel, or under a
bed ? and not to be set on a candlestick ?   For
there is nothing hid, which shall not be manifested; neither was any thing kept secret, but that
it should come abroad.   If any man have ears to
hear, let him hear.   And he said unto them, Take
heed what ye hear; with what measure ye mete,
it shall be measured to you ; and unto you that
hear shall more be given.   For he that hath, to

him shall be given; and he that hath not, from him shall be taken even that which he hath."

Jesus used the light of a candle to represent his doctrines, which illuminate the souls of those who accept them. This light is not to be hidden from the world, but should shine forth to enlighten and bless those who behold it. The instruction received by those who listened to Jesus was to be communicated by them to others, and thus handed down to posterity. He also declared that there was nothing hidden that should not be manifested. Whatever was in the heart would sooner or later be revealed by the actions; and these would determine whether the seed sown had taken root in their minds and borne goodly fruit, or whether the thorns and brambles had won the day. He admonished them to hear and understand him. To improve the blessed privileges then extended to them, would result in their own salvation and through them would benefit others.

And with what measure of sincere attention they listened to his instructions, they would receive like measure of knowledge in return. All who truly desired to understand his doctrines would be fully satisfied; their Heaven-given privileges would increase; their light would brighten unto the perfect day. But those who did not desire the light of truth would grope in darkness and be overcome by the powerful temptations of Satan. They would lose their dignity and self-control, and the little knowledge of which they had boasted when they declared that they had no need of Christ, and scorned the guidance of Him who left a throne in Heaven to save them.

Following the thread of his discourse, the Divine Teacher uses another parable, saying, "So is the kingdom of God, as if a man should cast seed into the ground; and should sleep, and rise night and day, and the seed should spring and grow up, he knoweth not how. For the earth bringeth forth fruit of herself; first the blade, then the ear, after that the full corn in the ear. But when the fruit is brought forth, immediately he putteth in the sickle, because the harvest is come." The seed here spoken of is the word of God sown in the heart and made fruitful by divine grace. If the truth takes root in the heart, it will sooner or later spring into life and bear fruit. The life and character will show the nature and quantity of the seed sown. But the work of cultivating is the work of a life-time. The principles of truth once planted in the soul, are to be carried out in the daily duties of life. The growth of Christian character is gradual— like the advancement of the natural plant through its various stages of development. But nevertheless the progress is continual. As in nature, so it is in grace, the plant must either grow or die.

Day by day the sanctifying influence of the Spirit of God almost imperceptibly leads those who love the ways of truth toward the perfection of righteousness, till finally the soul is ripe for the harvest, the life-work is ended, God gathers in his grain. There is no period in the Christian life when there is no more to learn, no higher attainments to reach. Sanctification is the work of a life-time. First the blade, then the ear, then the full corn in the ear, then the ripening and the harvest; for when the fruit is perfect, it is ready for the sickle.

This figure presented a most marked contrast to the condition of the Jews. Their religion was cold and formal, the Holy Spirit had no place in their hearts; therefore, instead of growing in grace, and advancing in the knowledge of God, they were continually becoming more callous and bigoted, retreating farther and farther from the presence of the Lord. The proud, caviling Pharisees looked around upon the vast numbers gathered to hear Jesus, and noted contemptuously how few there were who acknowledged him as the Messiah. There were many educated and influential men who had come to hear the prophet whose fame had spread far and near. Some of these looked with curious interest upon the throng, which was composed of all classes of society and every nationality. There were the poor, the illiterate, the ragged beggar, the robber with the seal of guilt upon his face, the sick, the maimed, the dissipated, high and low, rich and humble, jostling each other for a place to stand and hear the words of Jesus.

As they gazed, they asked themselves incredulously, Is the kingdom of God composed of such material as this? Jesus read their thoughts, and replied to them by another parable :—

"Whereunto shall we liken the kingdom of God? or with what comparison shall we compare it? It is like a grain of mustard seed, which, when it is sown in the earth, is less than all the seeds that be in the earth. But when it is sown, it groweth up, and becometh greater than all herbs, and shooteth out great branches; so that the fowls of the air may lodge under the shadow of it." Far and near the mustard lifted itself above the grass and grain, waving its branches lightly in the air. Birds flitted from twig to twig and sang amid its leafy foliage. Yet the seed from which sprang this giant plant, was the least of all seeds. At first it had sent up a tender shoot; but it was of strong vitality, and grew and flourished till it was of large proportions, and the birds lodged under its shadow.

The people look upon the mustard, growing so vigorously about them, and their minds are vividly impressed by the illustration Jesus has used to point the truths of his doctrine. He thus declares that not by force of arms, and the pomp and heraldry of war, is the kingdom of Christ to be set up. But the work is of gradual development. Though the beginning may be small, it will grow and strengthen till, like the grain of mustard seed, it will reach, through imperceptible stages of development, the majesty of greatness.

Jesus takes this poor little seed to illustrate his mighty truths. The merest trifle is not beneath the notice of the great Teacher. Many were there whose Christian experience began that day, and would be like the symbol he had used, growing into strength and beauty, trampled upon, yet still maintaining its vigorous life. This figure was indelibly written upon the minds of hundreds who listened to the words of Jesus. Never would they behold the rank-growing mustard, so plentiful in that region, but they would be reminded of this parable of the Saviour, and their hearts would remember the lesson that he taught concerning the mysterious influence of divine grace upon the human soul, and the quickening power of the word that declares itself in the daily life.

"Another parable spake he unto them: The kingdom of Heaven is like unto leaven, which a woman took, and hid in three measures of meal, till the whole was leavened." The leaven in the meal represents the progressive work of divine grace in the human heart. The leaven was not naturally in the meal, but being placed in it gave rise to fermentation which resulted in a radical change of the whole mass. So the principles of God's truth, hidden in the heart of an individual, change his entire nature, and influence his life. The natural feelings are transformed, the affections are consecrated, and the mind elevated. Physically, the man appears the same; but inwardly, he has become renewed by the heavenly principles that animate his life.

Again Jesus took the fields before him and the sowers and reapers to illustrate his truths, saying, "The kingdom of Heaven is likened unto a man which sowed good seed in his field. But while men slept, his enemy came and sowed tares among the wheat, and went his way. But when the blade was sprung up, and brought forth fruit, then appeared the tares also.

The tares were noxious weeds, very annoying to the cultivator of the soil, for they sprang up together with the good grain. There was danger of disturbing the roots of the wheat, and destroying the young blades, if the weeds were rudely pulled from among them; besides this, the tares so closely resembled the grain, while growing, that it was hard to distinguish the one from the other.

When the servants of the householder came and asked him from whence the tares had come, seeing he had sown good seed in his field, he told them that an enemy had sowed the weeds among his grain to injure him. Then they inquired if they might not gather out the tares and leave the wheat free. "But he said, Nay; lest while ye gather up the tares, ye root up also the wheat with them. Let both grow together until the harvest; and in the time of harvest I will say to the reapers, Gather ye together first the tares and bind them in bundles to burn them, but gather the wheat into my barn."

The enemy sowing the troublesome seeds, is an illustration of Satan's work upon the human mind. Christ is the Sower, who scatters the precious grain in the fallow ground of the heart; but the enemy of souls steals in secretly and sows the seeds of evil. These germs of error spring up abundantly and bear their noxious fruit, sometimes crowding out and destroying the precious plants about them. The soil that should have produced goodly grain for the nourishment of man, runs to waste, and the seeds of sin are carried from that to other fields.

The growth of the tares among the wheat would draw special attention to it. The grain would be subjected to severe criticism. Indeed, the whole field might be set down as worthless by some superficial observer, or by one who delighted to discover evil. The sower might be condemned by him, as one who had mingled the bad seed with the good for his own wicked purpose. Just so the erring and hypocritical ones who profess to follow Jesus bring reproach upon the cause of Christianity, and cause the world to doubt concerning the truths of Christ. As the presence of the tares among the wheat counteracted to a great degree the work of the sower, so sin among the people of God, frustrates, in a measure, the plan of Jesus to save fallen man from the power of Satan and render the barren ground of the human heart fruitful of good works.

The tares so closely resembled the wheat that the laborers might easily be deceived when the blades were green, and root out the good plants. But when the field was white for the harvest, then the worthless weeds bore no resemblance to the wheat that bowed under the weight of its full, ripe heads. Then the tares were ruthlessly plucked up and destroyed, while the precious grain was gathered into barns. Sinners who make false pretensions of piety mingle together for a time with the true followers of Christ, and this external semblance of Christianity is calculated to deceive many. But in the harvest of the world there will be no likeness between good and evil. The wicked will be gathered from the righteous, to trouble them no more forever.

After Jesus had sent the multitude away, and had retired with his disciples into the house, they asked him to explain the parable that he had given them, and he answered, " He that soweth the good seed is the Son of Man. The field is the world; the good seed are the children of the kingdom; but the tares are the children of the wicked one; the enemy that sowed them is the devil; the harvest is the end of the world; and the reapers are the angels. As therefore the tares are gathered and burned in the fire, so shall it be in the end of this world. The Son of Man shall send forth his angels, and they shall gather out of his kingdom all things that offend, and them which do iniquity, and shall cast them

into a furnace of fire; there shall be wailing and
gnashing of teeth. Then shall the righteous shine
forth as the sun in the kingdom of their Father.
Who hath ears to hear, let him hear."

These words of Christ are meaningless to those
who are looking for a temporal millennium, when
all the world will be converted. He expressly
states that the wheat and tares shall grow together till the harvest, which is the end of the
world. Then the tares are to be gathered out of
the field; but they are not to be transformed by
a mighty miracle into wheat. They are to remain
tares, and are to be cast into the fire and utterly
destroyed.

Jesus, in his explanation of the parable, brings
distinctly before his disciples the great difference
between the treatment of the wicked and the
righteous in that time when men shall be judged
for their deeds. Reaching down to the end of
time, he corrects the false doctrines of those
who rise up to deceive the people. He would
teach men that God, who rained a fiery tempest
upon the cities of the plains and destroyed them
because of the iniquity in their midst, will surely
punish the sinner. He holds the destiny of men
and nations in his hands, and he will not always
be mocked. Jesus himself declares that there is
a greater sin than that which brought destruction upon Sodom and Gomorrah; it is the sin of
those who see the Son of God and listen to his
teachings, yet turn from his salvation, and reject
his offered mercy. But the righteous shall be rewarded with eternal life.

Jesus, in his teachings on this occasion, spoke
many parables to the people, that he might forcibly impress his truths upon their minds. Our

Saviour's mission to the world was to bring to
light hidden mysteries which finite man could
never fathom, divine problems which the human mind is unable to solve. "Of which salvation the prophets have inquired and searched
diligently, who prophesied of the grace that
should come unto you." "Which things the angels desire to look into." The Son of God
came to be a light to the world, to reveal
wonders to the children of men that even the
angels had vainly longed to understand. He
patiently explains the marvelous transformation of sinful mortals into children of God and
heirs with himself in the kingdom of Heaven.
The introduction of sin had opened the door to
every species of suffering and wretchedness, till
moral darkness shrouded the earth like a funeral
pall; but Jesus, the Restorer, brings man into
connection with himself and re-creates him in the
divine image.

The Saviour continued his parables to the listening people, saying, "Again, the kingdom of
Heaven is like unto treasure hid in a field; the
which when a man hath found, he hideth, and
for joy thereof goeth and selleth all that he hath,
and buyeth that field. Again, the kingdom of
Heaven is like unto a merchant man, seeking
goodly pearls; who, when he had found one
pearl of great price, went and sold all that he
had, and bought it." In those days there were
many who searched for treasure which was supposed to be buried in certain localities where
great cities had once stood. In the great thoroughfare of travel, where Jesus was then teaching, it was not unusual to meet persons who had
come long distances on their way to where it

was supposed hidden treasure could be found. The desire for great riches led them upon a journey fraught with many perils. They had left their avocations upon a venture that seldom proved successful. But if they secured a small treasure they redoubled their exertions, hoping to realize still greater riches. Jesus had this class of his hearers in view, when he thus illustrated the mysterious riches of his grace, which, once having attracted the heart of man, lead him to seek higher attainments and greater blessings. The more he realizes of the peace of God, the more he desires to drink deeper at the fountain of his love. The thirst for righteousness, the longing and seeking for its treasures, continually increase.

In order to obtain a vast treasure that is supposed to be hidden in a field, or a gem that is of great and unknown value, the man who is seeking for riches invests all his substance in that field, or uses it to purchase the precious jewel, calculating that it will increase in value on his hands and bring him the fortune that he covets. So should the Christian, who desires the riches of Heaven, set aside all considerations that interfere with his eternal welfare, and put his soul into the work of securing the riches of Christ's love. His talents, his means, his energies, should all be applied in such a way as to win the approbation of God. Jesus directs the minds of his hearers to infinite riches, hidden where all may engage in searching for them, sure of being successful, never doomed to the disappointment of fruitless toil. He came from Heaven to direct the search. High and low, rich and poor, stand upon an equal footing, and none need seek in vain. Obedience to his will is the one condition of success, and well may the earnest seeker afford to sell all that he has to possess this blessing of divine love—the pearl of great price.

There were many fishermen in the assembly that listened to the teachings of Jesus; and therefore he spoke a parable that would bring his truth directly home to their minds by an illustration drawn from their daily lives. Said he, " Again, the kingdom of Heaven is like unto a net, that was cast into the sea, and gathered of every kind. Which, when it was full, they drew to shore and sat down, and gathered the good into vessels, but cast the bad away. So shall it be at the end of the world. The angels shall come forth, and sever the wicked from among the just, and shall cast them into the furnace of fire; there shall be wailing and gnashing of teeth." Here again the separation of the wicked from the righteous at the end of the world is impressed upon the minds of his hearers, in words that cannot be mistaken.

Jesus had a wise purpose in making use of so many parables by which to teach the same important truths. All classes were before him, for it was a place where many different people met in the pursuit of their business or in their journeys. By using a variety of illustrations he succeeded in reaching many minds. The parable of the sower and that of the wheat and tares, applied to all. The fields were before them, and the laborers scattering the seed, or harvesting the earlier grain. Also the mustard that grew so luxuriantly about them furnished a lesson for all.

But in order to press home his truths more closely, he also spoke other parables to suit par-

ticular cases.   The searcher for riches represented
a large class, who could not but be struck by the
parable of the hidden treasure.   And the leaven,
buried in the meal, while it was an illustration
that could be understood by all, brought home
the truth with added power to the minds of the
women, who knew so well the action of the leav-
en upon the meal, and were thus enabled to draw
a forcible comparison between that and the work-
ings of God's grace upon the human heart.   Jesus overlooked none in his teachings, and the
humblest were remembered with tender pity.

The Saviour inquired of his disciples if they
understood these things.   They answered, " Yea,
Lord.   Then said he unto them, Therefore every
scribe which is instructed unto the kingdom of
Heaven is like unto a man that is an householder, which bringeth forth out of his treasure things
new and old."   In this parable, Jesus presented before his disciples the responsibility of
those whose work it is to give to the world the
light which they have received from him.   The
Old Testament was all the Scripture then in existence ; but it was not written merely for the an-
cients ; it was for all ages and for all people.   Jesus would have the teachers of his doctrine diligently search the Old Testament for that light
which establishes his identity as the Messiah
foretold in prophecy, and reveals the nature of
his mission to the world.   The Old and the New
Testament are inseparable, for both are the
teachings of Christ.   The doctrine of the Jews,
who accept only the Old Testament, is not unto
salvation, since they reject the Saviour whose
life and ministry was a fulfillment of the law
and the prophecies.   And the doctrine of those who

discard the Old Testament is not unto salvation, because it rejects that which is direct testimony of Christ. Skeptics begin with discounting upon the Old Testament, and it takes but another step to deny the validity of the New, and thus both are rejected.

The Jews have little influence over the Christian world in showing them the importance of the commandments, including the binding law of the Sabbath, because in bringing forth the old treasures of truth, they throw aside the new ones in the personal teachings of Jesus. On the other hand, the strongest reason why Christians fail to influence the Jews to accept the teachings of Christ as the language of divine wisdom, is because, in bringing forth the treasures of his word, they treat with contempt the riches of the Old Testament, which are the earlier teachings of the Son of God, through Moses. They reject the law proclaimed from Sinai, and the Sabbath of the fourth commandment, instituted in the garden of Eden. But the minister of the gospel, who follows the teachings of Christ, will gain a thorough knowledge of both the Old and the New Testament, that he may present them in their true light to the people an inseparable whole—the one depending upon and illuminating the other. Thus, as Jesus instructed his disciples, they will bring forth from their treasure "things new and old."

In looking abroad over the various fields where he had labored, Jesus was filled with compassion for those scattered ones who had accepted him as their Saviour, and looked to him for the bread of life. They seemed to him like sheep to be left without a shepherd, when he should ascend to Heaven. Before his sufferings and death, it was necessary that he should commission his disciples to go forth as his representatives, that the believers might look to them as divinely appointed teachers, so that in the approaching time of darkness and discouragement they would not be left without counselors. Calling the twelve about him, he said to them ; " The harvest truly is great, but the laborers are few ; pray ye therefore the Lord of the harvest, that he would send forth laborers into his harvest." As yet the disciples had little experience in preaching the practical truths received from their Lord ; but they had been his companions for several months, and he had occasionally sent them forth to labor by themselves for a short time, to prepare them for their future mission when he should no longer be with them. But he now separated them in pairs, and sent them away from him in different directions. He delegated to them the power of working miracles, but they were in no case to employ this power for their own exaltation or advantage. They were to be gone but a few days, and they were not sent among strangers on this first tour, but among their brethren who were to prepare their way that they might have access to the people, many of whom earnestly desired to know more of the doctrines of Christ.

In sending out his disciples, Jesus instructed them, upon entering a town or city, to seek those who were of good repute and abide with them during the time in which they labored in that locality ; for the influence of such persons would be beneficial to the cause. But if the disciples were not received by those to whom they went, they were to shake off even the dust from their feet against the house that was closed against them, or the city that refused to hear their message. This act was calculated to impress the people with the importance of the gospel message, and with the fact that it could not be slighted or rejected with inpunity. The great Teacher declared to his disciples, with startling emphasis, that it would be more tolerable for Sodom and Gomorrah in the day of Judgment than for the city that refused to hear them.

Jesus enjoins his disciples to make known to others those truths which he had spoken to their ears alone, saying, "What I tell you in darkness, that speak ye in light; and what ye hear in the ear, that preach ye upon the house-tops." Knowing the rebuffs and persecution they are to meet in the ministry upon which they are now about to enter, he strengthens them for their work by assuring them that in all their coming toils and dangers, God will watch over them. They are to go on unmindful of the opposition of men, seeking only to please God in whose hands they are: "And fear not them which kill the body, but are not able to kill the soul; but rather fear Him which is able to destroy both soul and body in hell."

They are to go forward, bearing their testimony of truth, and leave their fate with their Heavenly Father. Jesus comforts them with a knowledge of the divine care that watches over their lives, saying, "Are not two sparrows sold for a farthing? and one of them shall not fall on the ground without your Father. But the very hairs of your head are all numbered. Fear ye not therefore; ye are of more value than many sparrows."

And finally, he crowns his instruction and encouragement with the grand assurance of eternal reward to those who accept the Son of God and obey his teachings, and of denunciation to those who reject them: "Whosoever therefore shall confess me before men, him will I confess also before my Father which is in Heaven. But whosoever shall deny me before men, him will I also deny before my Father which is in Heaven."

Thus the Saviour commissioned his disciples to go out into the world and preach his word, to heal the sick, and comfort the sorrowful as they had seen him do, and they went forth, working according to his directions. The mission of God's servants to-day is of the same vital importance as that of the apostles whom Christ sent from him with such solemn words of instruction. To accept or to reject the message of Christ will insure the results indicated by the Master to his disciples on that solemn occasion when he commissioned them to teach his word to the people.

CHAPTER XX.

THE LOAVES AND FISHES.

JESUS, to obtain a little season of repose, and for the benefit of his disciples, proposed that they should go with him into a desert place and rest awhile. There were suitable places for such retirement beyond the sea from Capernaum, and

they entered a boat to make their way thither.
But some who were searching for Jesus saw him
depart from the shore, and the anxious people
gathered together watching the slowly receding
boat.   The news spread from city to city that
Jesus was crossing the sea; and many who
were eager to see and hear him flocked to the
place where it was thought that his boat would
land, while others followed him over the water
in boats.   So when Jesus and his disciples landed they found themselves in the midst of a multitude of people, pressing forward on all sides to
meet them.

Hundreds of the sick and maimed had been
brought for Jesus to relieve, and were disposed
upon the ground in positions favorable to arrest
his attention.   The crowd had awaited his coming with intense anxiety, and their numbers were
continually increasing. The Saviour could not
here find the rest he sought, for the waiting company commanded his attention; their needs en-
listed his immediate sympathy and aid. He could
not steal away with his disciples to secure the
coveted retirement, and disappoint this expectant
people.   All maladies were represented among
the sick who claimed his notice. Some were
burning with fever and unconscious of the anxious friends that ministered to them. There
were the deaf, the blind, the palsied, the lame,.
and lunatic.   In looking upon this wretched
throng the heart of Jesus melted with compassion.

He was so pressed upon by the multitude that
he went a little apart upon a grassy eminence,
where he could be seen and heard by all the people.   Here he taught them through the entire

day, and healed all the sick and afflicted that were brought to him. Those who had been confused in their belief, and longed for some intelligent doctrine to relieve their uncertainty, found their darkness dispelled by the beams of righteousness from the presence of Christ, and were charmed with the simplicity of the truths he taught.

His discourse was often interrupted by the delirious ravings of some fever-stricken sufferer, or the piercing shriek of the insane, whose friends were trying to press through the crowd and bear the afflicted to the Healer. The voice of wisdom was also often lost in shouts of triumph as the victims of hopeless disease were instantly restored to health and strength. The great Physician patiently submitted to these interruptions, and spoke calmly and kindly to all. He came from the other side of the sea because he was weary, but lo, he found more pressing cases for his attention than at the place from which he had secretly departed.

At length the day was spent, the sun was sinking out of sight in the west, and yet the people lingered. Many had come miles to hear the words of Jesus and had eaten nothing all day. The Master had labored through all that time without food or repose, and the disciples, seeing him pale with weariness and hunger, besought him to rest from his toil and take some refreshment. Their entreaties being of no avail, they consulted together as to the propriety of forcibly removing him from the eager multitude, fearing that he would die of fatigue. Peter and John each took an arm of their blessed Master and kindly endeavored to draw him away. But he refused to be removed from the place. His work was imperative; every applicant for his mercy felt his own case to be the most urgent. The crowd press about the Saviour; they sway him hither and thither. In their efforts to more nearly approach him, they trample upon each other.

Jesus, perceiving all this, beckons to Peter, who is in his boat on the sea, to come nigh. The disciple obeys the signal, and comes to shore. Jesus presses through the throng, and steps into the boat, bidding Peter to thrust out a little from the land. He now sits in the rocking boat of the fisherman, and, in full sight and hearing of the crowd, finishes the long and toilsome day by speaking precious truths to them. The Son of God, leaving the royal courts of Heaven, takes not his position upon David's throne; but from the swaying seat of a fisherman's boat, speaks the words of eternal wisdom which are to be immortalized in the minds of his disciples and given to the world as the legacy of God.

As the sun was setting, Jesus saw before him five thousand people besides women and children, who had been all day without food. He inquired of Philip concerning the probability of obtaining bread for so large a number, that they might not return to their homes unrefreshed nor faint by the way. This he did to test the faith of his disciples, for he himself was at no loss how to provide food. He who would not work a miracle to satisfy his own hunger in the wilderness, would not allow the multitude to suffer for lack of food. Philip looked over the sea of heads and thought how impossible it would be to obtain sufficient food to satisfy the wants of such a crowd. He answered that two hundred penny-worth of bread would not be nearly enough to divide among them so that each one might have a little. Jesus inquired how much food could be found among the company. He was told that Andrew had discovered a lad who had with him five barley loaves, and two small fishes. But this was nothing among so many, and they were in a desert place, where no more could be obtained.

Jesus commanded that this meager store should be brought to him. This being done, he directed his disciples to seat the people upon the grass in parties of fifty, and one hundred, to preserve order, and that all might witness the miracle he was about to do. This marshaling of five thousand people into companies, was at length satisfactorily accomplished, and they were all seated in the presence of the Saviour. He then took the loaves and fishes, and, having given thanks, distributed them to the disciples and to the multitudes, in quantities sufficient to satisfy their appetites.

The people had arranged themselves in the required order wondering what was to be done, but their amazement knew no bounds when the problem was solved, and they beheld food portioned out to that vast assembly from the slender store scarcely sufficient for a score of persons. The food did not diminish, as Jesus handed it to his disciples, who in their turn served the people. As often as they returned to him for a fresh supply, it was furnished them. After all had been satisfied, he directed the disciples to gather up the fragments that nothing might be lost; and the broken fragments filled twelve baskets.

During this remarkable feast, there was much

earnest reflection among those who were so miraculously served. They had followed Jesus to
listen to words such as had never before fallen
upon their ears. His teachings had sunk into
their hearts. He had healed their sick, had comforted their sorrow, and, at last, rather than send
them away hungering, he had fed them bounte-
ously. His pure and simple doctrine laid hold of
their minds, and his tender benevolence won their
hearts. While eating the food he had provided
for them, they decided that this was indeed the
Messiah. No other one could do so mighty a
miracle. No human power could create from
five barley-loaves and two small fishes, food sufficient to feed thousands of hungry people. His
teachings and work of healing had already
nearly convinced them of his divinity, and this
miracle crowned their growing conviction with
entire belief.

They decided that this was the Prince of Life,
the promised Deliverer of the Jews. They perceive that he makes no effort to win the applause
of the people. In this he is essentially different
from the chief priests and rulers, who are ambitious for titles and the honor of men. They fear
that he will never claim his right as King of Israel and take his place on David's throne in Jerusalem. But they decide that what he will not assume for himself, they will claim for him. They
need no greater evidence of his divine power nor
will they wait for any further proof. They quietly consult among themselves, and arrange to take
him by force, and bear him upon their shoulders,
proclaiming him the King of Israel. The disciples unite with the people in declaring that the
throne of David is the rightful inheritance of

their Master. Let the arrogant priests and rulers be humbled, and compelled to yield honor to Him who comes clothed with the authority of God. They begin to devise means to accomplish their purpose; but Jesus discerns their plans, which, if followed out, would defeat the very work he designs to do, and put a period to his instruction and deeds of mercy and benevolence.

Already the priests and rulers look upon him as one who has turned the hearts of the people from them to himself. Already they so dread his growing influence among them that they seek to take his life. He knows that violence and insurrection would be the result of his exaltation as Israel's king. He did not come into the world to set up a temporal kingdom; his kingdom, as he had stated, was not of this world. The multitude do not perceive the dangers arising from the movement they contemplate; but the calm eye of divine wisdom discovers all the hidden evils. Jesus sees that it is time to change the current of feeling among the people. He calls his disciples to him and directs them to immediately take the boat and return to Capernaum, leaving him to dismiss the people. He promises to meet them that night or on the following morning. The disciples are loth to submit to this arrangement. They are ambitious that Jesus should receive his true merits, and be lifted above the persecutions of the priests and rulers. The favored moment seems to have arrived, when, by the unanimous voice of the people, Christ can be elevated to his true dignity.

They cannot feel reconciled that all this enthusiasm shall come to naught. The people were assembling from all quarters to celebrate the passover at Jerusalem. They were all anxious to see the great Prophet whose fame had spread through all the land. This, to the faithful followers of Jesus, seemed the golden opportunity to establish their beloved Master as Israel's king. It seemed, in the glow of this new ambition, a very hard thing for them to go away by themselves and leave their Master alone upon the desolate shore, surrounded by high and barren mountains.

They remonstrate against this arrangement; but Jesus is firm in his decision, and commands them to follow his directions with an authority that he had never before assumed toward them. They obey in silence. Jesus then turns to the multitude, and perceives that they are thoroughly decided to force him into becoming their king. Their movements must be checked at once. The disciples had already departed, and he now, standing before them with a grand dignity, dismisses them in so firm and decisive a manner that they dare not disobey his commands. The words of praise and exaltation die upon their lips. Their steps are stayed as they are in the very act of advancing to seize him, and the glad and eager looks fade from their countenances. There were men of strong minds and firm determination in that throng, but the kingly bearing of Jesus, and his few quiet words of authority quelled the tumult in a moment and frustrated all their designs. Like meek, submissive children, they obey the command of their Lord, submitting humbly, and without question, to a power that they recognize as above all earthly authority.

Jesus looked upon the retreating multitude
with yearning compassion. He felt that they
were as scattered sheep without a shepherd.
The priests, who should have been teachers in
Israel, were but machines for performing un-
meaning ceremonies and repeating the law they
did not themselves understand nor practice.
When he was left alone he went up into the
mountain, and, for many hours, bent in supplication before the Father with bitter agony and
tears. Not for himself were those earnest prayers, but for man, depraved and lost but for re-
deeming grace. It was for man that the Son of
God wrestled with his Father, asking that the
poor sinful creature might turn from his guilt to
the light of salvation.

The Saviour knew that his days of personal
effort for men upon earth were numbered. He
who read the hearts of men knew that comparatively few would accept him as their Redeemer,
acknowledging themselves lost without his divine aid. The Jews were rejecting the very help
that God had sent to save them from utter ruin.
They were fastening the chains that bound them
in hopeless night. They were bringing upon
themselves the certain wrath of God for their
blind and obstinate wickedness. Hence the grief
of Jesus, and his tears and strong cries for his mistaken people, who spurned his love that would
shelter them, and his mercy that would save
them from the retribution of their sins. Deep
emotion shakes that noble form as he keenly realizes the doom of the people he has come to
save. In every trial and emergency, Jesus went
to his Heavenly Father for help, and, in those secret interviews, received strength for the work

that lay before him. Christians should follow
the example of their Saviour, and seek in prayer
the strength that will enable them to endure the
trials and duties of life. Prayer is the Christian's defense, the safeguard of his integrity and
virtue.

CHAPTER XXI.

WALKING ON THE WATER.

MEANWHILE, the disciples were in trouble. A
storm had arisen, and the lake was lashed into
fury. Hour after hour they labored at the oars,
being driven hither and thither by the resistless
force of the waves. All night they were tossed
upon the raging billows, feeling liable at any moment to be engulfed beneath them. It was but
a few hours' work, in ordinary weather, to reach
the opposite shore, from the place they had left;
but their frail bark was driven farther and farther from the port they sought, the plaything of
the angry tempest. They had left Jesus with
dissatisfied hearts. They had set out, murmuring among themselves because their wishes had
not been gratified in the matter of exalting their
Lord to be the King of Israel. They had blamed
themselves for being so easily turned from their
purpose, and yielding so readily to the commands
of Jesus. They reasoned that if they had remained and persisted in their intention, they
might have finally gained the point.

When the storm arose they still more deeply
regretted having left Jesus. Had they remained

this peril would have been avoided. This was a severe trial of their faith. In the darkness and tempest they sought to gain the point where he had promised to meet them, but the driving wind forced them from their course and made all their efforts futile. They were strong men and accustomed to the water, but now their hearts failed them with terror; they longed for the calm commanding presence of the Master, and felt that were he with them they would be secure. But Jesus had not forgotten his disciples. From the distant shore, his eye pierced the darkness, saw their danger, and read their thoughts. He would not suffer one of them to perish. As a fond mother watches the child she has in kindness corrected, so the compassionate Master watched his disciples; and when their hearts were subdued, their unholy ambition quelled, and they humbly prayed for help, it was given them. At the very moment they believed themselves lost, a flash of lightning revealed the figure of a man walking toward them upon the water. An unspeakable terror seized them. The hands that had grasped the oars with muscle like iron, relaxed their hold, and fell powerless by their sides. The boat rocked at the will of the waves, while their eyes were riveted upon this vision of a man stepping firmly upon the white-capped billows.

They thought it must be a spirit, which omened their immediate destruction. Jesus calmly advanced as though he would pass them, but they recognize his form, and feel that he will not leave them in their distress. They cry out, supplicating his help! The figure turns! It is their beloved Master, whose well-known voice speaks,

silencing their fear, "Be of good cheer. It is I,
be not afraid." Were ever words so welcome, so
reassuring as these! The disciples are speechless
with joy. Their apprehensions are gone. The
storm is forgotten. They hail Jesus as their
Deliverer!

Ardent Peter is nearly beside himself with delight. He sees his Master boldly treading the
foam-wreathed waves, coming to save his followers, and he loves his Lord as never before. He
yearns to embrace and worship him. He longs
to meet him and walk by his side upon the
stormy water. He cries, "Lord, if it be thou,
bid me come unto thee on the water." Jesus
granted his request; but Peter had taken only a
step upon the surface of the boiling deep, when
he looked back proudly toward his companions
to see if they were watching his movements, and
admiring the ease with which he trod upon the
yielding water.

In taking his eyes from Jesus, they fell upon
the boisterous waves that seemed greedily threatening to swallow him; their roaring filled his ears,
his head swam, his heart failed him with fear. As
he is sinking, he recovers presence of mind sufficient to remember that there is One near who
can rescue him. He stretches out his arms toward Jesus, crying, "Lord, save me, or I perish!"
The pitying Saviour grasps the trembling hands
that are reached toward him, and lifts the sinking form beside his own. Never does that kindly face and that arm of strength turn from the
supplicating hands that are stretched out for
mercy. Peter clings to his Lord with humble
trust, while Jesus mildly reproaches him: "O
thou of little faith! wherefore didst thou doubt?"

The trembling disciple now clings firmly to the hand of the Master till they are both safely seated in the boat among their joyful companions. But Peter was subdued and silent; he had no reason to boast over his fellows, for he had very nearly lost his life through exaltation and unbelief. When he took his eyes from Jesus in order to note the admiration of others, he lost guidance, and doubt and fear seized upon him. So it is in the Christian life; nothing but an eye firmly fixed upon the Saviour will enable us to tread the stormy billows of the world. Immediately upon Jesus taking his place in the boat they were at the land. The tempest had ceased, and the night of horror was succeeded by the light of dawn. The disciples, and others who were also on board, bowed at the feet of Jesus with thankful hearts, saying, "Of a truth thou art the Son of God!"

The multitude that had been fed the preceding day had left Jesus on the barren shore, and they knew that there was no boat left by which he could depart. They therefore on the following morning returned to the spot where they had last seen him watching their departure with compassionate eyes. The news of his wonderful miracle of feeding the multitude had spread far and near, and at an early hour they began to arrive, by land and water, in large numbers. But they searched in vain for the great Teacher, and finally returned to Capernaum, still seeking him.

Meanwhile, the Master, with his disciples, had found the seclusion they sought the previous day. Jesus felt that it was necessary to give his disciples some special instruction, but he was followed so closely by the crowds that it was ex-

tremely difficult to secure such seasons of retirement. He could not obtain the time for prayer
in the day-time, but frequently devoted the entire night to communion with his Heavenly Father, wrestling in supplication for the erring children of men. The Saviour, oppressed by the unbelief of humanity, bearing the burden of the
world's iniquity, was indeed a Man of sorrows,
and acquainted with grief.

Jesus made use of the few hours of seclusion
with his disciples in praying with them, and
teaching them more definitely concerning the
nature of his kingdom. He saw that, in their
human weakness, they were inclined to desire
that his reign should be a temporal one. Their
earthly ambition had caused them to become
confused as to the real mission of Christ. He
now reproved them for their misconception, and
taught them that instead of worldly honor it
was shame that awaited him, and instead of a
throne, the pitiless cross. He taught them that
for his sake, and to win salvation, they must also
be willing to endure reproach and contumely.

The time drew near when Jesus was to die,
and leave his disciples to face the cold and cruel
world alone. He knew how bitter hate and unbelief would persecute them, and he wished to
encourage and strengthen them for their trials.
He accordingly went away by himself and prayed
for them, interceding with the Father, that in the
time of that fearful test which awaited them,
their faith would prove steadfast, and his sufferings and death might not utterly overwhelm them
with despair. What tender love was this, that,
in view of his own approaching agony, reached
forward to shield his companions from danger!

When he again joined his disciples, he asked them: "Whom do men say that I, the Son of Man, am? And they said, Some say that thou art John the Baptist; some, Elias; and others, Jeremias, or one of the prophets." Questioning still closer, he inquired, "But whom say ye that I am?" Peter, ever ready to speak, answered for himself and his brethren: "Thou art Christ, the Son of the living God. And Jesus answered and said unto him, Blessed art thou, Simon Bar-jona; for flesh and blood hath not revealed it unto thee, but my Father which is in Heaven."

Notwithstanding the faith of many had utterly failed, and the power of the priests and rulers was mighty against them, the brave disciple thus boldly declared his belief. Jesus saw, in this acknowledgment, the living principle that would animate the hearts of his believers in coming ages. It is the mysterious working of God's Spirit upon the human heart, that elevates the humblest mind to a knowledge above all earthly wisdom, an acquaintance with the sacred truths of God. Ah, indeed, "blessed art thou, Simon Barjona, for flesh and blood hath not revealed it unto thee."

Jesus continued: "And I say also unto thee, That thou art Peter, and upon this rock I will build my church; and the gates of hell shall not prevail against it." The word Peter signifies rolling stone. Christ did not refer to Peter as being the rock upon which he would found his church. His expression, "this rock," applied to *himself* as the foundation of the Christian church. In Isaiah 28:16, the same reference is made: "Therefore thus saith the Lord God, Behold, I lay in Zion, for a foundation, a stone, a tried stone, a precious corner stone, a sure foundation." It is the same stone to which reference is made in Luke 20:17, 18: "And he beheld them, and said, What is this then that is written, The stone which the builders rejected, the same is become the head of the corner? Whosoever shall fall upon that stone shall be broken; but on whomsoever it shall fall, it will grind him to powder." Also in Mark 12:10, 11: "And have ye not read this scripture, The stone which the builders rejected is become the head of the corner. This was the Lord's doing, and it is marvelous in our eyes?"

These texts prove conclusively that Christ is the rock upon which the church is built, and, in his address to Peter, he referred to himself as the rock which is the foundation of the church. He continues:—

"And I will give unto thee the keys of the kingdom of Heaven; and whatsoever thou shalt bind on earth shall be bound in Heaven; and whatsoever thou shalt loose on earth shall be loosed in Heaven." The Roman church makes a wrong application of these words of Christ. They claim that he addressed them specially to Peter. Hence he is represented in works of art as carrying a bunch of keys, which is a symbol of trust and authority given to ambassadors and others in high positions. The words of Christ: "I will give unto thee the keys of the kingdom of Heaven," were not addressed to Peter alone, but to the disciples, including those who compose the Christian church in all ages. Peter was given no preference nor power above that of the other disciples. Had Jesus delegated any special authority to one of them, we would not find them so frequently contending among themselves as to who should be greatest. They would have at once submitted to the wish of their Master, and paid honor to the one whom he had selected as their head.

But the Roman Catholic church claims that Christ invested Peter with supreme power over the Christian church, and that his successors are divinely authorized to rule the Christian world. In still another place Jesus acknowledges the same power to exist in all the church that is claimed to have been given to Peter alone, upon the authority of the text previously quoted: "Verily I say unto you, Whatsoever ye shall bind on earth shall be bound in Heaven; and whatsoever ye shall loose on earth shall be loosed in Heaven."

CHAPTER XXII.

CHRIST IN THE SYNAGOGUE.

THIS interview of Jesus with his disciples, in which they had received much precious instruction, was interrupted by those who had been searching for him. As the people began to flock about him, bringing their sick and afflicted, he repaired to the synagogue. While he was teaching there, many others of those who had left him on the other side of the lake came to the synagogue, and were surprised to see Jesus and his disciples there before them, knowing that there was no boat by which he could pass to the other side.

They began to inquire how and when he had crossed the sea. They were astonished when the disciples related to them the events of the preceding night. The fury of the storm and the many hours of fruitless rowing against the fury of adverse winds, the appearance of Christ walking upon the water, the fears thus aroused, his reassuring words, the adventure of Peter and its result, with the sudden stilling of the tempest and landing of the boat, were all faithfully recounted to the wondering crowd, amid frequent interruptions and exclamations of amazement.

But their attention was now directed to the lessons of Jesus, so full of solemn interest. Many were deeply affected; but the minds of some were entirely engrossed with curiosity regarding the wonderful relation they had heard. As soon as the discourse was ended, they gathered around the Saviour, questioning him, hoping to receive from his own lips a fuller account of his mighty work of the previous night. But Jesus did not gratify their idle curiosity. He was also beset by the Pharisees, to show them a sign from Heaven that he was the Son of God. They asked an evidence of his miraculous power, such as had been given on the other side of the sea. They importuned him to repeat his wonderful works before them.

Jesus declared to them that they did not seek him from any worthy motive; that they did not desire to learn how to please God in their daily lives; but they asked him to work miracles, sometimes in a spirit of unbelief, and sometimes because they hoped to be benefited by temporal favors which he might thus bestow upon them. He bade them not to labor for the meat which perishes, but to seek for spiritual food, that wisdom which endures unto everlasting life. This the Son of God alone could give, for he has the seal of the Father. With solemn earnestness he sought to impress upon them that temporal favors are of little consequence compared with the heavenly grace offered by the Son of God.

"Then said they unto him, What shall we do, that we might work the works of God? Jesus answered and said unto them, This is the work of God, that ye believe on Him whom he hath sent. They said therefore unto him, What sign showest thou then, that we may see, and believe thee? what dost thou work? Our fathers did eat manna in the desert; as it is written, He gave them bread from heaven to eat." It was Christ himself who conducted the Hebrews in their travels through the wilderness. It was he who had daily fed them manna from heaven; yet they blindly referred him to this miracle, wrought for their fathers, in a spirit of caviling unbelief. Jesus declared to them that as God had given them manna to preserve their lives, so he had sent to them this gift of his Son, that through him they might eat of the bread of life and become immortal.

"Then said Jesus unto them, Verily, verily, I say unto you, Moses gave you not that bread from heaven; but my Father giveth you the true bread from Heaven. For the bread of God is He which cometh down from Heaven, and giveth life unto the world. Then said they unto him, Lord, evermore give us this bread." Jesus used bread as a figure to illustrate the vitalizing power of his Spirit. The one sustains physical life, while the other satisfies the heart, and strengthens the moral powers. Said he, " I am the bread of life; he that cometh to me shall never hunger; and he that believeth on me shall never thirst. But I said unto you, That ye also have seen me, and believe not." Those who experience the spiritual union with Christ never hunger for higher enjoyment. All uncertainty is gone, the weary soul finds continual refreshment in the Saviour. The feverish thirst for wealth and honor is gone. He is in them a well of water springing up into everlasting life.

Jesus assured the Jews that they had seen him and his works yet believed not. He did not refer to their seeing him with their natural eyes; but he meant that their understanding had been convinced, while their proud and stubborn hearts refused to acknowledge him as the Messiah. The Saviour had been doing in their midst works that no man had ever done. The living evidences of his divine power had been before them day after day; yet their hard and caviling hearts asked for still another sign of his divinity before they would believe. Had this been given them they would still have remained as unbelieving as before. If they were not already convinced of his Messiahship by what they had seen and heard, it was useless to show them more marvelous works. The dignity of God's holy Son was not to be compromised to gratify a questioning crowd.

Said Jesus, " For this people's heart is waxed gross, and their ears are dull of hearing, and their eyes they have closed; lest at any time they should see with their eyes, and hear with their ears, and should understand with their heart, and should be converted, and I should heal them." Unbelief will ever find cause to doubt and reason away the most positive proof. The Jews stood constantly upon guard, lest they should be forced by overwhelming evidence to yield their prejudice and unbelief. Though their understanding was convinced, they refused to surrender their pride and self-righteousness, admitting that they, who had boasted of their wisdom over all the rest of the world, themselves needed a teacher.

The Jews had assembled to celebrate the passover. In eating the flesh of the lamb, they were to remember that it represented the Lamb of God, and their protection when the first-born of their enemies were slain in Egypt. The blood that the Hebrews were commanded to have upon their door-posts, and which was a sign of safety to them, also represented the blood of Christ, which was to be shed for the sins of the world. The Saviour has power to finally raise from the dead all those who, by faith, eat of his flesh and drink of his blood. This spiritual food gives to the believers a well-founded hope of the resurrection to immortal life in the kingdom of God.

These precious truths Jesus declared to the incredulous multitude, saying, "All that the Father giveth me shall come to me; and him that cometh to me I will in no wise cast out. For I came down from Heaven, not to do mine own will, but the will of him that sent me. And this is the Father's will which hath sent me, that of all which he hath given me I should lose nothing, but should raise it up again at the last day. And this is the will of Him that sent me, that every one which seeth the Son, and believeth on him, may have everlasting life, and I will raise him up at the last day."

He spoke of his future sacrifice in these words: " And the bread which I will give you, is my flesh, which I will give for the life of the world." He offered his salvation to all who would accept him, clothed in humanity, as their Redeemer, having access to the Father, and being invested by him with divine authority.

But the Jews were displeased that Jesus should claim to be the bread of life come down from Heaven. "And they said, Is not this Jesus, the son of Joseph, whose father and mother we know ? how is it, then, that he saith, I came down from Heaven ?" They so clung to their bigotry and pride that it now seemed impossible for them to believe evidence that was plain as the noonday sun. Their jealousy was aroused that this man of humble birth was able to work wonders that they could not explain away, and teach truths that could not be contradicted. So they endeavored to awaken the prejudice and unbelief of the people by referring scornfully to the lowly origin of Jesus, and by reason of his mysterious birth, insinuating that he was of doubtful parentage. They contemptuously alluded to his life as a Galilean laborer, and to his family as being poor and lowly. They declared that the lofty claims of this uneducated carpenter should be at once repudiated.

But Jesus heard their murmurings and reproved them. He again, in more forcible language, declared his connection with the Father, and the necessity for the heart to be enlightened by the Spirit of God before it can feel the need of a Saviour. " No man can come to me, except

the Father which hath sent me draw him; and
I will raise him up at the last day.   It is written
in the prophets, And they shall be all taught of
God.   Every man, therefore, that hath heard, and
hath learned of the Father, cometh unto me."
He here refers to the prophecy of Isaiah: "And
all thy children shall be taught of the Lord, and
great shall be the peace of thy children."

This was not a new doctrine which Jesus
taught.   It was the fulfillment of prophecy,
which, as expounders of the word, the priests
and elders should have thoroughly understood.
In declaring that none come to him unless the
Father draws them, the Saviour wished them to
understand that God would never appear in person to teach them concerning the way of life.
Humanity could not endure the vision of his
glory for a moment; only through the Son could
they come to him.   In seeing and hearing the Son,
they saw and heard the Father.   He is Mediator between God and his disobedient children.
The Jews claimed God as their teacher, but
Christ declared such profession vain, for, said he,
"Every man, therefore, that hath heard, and hath
learned of the Father, cometh unto me."

Jesus did not attempt to answer the questions
raised regarding his birth any more than he had
answered those concerning his crossing the sea.
He did not desire to magnify himself, nor the
miracles that marked his life.   The prejudice
of the Pharisees lay deeper than their questions would indicate, and had taken root in the
bitter perversity of their sinful hearts.   His sayings and doings had not created such feelings, but
only called them into action, because his pure
and elevated doctrine was not in harmony with

their selfish hearts. Said he, " Verily, verily, I say unto you, He that believeth on me hath everlasting life. I am that bread of life." There were conflicting views and much uncertainty in regard to the resurrection of the dead. Aside from the dissension between the Sadducees and Pharisees, the Jews were in great darkness concerning the future life and the resurrection of the body. Jesus pitied them in their benighted condition, and bade them accept him, who was their only hope, the great Life-giver, even the " bread of life."

They had referred him to the manna which their fathers ate in the wilderness, as if the furnishing of that food was a greater miracle than Jesus had wrought; but he now declared unto them that the temporal food then given from Heaven was but a meager gift compared with the blessing of eternal life which he now offered them. The food eaten then sustained the strength, but did not prevent the approach of death, nor insure immortal life. The bread that the Son of God offered to man was death-destroying, giving in the end immortal life to the body. Said he, " Your fathers did eat manna in the wilderness, and are dead. This is the bread which cometh down from Heaven, that a man may eat thereof, and not die. I am the living bread which came down from Heaven; if any man eat of this bread, he shall live forever; and the bread that I will give is my flesh, which I will give for the life of the world."

Our Lord here points forward to his approaching death, the only true propitiation for the sins of humanity. The Jews were about to celebrate with great display the feast of the passover. The lamb to be eaten there, was a symbol of Christ's body; yet the very person that it represented stood in their midst, presenting himself as their Saviour, whose blood would preserve them from the wrath of a sin-hating God, and they refuse his offers of mercy.

The miracle Jesus had performed in feeding the multitude, furnished him a forcible figure by which to illustrate his work upon earth. He declared that, as temporal bread imparts health and strength to the body, so will faith in Christ, and obedience to his teachings, give spiritual vigor to the soul, and life everlasting. But the Jews, determined to misinterpret his words, now engaged in angry contention, asking, "How can this man give us his flesh to eat?" They affected to understand his words in the same literal sense as did Nicodemus, when he asked, "How can a man be born when he is old?" They comprehended the meaning of Jesus, but were not willing to acknowledge it. They thought it a favorable opportunity to prejudice the people against him, by presenting his words to them in the most unfavorable light. "Then Jesus said unto them, Verily, verily, I say unto you, Except ye eat the flesh of the Son of Man, and drink his blood, ye have no life in you. Whoso eateth my flesh, and drinketh my blood, hath eternal life; and I will raise him up at the last day. For my flesh is meat indeed, and my blood is drink indeed. He that eateth my flesh, and drinketh my blood, dwelleth in me, and I in him. As the living Father hath sent me, and I live by the Father, so he that eateth me, even he shall live by me. This is that bread which came down from Heav-

en ; not as your fathers did eat manna, and are
dead ; he that eateth of this bread shall live forever."

The Jews appeared to be horrified at these
sayings of Christ. Their law strictly forbade
them to taste blood, and they construed his language into a sacrilegious speech, and contended
and disputed over his words among themselves.
Jesus gave his disciples, and the people, lessons
which they could not at the time fully comprehend, because of their moral darkness. Many
things which his followers did not fully understand when he uttered them, were made plain by
subsequent events. His words were a stay to
their hearts when he walked no more with them.

Even the disciples murmured at these last
words of Jesus. They said, " This is a hard saying ; who can hear it ? " The Saviour heard
their complaints and answered them : " Doth this
offend you ? What and if ye shall see the Son
of Man ascend up where he was before ? It is
the spirit that quickeneth ; the flesh profiteth
nothing ; the words that I speak unto you, they
are spirit, and they are life." Thus he instructed
them that it was not his human flesh that would
give life eternal, but faith in his words and in
the efficacy of the sacrifice he was to make for
the world. His teaching and example, his life
and death, were the heavenly food that was to
give them spiritual life and vigor. He reproved
them because they had murmured when he said
that he had come down from Heaven. If they
were not able to receive this truth, how would
it be when he ascended before their eyes to that
Heaven from whence he came ?

Jesus knew that many followed him who

hoped to receive temporal favors thereby. They looked for him to work some miracle that would benefit them; but especially did they hope that he would eventually free them from the Roman yoke. He also knew that there was one near who would betray him. He told them that there were some among them who believed not. "And he said, Therefore said I unto you, that no man can come unto me, except it were given unto him of my Father."

He wished them to understand that their hearts must be open to the Spirit of God before they could be drawn to him by faith. They must be willing to have their errors reproved, to eschew evil, and lead holy lives. The unbelief existing among the priests and rulers influenced the people to be hesitating and doubtful. Jesus had given them sufficient proof of his divinity; but their incredulous minds were ever seeking to explain away his wonderful works. They reasoned that the disciples might have been under a delusion when they saw him walking upon the water.

True, they could not but admit that he had performed many miraculous cures, and plentifully fed a vast multitude from five loaves and two small fishes; but their dissatisfied hearts queried, if he could do these wonders, why might he not give health, strength, and riches to all his people, free them from their oppressors, and exalt them to power and honor? Then they would believe on him and glorify his name. Thus they allowed themselves to be bound by unbelief and discontent. Their gross minds refused to comprehend the meaning of his words, "I am the bread which came down from Heaven." His doctrine was too pure and exalted to attract their carnal hearts.

This discourse of Jesus cooled the enthusiasm of the people. If, by becoming his disciples, they must live righteous lives, deny self, and suffer humiliation, they had no desire to rally under his banner. Alas for Israel! They knew not the time of their visitation! They refused their Saviour, because they longed for a conqueror who would give them temporal power. They wanted the meat which perishes, and not that which endures unto everlasting life. Their ambition was for earthly riches and glory, and they had no relish for the words of Christ that taught personal purity, and a thorough reformation of life.

Many of the words and dealings of Jesus appear mysterious to finite minds; but all his purposes were clear to his divine understanding. His whole plan was mapped before him, perfect in all its details. Every act was calculated to produce its individual results. The history of the world from its creation to the end of time was fully known to Christ. Were the mind of man capable of understanding his dealings, every act of his earthly life would stand forth important, complete, and in harmony with his divine mission.

The murmuring of his followers grieved the heart of the Saviour. In openly rebuking their unbelief before the multitude, he had increased their disaffection, and many of them went back and walked no more with Jesus. He looked after these erring ones with eyes of pitying tenderness. They were greatly displeased, and, wishing to wound Jesus and gratify the malice of the Pharisees, they turned their backs upon him and left him with disdain. In doing this they made the fatal mistake of rejecting God's counsel to them. It was such developments as these that made the Saviour a Man of sorrows and acquainted with grief. The consciousness that his kindness and compassion were unappreciated, his love unrequited, his mercy slighted, his salvation rejected, filled his divine soul with a grief that was inexpressible. Could these ungrateful disciples have discerned how God viewed their behavior to his dear Son, they would hardly have walked away so proudly and defiantly. They were choosing darkness rather than light, because they were too vain and self-righteous to receive a merited rebuke, and too worldly to accept a life of humility in order to secure salvation. In the face of all his wonderful works they turned away from Him, who, by the beauty of his doctrine and his mercy and benevolence, had called thousands to his side ; who had relieved suffering humanity, so that entire cities and villages were freed from disease, and there was no work for a physician among them.

When we view the generosity of Christ to the poor and suffering, his patience with the rude and ignorant, his self-denial and sacrifice, we are lost in admiration and reverence. What a gift has God lavished upon man, alienated from him by sin and disobedience ! Well may the heart break and the tears flow in contemplation of such inexpressible love ! Christ abased himself to humanity that he might reach man sunken into the depths of woe and degradation, and lift him into a nobler life, give him moral strength to resist the power of Satan and overcome sin in his name.

Sad was the recompense he met for his marvelous condescension.

The words of Jesus were scorned because he declared that outward professions and observances of forms would not avail; the work must reach the heart and bring forth fruit meet for repentance. The words that he addressed to his disciples are also spoken to the followers of Christ today. The same necessity exists for a clean heart and a pure life. Yet how many reject the warning of God, spoken by his servants, and the close, practical truths pressed home to their hearts, because their lives are not in accordance with the will of God, because they perceive that an entire reformation is necessary, and are unwilling to take up the self-denying work, and are therefore angry because their sins have been discovered. They go away offended, even as the disciples left Jesus, murmuring, "This is a hard saying; who can hear it?"

Those who profess godliness, yet do not heed the admonitions of the Lord, nor regulate their lives in harmony with his holy will, fasten themselves more and more firmly by chains of darkness. Many who now profess to believe the truth of Christ, endure the test no better than those who turned away from following him. Many, while professing the faith, are so separated from Christ by hearts of unbelief, that they reject the words and works of God shown through his servants. If the divine revelation does not harmonize with their views, they feel at liberty to turn from its teachings. If it rebukes their sins they are offended. Praise and flattery would be grateful to their ears, but the truth is disagreeable, they cannot hear it. When the crowds follow, and the multitudes are fed, and the cries of triumph go up, their voices are loud in praise; but when the searching of God's Spirit reveals to them their sin and bids them leave it, they turn their backs upon the truth, and "walk no more with Jesus."

God does not propose to be called to account for his ways and works. It is for his glory to conceal his purposes now; but by and by they will be revealed in their true importance. But he has not concealed his great love, which lies at the foundation of all his dealings with his children. He has revealed his love in the gift of his Son, and in the many providences by which he manifests himself. He who lives near to Jesus may understand much of the mystery of godliness, and comprehend the love that administers merited reproof. Humanity, alienated from God, can only be reconciled to him by partaking spiritually of the flesh and blood of his dear Son.

The Saviour did not attempt to prevent the disaffected disciples from leaving him, but, turning to the twelve chosen ones, said sorrowfully, "Will ye also go away?" Peter promptly replied by asking in turn "Lord, to whom shall we go? Thou hast the words of eternal life, and we believe and are sure that thou art that Christ, the Son of the living God." How full of meaning are these words, "To whom shall we go?" The teachers of Israel were slaves to cold formality. The Pharisees and Sadducees were in constant contention concerning the doctrine of the resurrection and other points of difference. To leave Jesus was to fall among sticklers for rites and ceremonies, and ambitious men who sought their own glory. The disciples had felt more peace and joy since they had accepted Christ than in all their previous lives. They had looked back with horror upon their former course of carelessness and iniquity. How could they, whose eyes had been opened to discern the malice and bigotry of the Jews, go back to them who had scorned and persecuted the Friend of sinners? Long had their faith sustained them in looking for the Messiah, and now that he had come, they could not turn from his presence to those who were hunting his life and had persecuted them for obeying him.

"To whom shall we go?" Not from the doctrine of Christ, his lessons of love and charity, to the darkness of unbelief, the wickedness of the world. While many were turning from the Saviour who had witnessed his miraculous works, who had seen him heal the sick and comfort the distressed, who had been electrified by the heavenly majesty of his bearing, Peter expresses the faith of the disciples, "Thou art that Christ." Never will they deny that he is the world's Redeemer, the Son of God. The very thought of losing this anchor of their souls thrilled their hearts with anguish. To be again destitute of a Saviour, subject to fear and superstition, would be to be adrift upon a dark and stormy sea.

Some may question the wisdom of Jesus in introducing a subject so easily misunderstood as that which had turned so many from him on this occasion. But he had a purpose in view. He saw that a most trying ordeal awaited his disciples in his betrayal, his agony in Gethsemane, and his crucifixion. He knew who among his followers were unbelieving and who were of weak faith. Had no test been given them, Jesus would have had many among his followers who were weak in character, and undecided. When the great trial came, and their Lord was betrayed and condemned in the Judgment Hall; when he was humiliated, and the multitude, who had hailed him as their king, hissed at him and reviled him; when the cruel, jeering crowd cried, "Crucify him!"—then these faint-hearted ones would have sunk beneath their fear and disappointment.

The apostasy of these professed followers of Christ at such a time, would have been more than the twelve could have endured in addition to their great grief and the terrible ruin of their fondest hopes. The example of those who turned from him, might, in that hour of horror, have carried all the rest with them. But Jesus brought about this crisis while he was still present to comfort and strengthen his chosen, and prepare them for what was to follow. When the hooting rabble scorned Him who was doomed to the cross, the disciples were not overwhelmed with surprise at this insult to their Master, for they had seen the fickleness of those who had once followed him. When those who had professed to love the Master turned from him in the time of his trouble, the disciples remembered that the same thing had occurred before, for less reason. They had tested the inconstant favor of the world, and hung not their faith upon the opinions of others. Jesus wisely prepared the minds of his faithful few for the great trial of his betrayal and death.

Peter had great faith in Jesus. From the first he had believed that he was the Messiah. He had seen and heard John, who was the forerunner of Christ, proclaim him to be the Lamb of God that taketh away the sins of the world. He had been closely connected with Jesus, had witnessed his miracles, listened to his teachings, and was convinced that he was the Son of God Many who had been convicted by the preaching of John, and had accepted Christ, began to doubt as to the mission of John, when he was imprisoned and put to death. They also doubted if Jesus was really the Messiah, whom they had looked for so long.

But the faith of Peter never flagged; he followed his Master with unwavering devotion. When those of the disciples who had ardently expected Jesus to make a great display of power, and take his place on David's throne, left him because they perceived that he had no such intention, Peter and his companions faltered not in their allegiance. The vacillating course of those who praised yesterday, and condemned to-day, did not affect the faith of the true follower of the Saviour. Peter declares, "Thou art the Son of the living God." He waited not for kingly honors to crown his Lord, but accepted him in his humiliation. Peter, in his confession of Christ, expressed the faith of the disciples. But notwithstanding this, Jesus knew that neither his believing followers nor any of the Jews had any idea of associating humiliation, suffering and death, with their Messiah. Compassionate Redeemer, who, in the full knowledge of the doom that awaited him, tenderly smoothed the way for his disciples, prepared them for their crowning trial, and strengthened them for the final test!

CHAPTER XXIII.

THE PARALYTIC.

AGAIN the mission of Christ brought him to Capernaum. When the news spread abroad that Jesus was a guest at the house of Peter, men, women, and children flocked from every direction to hear the wonderful Teacher. There was a man in the vicinity who was reduced to utter helplessness by the incurable disease of palsy. He had given up all hope of recovery. But his friends and relatives had heard the gracious instruction of Jesus; they had witnessed his wonderful miracles; they saw that he turned none away, that even the loathsome lepers found access to his presence, and were healed, and they began to hope that the paralytic might be relieved if he could be brought under the notice of Jesus.

They tried to encourage the sufferer, telling him of the miraculous power of Jesus to cure every malady, of the words of mercy he had spoken to the despairing, and of those who are set free from the power of Satan by a word of his sublime authority. As the palsied man listened to the good tidings, hope revived in his heart that he might be relieved of his terrible infirmity. He longed to see Jesus and place himself in his hands. But when he reflected that dissipation had been the main cause of his affliction, hope sank for he feared that he would not be tolerated in the presence of the pure Physician. He had loved the pleasures of sin, his life had been a transgression of the law of God, and his bodily affliction was the penalty of his crime.

He had long before placed his case in the hands of the Pharisees and doctors, entreating their interest and sympathy, hoping that they would do something to relieve his tortured mind and physical sufferings. But they had looked coldly upon him and pronounced him incurable. They had added to his woe by telling him that he was only suffering the righteous retribution of God for his misdemeanors. It was the custom of the Pharisees to hold themselves aloof from the sick and needy. They held that sickness and distress were always an evidence of God's anger toward the transgressor. Yet frequently these very men, who exalted themselves as holy and enjoying the peculiar favor of God, were more corrupt in heart and life than the poor sufferers whom they condemned.

The palsied man had sunk into despair seeing no help from any quarter, till news of the miracles of mercy performed by Jesus had aroused hope again in his breast. Yet he feared that he might not be allowed in his presence; he felt that if Jesus would only see him and give him relief of mind by pardoning his sins, he would be content to live or die according to his righteous will. His friends assured him that Jesus had healed others who were in every respect as sinful and helpless as himself, and this encouraged him to believe that his own petition would be granted.

He felt that there was no time to lose; already his wasted flesh was beginning to decay. If anything could be done to arrest mortality, it must be done at once. The despairing cry of the dying man was, Oh that I might come into his presence! His friends were anxious to assist him in gratifying his wish, and several projects were suggested to bring about this result, but none of them seemed feasible. The sick man, although racked with bodily pain, preserved the full strength of his intellect, and he now proposed that his friends should carry him on his bed to Jesus. This they cheerfully undertook to do.

As they approached the dense crowd that had assembled in and about the house where Jesus was teaching, it seemed doubtful that they could accomplish their purpose. However, they pressed on with their burden, till their passage was completely blocked up and they were obliged to stop before they arrived within hearing of the Saviour's voice. Jesus was within, and, as was customary, his disciples sat near him; for it was most important that they should hear his words, and understand the truths which they were to proclaim by word or pen over all lands and through all ages.

The haughty Pharisees, the doctors and the scribes, were also gathered near with wicked purposes in their hearts, and a desire to confuse and confound the sacred Teacher, that they might accuse him of being an impostor, and condemn him to death. Jealous of his power and wisdom, they concealed their intense hatred, for the purpose of closely watching his words, and calling him out upon various subjects with the hope of surprising him into some contradiction or forbidden heresy that would give them an excuse to prefer charges against him. They were present when Jesus healed the withered hand upon the Sabbath day, and these men, who claimed to enjoy the special favor of God, were filled with madness because he had presumed to do this good work upon the Lord's day.

Outside of these magnates thronged the promiscuous multitude, drawn there from various motives. Some felt an irresistible impulse to hear the words of Jesus, yet dimly comprehended their import. They were eager to catch every syllable of the sacred utterances; and, in many cases, seeds of life lodged in their hearts, to spring up afterward and bear blessed fruit. Others came from wonder and curiosity, or a love of excitement,—the desire to see and hear some new thing. All grades of society were represented there, and many different nationalities.

Through this surging crowd, the bearers of the paralytic seek to push their way; but the attempt is useless. They urge the necessity of their case, in order to prevail upon the people to fall back, but it is of no avail. The sufferings of the invalid are increased by his anxiety, and his friends fear that he will die in this scene of confusion. The sick man gazes about him with inexpressible anguish. Must he relinquish all hope when the longed-for help is so near? He feels that he cannot endure so bitter a disappointment. He suggests that they bear him to the rear of the house, and break through the roof and let him down into the immediate presence of Jesus.

Seeing that it is his only chance of life, and fearing that he cannot live to be taken home, his friends follow his suggestion. The roof is opened, and the sick man is let down at the very feet of Christ. The discourse is interrupted; the Saviour looks upon that mournful countenance, and sees the pleading eyes fixed upon him with a silent entreaty. He understands the case, for it was he who had led the perplexed and doubting spirit to himself. He had come to the world to give hope to the guilty and wretched. John had pointed to him as "the Lamb of God, that taketh away the sin of the world." The divine spirit of Jesus stirred the heart of this poor sinner, and while he was yet at home, had brought conviction to his conscience. He had watched the first glimmer of faith deepen into a belief that Jesus was his only helper, and had seen it grow stronger with every effort to come into his presence.

The sufferer had wealth, but it could not relieve his soul of guilt, nor remove disease from his body. But divine power attracted him to the Friend of sinners, who alone could relieve him. Jesus acknowledges the faith that is evidenced by the sick man's efforts, under such perplexing difficulties, to reach the presence of his Lord, and lifting up his voice in melodious tones, addressed him: "Son, be of good cheer, thy sins are forgiven thee." The burden of darkness and despair rolls from the sick man's soul; the peace of perfect love and forgiveness rests upon his spirit and shines out upon his countenance. His physical pain is gone, and his whole being is transformed before the eyes of the astonished multitude. The helpless paralytic is healed, the guilty sinner is pardoned! He has now received the evidence he so much desired. Yet not here, but at home, when he had repented of his sins and believed in the power of Jesus to make him whole, had the life-giving mercies of the Saviour first blessed his longing heart.

The simple faith of the paralytic accepted the

words of the Master as the boon of new life. He preferred no further request, he made no noisy demonstration, but remained in blissful silence too happy for words. The light of Heaven irradiated his countenance, and the people looked with awe upon the scene before them. Christ stood with a serene majesty that lifted him above the dignitaries of the synagogue and the doctors of the law. The Pharisees, the scribes, and the doctors had waited anxiously to see what disposition Jesus would make of this case. They recollected that the sufferer had appealed to them for help, and that they had entrenched themselves in the sanctity of their office and refused him one ray of encouragement. They had even expressed annoyance at being troubled with so disagreeable a matter. They had looked with horror upon his shriveled form, and said, We cannot raise one from the dead; dissolution has already commenced.

Not satisfied with the agony thus inflicted, they had declared that he was suffering the curse of God for his sins. All these things came fresh to their minds when they saw the sick man before them. They also perceived that the people, most of whom were acquainted with these facts, were watching the scene with intense interest and awe. They felt a terrible fear that their own influence would be lost, not only over the multitude present, but also over all who should hear the news of this marvelous event.

These lofty men did not exchange words together, but looking into one another's faces, they read the same thought expressed upon every countenance: Something must be done to arrest

the tide of popular sentiment. Jesus had declared that the sins of the paralytic were forgiven. The Pharisees caught at these words as
an assumption of infinite power, a blasphemy
against God, and conceived that they could present this before the people as a crime worthy of
death. They did not express their thoughts, but
these worshipers of forms and symbols were saying in their minds, He is a blasphemer! Who
can forgive sins but God alone? They were laying hold of the Saviour's words of divine pardon,
to use as a means by which to accuse him. But
Jesus read their thoughts, and, fixing his reproving glance upon them, beneath which they cow-
ered and drew back, addressed them thus: "Why
reason ye these things in your hearts? Whether
is it easier to say to the sick of the palsy, Thy
sns be forgiven thee; or to say, Arise, and take
up thy bed, and walk? But that ye may know
that the Son of Man hath power on earth to forgive sins (he saith to the sick of the palsy), I say
unto thee, Arise, and take up thy bed, and go
thy way into thine house."

Then he who had been borne to Jesus on a
litter, and whose limbs were then useless, rises to
his feet with the elasticity and strength of youth.
The life-giving blood bounds through his veins,
seeking its natural channels with unerring precision. The lagging human machinery springs
into sudden activity, the animating glow of health
succeeds the pallor of approaching death. "And
immediately he arose, took up the bed, and went
forth before them all; insomuch that they were
all amazed, and glorified God, saying, We never
saw it on this fashion."

Oh! wondrous love of Christ, stooping to heal

the guilty and the afflicted! Divinity sorrowing
over and soothing the ills of suffering humanity!
Oh! marvelous power thus displayed to the children of men! Who can doubt the message of
salvation! Who can slight the mercies of a compassionate Redeemer!

The effect of this wonderful miracle upon the
people was as if Heaven had opened and revealed
the glories of the better world. As the man who
had been cured of palsy passed through the crowd,
blessing God at every bounding step, and bearing
his burden as if it were a feather's weight, the
people fell back to give him room, and with awe-
struck faces gazed upon him, and whispered softly
among themselves, saying, "We have seen strange
things to-day." The Pharisees were dumb with
amazement, and overwhelmed with defeat. They
saw that here was no opportunity for their prejudice and jealousy to inflame the multitude.
The wonderful work wrought upon the man
whom they, in their arrogance, had given over to
death and the wrath of God, had so impressed
the minds of the people that the influence of
these leading Jews was, for the time, forgotten.
They saw that Christ possessed a power, and
claimed it as his own prerogative, which they
thought belonged to God alone. The gentle dignity of his manner, united with his miraculous
works, was in such marked contrast with their
own proud and self-righteous bearing that they
were disconcerted and abashed, recognizing, but
not confessing, the presence of a Superior Being.

Had the scribes and Pharisees been honest before God, they would have yielded to the con-
clusive evidence they had witnessed that Jesus
was the Promised One of Israel. But they were

determined that nothing should convince them of this fact. They were in haughty and determined opposition to this meek and humble Teacher, who came from the workshops of Nazareth, yet by his wonderful works threatened to annihilate their dignity and station. So they yielded in no degree their hatred and malice, but went away to invent new schemes for condemning and silencing the Son of God.

These men had received many and repeated proofs that Jesus was the promised Saviour, but none had been so convincing and unquestioned as this miracle of mercy. Yet the stronger the evidence that was presented to their minds that Jesus had power on earth to forgive sins, as well as to heal the sick, the more they armed themselves with hatred and unbelief, till God left them to the forging of chains that would bind them in hopeless darkness. There was no reserve power to reach hearts so hardened with malice and skepticism.

Many in these days are taking the same course as the unbelieving Jews. God has given them light which they refuse to accept. His Spirit has rebuked them; but they have made his reproofs a stumbling-block in their way, over which they trip and fall. They have rejected his offered mercies, they have scorned to believe his truth, till they are left unrestrained to pursue their downward course.

There was great rejoicing in the home of the healed paralytic, when he came into the midst of his family, carrying with ease the couch upon which he had been slowly borne from their presence but a short time before. They gathered round with tears of joy, scarcely daring to be-

lieve their eyes. He stood before them in the
full vigor of manhood. Those arms that they
had seen lifeless were quick to obey his will; the
flesh that had been shrunken and leaden-hued
was now fresh and ruddy with health; he
walked with a firm, free step; hope was written
in every lineament of his countenance; all gloom
had disappeared, and an expression of peace and
purity had taken the place of the marks of sin
and suffering. Glad thanksgivings went up from
that house, and God was glorified through his
Son, who had restored hope to the hopeless, and
strength to the stricken one. This man and his
family were ready to lay down their lives for
Jesus. No doubt could dim their faith, no unbelief could mar their perfect fealty to Christ,
who had brought light into their darkened home.

CHAPTER XXIV.

WOMAN OF CANAAN.

JESUS now left the vicinity of Jerusalem and
went to the coasts of Tyre and Sidon. Here a
woman who was a Canaanite met and besought
him to heal her daughter, who was grievously
vexed with a devil. The woman well knew that
the Jews had no dealings with the Canaanites
and that they refused even to speak to them; but
having heard of the miracles of mercy which Jesus
had performed, she resolved to appeal to him to
relieve her daughter from the terrible affliction
that was upon her. The poor woman realized
that her only hope was in Jesus, and she had

perfect faith in his power to do that which she asked of him.

But Jesus received the importunities of this representative of a despised race in the same manner as the Jews would have done; this was not only to prove the faith and sincerity of the woman, but also to teach his disciples a lesson of mercy, that they might not be at a loss how to act in similar cases after Jesus should leave them and they could no longer go to him for personal counsel. Jesus designed that they should be impressed with the contrast between the cold and heartless manner in which the Jews would treat such a case, as evinced by his reception of the woman, and the compassionate manner in which he would have them deal with such distress, as manifested by his subsequent granting of her petition in the healing of her daughter.

Although Jesus was apparently indifferent to her cries, yet she did not become offended and leave him, but still had faith that he would relieve her distress. As he passed on, as if not hearing her, she followed him, continuing her supplications. The disciples were annoyed at her importunity and asked Jesus to send her away. Their sympathies were not aroused by her distress. They saw that their Master treated her with indifference, and they therefore supposed that the prejudice of the Jews against the Canaanites was pleasing to him. But it was a pitying Saviour to whom the woman made her plea, and, in answer to the request of the disciples to send her away, Jesus said, "I am not sent but unto the lost sheep of the house of Israel." Although this answer was in accordance with the prejudice of the Jews, it was an implied rebuke to the disciples, which they afterward understood as reminding them of what he had often told them: That he came to the world to save all who would accept him. Whoever sought the Saviour, ready to believe on him when he should be manifested to them, were of the lost sheep whom he had come to gather in his fold.

The woman was encouraged that Jesus had noticed her case sufficiently to remark upon it, although his words conveyed no definite hope to her mind, and she now urged her case with increased earnestness, bowing at his feet and crying, "Have mercy on me, O Lord, thou Son of David; my daughter is grievously vexed with a devil." Jesus, still apparently rejecting her entreaties, according to the unfeeling prejudice of the Jews, answered, "It is not meet to take the children's bread, and to cast it to dogs." This was virtually asserting that it was not just to lavish the blessings brought to the favored people of God upon strangers and aliens from Israel. This answer would have utterly discouraged a less earnest seeker. Many would have given up all further effort upon receiving such a repulse, and would have gone away feeling humiliated and abused, beyond all patience; but the woman meekly answered, "Truth, Lord; yet the dogs eat of the crumbs which fall from their masters' table."

From the abundance upon which the rightful family feasts, the crumbs fall to the floor and are devoured by the dogs that watch for them under the table. She acknowledged that she occupied a like position to that of the brutes that accept thankfully whatever falls from their master's hand. While favoring God's people with rich

and bountiful gifts, would not Jesus bestow upon
her one of the many blessings he gave so freely to
others? While confessing that she had no claim
upon his favor, she still plead for a crumb from
his bounty. Such faith and perseverance were
unexampled. Few of the favored people of God
had so high an appreciation of the Redeemer's
benevolence and power.

Jesus had just departed from Jerusalem because the scribes and Pharisees were seeking to
take his life; but here he meets one of an unfortunate and despised race, that had not been favored with the light of God's word; yet she
yields at once to the divine influence of Christ,
and has implicit faith in his ability to grant her
the favor she asks. She has no national nor religious prejudice or pride to influence her course
of action, and she unconditionally acknowledges
Jesus as the Redeemer, and able to do all that she
asks of him. The Saviour is satisfied, he has
tested her confidence in him, and he now grants
her request and finishes the lesson to his disciples.
Turning to her with a countenance of pity and
love, he says, "O woman, great is thy faith. Be
it unto thee even as thou wilt." From that hour
the daughter became whole, and the demon troubled her no more. The woman departed acknowledging her Saviour, and happy in the granting of
her prayer.

This was the only miracle that Jesus wrought
while on this journey. It was for the performance of this very act that he went into the coast
of Tyre and Sidon. He wished to relieve the afflicted woman, and at the same time to leave an
example, in this work of mercy toward one of a
despised people, for the benefit of his disciples

when he should be no longer with them. He wished to lead them from their Jewish exclusiveness to be interested in working for others besides their own people. This act of Christ opened their minds more fully to the labor that lay before them among the Gentiles. Afterward, when the Jews turned still more persistently from the disciples because they declared Jesus to be the Saviour of the world, and when the partition wall between Jew and Gentile was broken down by the death of Christ, this lesson, and similar ones which pointed to a gospel work unrestricted by custom or nationality, brought a powerful influence to bear upon the representatives of Christ in directing their labors.

CHAPTER XXV.

CHRIST STILLS THE TEMPEST.

JESUS had been teaching and healing uninterruptedly all day, and he greatly desired retirement and rest for himself and his disciples. He therefore instructed them to accompany him to the other side of the sea. But before he embarked he was accosted by a scribe who had listened to his words, representing the jewels of truth as being of far greater value than hidden treasure. In the grossness of his darkened mind, the scribe conceived that Jesus designed to enrich his followers with worldly treasure. He therefore eagerly addressed him, as had Judas, saying, "Master, I will follow thee whithersoever thou

goest." The Saviour read the unworthy thought
that actuated his heart, and answered him as he
had answered Judas, "The foxes have holes, and
the birds of the air have nests; but the Son of
Man hath not where to lay his head." This Jewish teacher had only his own selfish interest in
view when he proposed to follow Jesus. He
hoped that the Saviour would soon establish his
kingdom on earth, and that the wealth and station which would then accrue to his disciples,
were the riches of which Jesus had spoken. But
only a mind blinded by avarice and the lust of
the world could so have misinterpreted the words
of the Saviour.

If it were not for the poverty of Christ, and
the fact that the poor and humble are ranked
beneath his banner, many would connect themselves with him and glorify his name. If he had
bestowed honors and riches upon those who became his disciples, how gladly would the proud
Pharisees, the chief priests and scribes, have
paid him homage. Many in these days would
accept the truth if there was no self-denial connected with it. If they could have the world
with Christ, they would enlist in his army. But
to follow him in his humiliation, with no prospect of an earthly reward thereby, is more than
their feeble faith can endure. They turn back
crest-fallen, as did the scribe from the rebuke of
Jesus.

After dismissing the multitude, Jesus and his
disciples took ship for the other side of the sea,
which was a desert in comparison with the shore
that they were leaving; but for this very reason
they hoped to find rest from the fatigue of their
labors, being removed from the dwellings of men.

However, as they were moving off, a number of boats loaded with people followed Jesus, desirous of learning more concerning the doctrine that he taught.

The Saviour was wearied from his long and arduous labors, and being now for a time relieved from the claims of the multitude, he stretched himself upon the hard plank of the fishermen's boat and fell asleep. Soon after, the weather, which had been calm and pleasant, changed. The clouds gathered darkly over the sky, and a furious storm, such as frequently visited those parts, burst upon the sea. The sun had set, and the blackness of night settled down upon the water. The angry waves dashed against the ship, threatening every moment to engulf it. First tossed upon the crest of a mountain billow, and then as suddenly plunged into the trough of the sea, the ship was the plaything of the storm. Finally, it was discovered that it had sprung a leak and was fast filling with water. All was now hurry and confusion in the darkness and amid the roaring of the angry waves. The strong and courageous fishermen were skilled in managing their craft; but, experienced as they were to the changing moods of the sea, they knew not what to do in so terrible a gale, and their hearts filled with despair as they perceived that the boat was sinking.

They had been so engaged in their efforts to save themselves and keep the ship afloat, that they had forgotten that Jesus was on board. But now, as their courage fails them, and they think themselves lost, they remember that it was he who commanded them to cross the sea. In their agony of fear they turn to him, remember-

ing how he had once saved them in a like peril.
They call, "Master ! Master !" but the roaring of
the tempest drowns their voices, and there is no
reply. The waves break over them, and each
one threatens them with destruction.

Despair seizes them, and they call again ; but
there is no answer save the shrieking of the angry blast. Has the Master deserted them ? Has
he walked away upon the foam-capped billows
and left them to their fate ? They remembered
that he had once walked upon the water to come
and rescue them from death. Has he now given
them up to the fury of the tempest ? They
search for him distractedly, for they can do no
more to save themselves. The storm has so increased that all their efforts to manage the ship
are vain ; in Jesus is their only hope. Presently
a flash of lightning reveals him fast asleep, undisturbed amid the noise and confusion.

They rush to him, and bending over his prostrate form, cry out reproachfully, "Master, Master, carest thou not that we perish ?" Their
hearts are grieved that he should rest so peace-
fully, while danger and death threaten them,
and they have been laboring so hard against the
fury of the storm. This despairing cry arouses
Jesus from his refreshing sleep. As the disciples
rush back to their oars, to make a last effort,
Jesus rises to his feet. In his divine majesty he
stands in the humble vessel of the fishermen, amid
the raging of the tempest, the waves breaking
over the bows, and the vivid lightning playing
about his calm and fearless countenance. He
lifts his hand, so often employed in deeds of
mercy, and says to the angry sea, "Peace, be
still." The storm ceases, the heaving billows

sink to rest. The clouds roll away, and the stars shine forth; the boat sits motionless upon a quiet sea. Then, turning to his disciples, Jesus rebukes them, saying, "Why are ye so fearful? how is it that ye have no faith?"

A sudden hush crept over the disciples. Not a word was spoken; even impulsive Peter did not attempt to express the reverential awe that filled his heart. The boats that had set out to accompany Jesus had been in the same peril with that of the disciples. Fear and finally despair had seized their occupants; but the command of Jesus brought quiet where but a moment before all was tumult. All fear was allayed, for the danger was over. The fury of the storm had driven the boats into close proximity, and all on board beheld the miracle of Jesus. In the hush that followed the stilling of the tempest, they whispered among themselves, "What manner of man is this, that even the wind and the sea obey him?" Never was this impressive scene forgotten by those who witnessed it. Never will its wonderful majesty fail to inspire the children of God with reverence and awe.

When he was rudely aroused by the terrified fishermen, the Saviour had no fears for himself; his anxiety was for his disciples, who had distrusted him in the time of danger. He reproved their fears, which manifested their unbelief. They should have called upon him at the first appearance of danger, and he would have relieved their anxiety. But in their effort to save themselves they forgot that Jesus was on board. How many, in the trying scenes of life, amid perplexities and danger, fight against the storms of adversity alone, forgetting that there is One who

can help them.   They trust in their own strength
and skill, till, baffled and discouraged, they remember Jesus, and humbly call upon him to save
them.   Though he sorrowfully reproves their unbelief and self-confidence, he never fails to hear
their earnest cry, and give them the help they
need.

Tossed on the raging billows of the deep, the
weary voyager should remember that Jesus was
on the sea in a time of like peril; that his voice
commanded the terrible storm to cease; that the
angry elements obeyed the mandate, and his
faithful followers were saved.   When the waves
break over our sinking bark, and the lightning
reveals the foam-capped breakers that threaten
us with instant destruction, we may remember
in our peril that Jesus is on board.   He hears
our agonizing cry, and he will never forsake
those who put their trust in him.

Whether on the land or on the sea, sleeping or
waking, if we have the Saviour in our hearts there
is no need of fear.   The call of faith will always
meet with a response.   We may be rebuked because we have not sought him at the very beginning of trial, but nevertheless, he will accept our
humble petitions, wearied as we are in our efforts
to save ourselves.   Living faith in the Redeemer
will smooth the sea of life, and will deliver us
from danger in the way that he knows to be
the best.

CHAPTER XXVI.

MEN FROM THE TOMBS.

THE night upon the water was over, and in the early morning Jesus and the disciples landed, together with those who had followed them across the sea. But no sooner had they stepped upon the beach than two men possessed with devils rushed fiercely toward them as though they desired to tear them in pieces. Still clinging to them were parts of chains which they had broken, in escaping from confinement. They were cutting and bruising themselves with sharp stones and other missiles that they could lay their hands upon. They had been dwelling among the graves, and no traveler had been safe to pass that way; for they would rush upon him with the fury of demons and kill him if they could. Their faces glared out from their long and matted hair, and they looked more like wild beasts than men.

When the disciples and the others saw these fearful creatures rushing toward them, they fled in terror. But presently they discovered that Jesus was not with them, and they turned to see what had been his fate. They beheld him standing calmly where they had left him. He who stilled the tempest, he who had met Satan before and conquered him, did not flee before these demons. When the men, gnashing their teeth, and foaming at the mouth, approached him within a few feet, Jesus raised that hand which had beckoned the waves to rest, and the men could come no nearer. They stood raging but helpless before him.

In accents of authority he bade the unclean spirits come out of them. The words of Jesus penetrated the darkened minds of the men enough for them to dimly realize that One was near who could save them from the demons that tormented them. They fell at the feet of Jesus, worshiping him. But when they opened their mouths to entreat his mercy, the demon spoke through them and cried vehemently, "What have I to do with thee, Jesus, thou Son of the Most High God, I adjure thee by God, that thou torment me not!"

Jesus asked, "What is thy name?" and the answer was, "My name is Legion; for we are many." Using the afflicted men as mediums of communication between themselves and Jesus, they besought him not to send them away out of the country, but to let them enter into a herd of swine that was feeding near. Their request was granted; but no sooner did this occur than the swine rushed headlong down a steep precipice, and were drowned in the sea. Light dawned upon the minds of the restored lunatics. Their eyes beamed with an intelligence to which they had long been strangers. The countenances, so long deformed into the image of Satan, became suddenly mild, the blood-stained hands were quiet, and the men praised the Lord for their deliverance from the bondage of demons.

The design of Satan, in requesting that the demons might enter into the swine, was to hedge up the way of Jesus in that region. By causing the swine to be destroyed, considerable loss was brought upon their owners; and the enemy was not deceived in thinking that this circumstance would occasion Jesus to be held in disfavor throughout that country. The keepers of the swine had seen with amazement the whole transaction. They had seen the raving madmen suddenly become sane and calm; they had beheld the whole drove of swine instantly afterward charge recklessly into the sea where they were immediately drowned. They were obliged to account to the owners for their loss ; and they immediately hurried to publish the news to their employers, and to all the people. This destruction of property seemed, to the owners, of far greater magnitude than the joyful fact that two lunatics had been restored to reason, and no longer endangered the people who came in their way, nor needed the restrictions of bolts and chains.

These selfish men cared not that these unfortunate beings were now liberated, and sat calmly and intelligently at the feet of Jesus, listening to his words of instruction, filled with gratitude and glorifying the name of Him who had made them whole. They only cared for the property they had lost, and they were fearful of still greater calamities following the presence of this stranger in their midst. A panic spread far and near; the citizens apprehended financial ruin. A crowd came to Jesus, deploring the recent loss of propty and begging him to leave their vicinity. They looked with indifference upon the lunatics who had been healed, and were then conversing intelligently with Jesus. They knew them perfectly well, for they had long been the terror of the community. But the miraculous cure of these men seemed of lesser importance than their own selfish interests. They were thoroughly alarmed and displeased at their loss; and the prospect of Jesus remaining among them filled them with apprehension. They implored him to depart from their coast. The Saviour complied with their demands, and immediately took ship with his disciples and left them to their avarice and unbelief.

The inhabitants had before them living evidences of the power and mercy of Him whom they drove from their midst. They saw that the lunatics had been restored to reason; but they were so fearful of incurring pecuniary loss that the Saviour, who had baffled the Prince of Darkness before their eyes, was treated as an unwelcome invader, and they turned the priceless Gift of Heaven from their doors, and blindly rejected his visit of mercy. We have not the opportunity of turning from the person of Christ, as did the Gadarenes; but there are many in these days who refuse to follow his teachings, because in so doing they must sacrifice some worldly interest. Many, in the various pursuits of life, turn Jesus from their hearts, fearful that his presence may cost them pecuniary loss. Like the selfish Gadarenes, they overlook his grace, and ruthlessly drive his Spirit from them. To such his words apply: "Ye cannot serve God and mammon."

Some may reason that the course pursued by Jesus in this matter prevented the people of that region from receiving his doctrine, that this startling exhibition of his power turned them away from his teachings, and cut them off from his influence. But such minds fail to penetrate the plans of the Saviour. At the time that the Gadarenes besought Jesus to leave their coast, there was also a petition offered by the restored lu-

natics. It was that they might accompany their
Deliverer. In his presence they felt secure from
the demons that had tormented their lives and
wasted their manhood. They kept close to his
side as he was about to enter the boat, knelt at
his feet and implored him to take them with him
and teach them his truth. But Jesus directed
them to go home to their friends, and tell them
what great things the Lord had done for them.

Here a work was given them to do,—to go to
a heathen home, and impart to their friends the
light that they had received from Jesus. They
might have plead that it was a great trial to be
separated from their Benefactor at this early
stage of their experience, and that it was more
congenial to their feelings to remain with him
than to be exposed to the trials and difficulties
that were sure to beset them in the course he directed them to pursue. They might also have
plead that their long isolation from society disqualified them for the task he had given them.

But instead of this, as soon as Jesus pointed
out the path of duty, they prepared to follow it.
Not only did they enlighten their own households
and neighbors in regard to Jesus, but they proclaimed his power to save throughout the region
of Decapolis, among the Gentiles, telling the
wonderful work of Christ in casting out the demons. The people of that region had refused
to receive the Saviour because he was the
means of destroying their property, yet they
were not left in utter darkness; for they had not
committed the sin of rejecting his doctrine, since
they had not heard it when they bade him leave
their coast. His words of life had not fallen upon
their ears. Therefore he commissioned those who

were so recently the mediums of Satan to communicate the light they had received from him to those benighted people. Those who had so lately been the representatives of the Prince of Darkness were converted into channels of truth, servants of the Son of God.

Men marveled as they listened to the wondrous news. They became interested and anxious to have part in this kingdom of which Jesus taught. Nothing could have awakened the people of this country so thoroughly as did this occurrence happening in their midst. They had only cared for the advantages of the world, and had thought little of their eternal interests. Jesus cared much more for their real good than they did themselves. He had permitted the devil's request to be granted, and the result was the destruction of their property. This loss raised the indignation of the people, and brought Jesus directly before the public notice. Although they entreated him to depart from them, they nevertheless saw and heard the men whom he had healed. When these persons, who had been the terror of the community, became the messengers of truth and taught the salvation of Jesus, they wielded a powerful influence to convince the people of that region that Jesus was the Son of God.

They sent Jesus from their coast because they feared additional loss of property, notwithstanding those who had crossed the lake with him told them the peril of the previous night, and the miracle performed by the Saviour in stilling the tempest. Their eyes, blinded by worldliness, only saw the magnitude of their loss. They refused to consider the advantage of having One among them who could control the very elements by the

lifting of his finger, cast out demons, and heal the
diseased and imbecile by a word or the touch of
his hand. The visible evidence of Satan's power
was among them. The Prince of Light and the
Prince of Darkness met, and all present beheld
the supremacy of the one over the other. Yet
seeing this they begged the Son of God to depart
from them. He gratified their wish; for he never
urges his presence where he is unwelcome.

Satan is the god of the world; his influence is
to pervert the senses, control the human mind
for evil, and drive his victims to violence and
crime. He sows discord and darkens the intellect.
The work of Christ is to break his power over
the children of men. Yet how many in every
department of life, in the home, in business trans-
actions, and in the church, turn Jesus from their
doors but let the hateful monster in.

It is no wonder that violence and crime have
spread over the earth, and moral darkness, like
the pall of death, shrouds the cities and habita-
tions of men. Satan controls many households,
people, and churches. He watches the indica-
tions of moral corruption, and introduces his spe-
cious temptations, carefully leading men into worse
and worse evils, till utter depravity is the result.
The only safety is to watch unto prayer against
his devices; for he goes about, in the last days,
like a roaring lion seeking whom he may devour.
The presence of Jesus is a safe-guard against his
advances. The Sun of Righteousness discloses
the hideous blackness of the enemy of souls, and
he flies from the divine presence.

Many professed Christians of our time banish
Jesus from them for the sake of worldly gain.
They may not use the exact words of the Gada-

renes, but their acts plainly indicate, that, in their various avocations, they do not desire his presence. The world is exalted above his mercy. The love of gain crowds out the love of Christ. They heed not his injunctions, they slight his re-proofs. By dishonesty and avaricious scheming, they virtually petition the blessed Saviour to de-part from them.

CHAPTER XXVII.

JAIRUS' DAUGHTER.

WHEN Jesus returned across the sea with his disciples, a great crowd were waiting to receive him, and they welcomed him with much joy. The fact of his coming being noised abroad, the people had collected in great numbers to listen to his teaching. There were the rich and poor, the high and low, Pharisees, doctors, and lawyers, all anxious to hear his words, and witness his miracles. As usual, there were many of the sick and variously afflicted entreating his mercy in their behalf.

At length, faint and weary with the work of teaching and healing, Jesus left the multitude in order to partake of food in the house of Levi. But the people pressed about the door, bringing the sick, the deformed, and the lunatic, for him to heal. As he sat at the table, one of the rulers of the synagogue, Jairus, by name, came and fell at his feet, beseeching him : "My little daughter lieth at the point of death. I pray thee, come and lay thy hands on her, that she may be healed; and she shall live."

The father was in great distress, for his child had been given up to die by the most learned physicians. Jesus at once responded to the entreaty of the stricken parent, and went with him to his home. The disciples were surprised at this ready compliance with the request of the haughty ruler. Although it was only a short distance, their progress was very slow; for the people pressed forward on every side eager to see the great Teacher who had created so much excitement, begging his attention and his aid. The anxious father urged his way through the crowd, fearful of being too late. But Jesus, pitying the people, and deploring their spiritual darkness and physical maladies, stopped now and then to minister to their wants. Occasionally he was nearly carried off his feet by the surging masses.

There was one poor woman among that crowd who had suffered twelve long years with a disease that made her life a burden. She had spent all her substance upon physicians and remedies, seeking to cure her grievous malady. But it was all in vain; she was pronounced incurable, and given up to die. But her hopes revived when she heard of the wonderful cures effected by Jesus. She believed that if she could come into his presence, he would take pity on her and heal her. Suffering with pain and weakness, she came to the sea-side where he was teaching, and sought to press through the crowd that encompassed him. But her way was continually hedged up by the throng. She began to despair of approaching him, when Jesus, in urging his way through the multitude, came within her reach.

The golden opportunity had come, she was in the presence of the great Physician! But amid the confusion, she could not be heard by him nor catch more than a passing glimpse of his figure. Fearful of losing the one chance of relief from her illness, she pressed forward, saying to herself, If I but touch his garment I shall be cured. She seized the opportunity as he was passing and reached forward, barely touching the hem of his garment. But in that moment she felt herself healed of her disease. Instantly health and strength took the place of feebleness and pain. She had concentrated all the faith of her life in that one touch that made her whole.

With a thankful heart she then sought unobtrusively to retire from the crowd; but suddenly Jesus stopped, and all the people, following his example, also halted. He turned, and looking about him with a penetrating eye, asked in a voice distinctly heard by all, "Who touched me?" The people answered this query with a look of amazement. Jostled upon all sides, and rudely pressed hither and thither as he was, it seemed indeed a singular inquiry.

Peter, recovering from his surprise, and ever ready to speak, said, "Master, the multitude throng thee, and press thee, and sayest thou, Who touched me?" Jesus answered, "Somebody hath touched me; for I perceive that virtue is gone out of me." The blessed Redeemer could distinguish the touch of faith from the casual contact of the careless crowd. He well knew all the circumstances of the case, and would not pass such confidence and trust without comment.

He would address to the humble woman words of comfort that would be to her a well-spring of joy.

Looking toward the woman, Jesus still insisted upon knowing who had touched him. Finding concealment vain, she came forward tremblingly and knelt at his feet. In hearing of all the multitude, she told Jesus the simple story of her long and tedious suffering, and the instant relief that she had experienced in touching the border of his garment. Her narration was interrupted by her grateful tears as she experienced the joy of perfect health, which had been a stranger to her for twelve weary years. Instead of being angered at her presumption, Jesus commended her action, saying, "Daughter, be of good comfort. Thy faith hath made thee whole; go in peace." In these words he instructed all present that it was no virtue in the simple act of touching his clothes that had wrought the cure, but in the strong faith that reached out and claimed his divine help.

The true faith of the Christian is represented in this woman. It is not essential to the exercise of faith that the feelings should be wrought up to a high pitch of excitement; neither is it necessary, in order to gain the hearing of the Lord, that our petitions should be noisy, or attended with physical exercise. It is true that Satan frequently creates in the heart of the suppliant such a conflict with doubt and temptation that strong cries and tears are involuntarily forced from him; and it is also true that the penitent's sense of guilt is sometimes so great that a repentance commensurate with his sin causes him to experience an agony that finds vent in cries and

groans, which the compassionate Saviour hears
with pity.   But Jesus does not fail to answer the
silent prayer of faith.   He who simply takes God
at his word, and reaches out to connect himself
with the Saviour, will receive his blessing in return.

Faith is simple in its operation and powerful
in its results.   Many professed Christians, who
have a knowledge of the sacred word, and believe its truth, fail in the childlike trust that is
essential to the religion of Jesus.   They do not
reach out with that peculiar touch that brings
the virtue of healing to the soul.   They allow
cold doubt to creep in and destroy their confidence.   He who waits for entire knowledge before he can exercise faith, will never be blessed of
God.   "Faith is the substance of things hoped
for, the evidence of things not seen."

The diseased woman believed that Jesus could
heal her, and the more her mind was exercised in
that direction, the more certain she became that
even to touch his garment would relieve her malady.   In answer to her firm belief, the virtue of
divine power granted her prayer.   This is a lesson of encouragement to the soul defiled by sin.
In like manner as Jesus dealt with bodily infirmities, will he deal with the repentant soul that
calls on him.   The touch of faith will bring the
coveted pardon that fills the soul with gratitude
and joy.

The delay of Jesus had been so intensely in-
teresting in its results that even the anxious
father felt no impatience but watched the scene
with deep interest.   As the healed woman was
sent away comforted and rejoicing, it encouraged
him to believe still more firmly that Jesus was

able to grant his own petition and heal his daughter. Hope grew stronger in his heart, and he now urged the Saviour to hasten with him to his home. But, as they resumed their way, a messenger pressed through the crowd to Jairus, bearing the news that his daughter was dead, and it was useless to trouble the Master further. The sympathizing ear of Jesus caught the words that smote the father's heart like the death-knell of his hopes. The pity of the Saviour was drawn out toward the suffering parent. He said to him, in his divine compassion, "Fear not; believe only, and she shall be made whole."

Hearing these words of hope, Jairus pressed closer to the side of Jesus; and they hurried to the ruler's house. The Saviour suffered no one to enter the room with him where the child lay dead, except a few of his most faithful disciples, and the parents themselves. The mourners were making a great show of grief, and he rebuked them, saying, "Weep not; she is not dead, but sleepeth." The women, who, according to the custom of the country, were employed to make this external display of sorrow, were indignant at this remark made by a humble stranger, and they began to inquire by what authority this person came, commanding them to cease lamenting for the dead and asserting that the girl still lived. They had seen the touch of death change the living child to a pulseless and unconscious form. They laughed the words of Jesus to scorn, as they left the room at his command. Accompanied by the father and mother, with Peter, James, and John, the Saviour approached the bedside, and, taking the child's hand in his own, he pronounced softly, in the familiar language of her home, the words, "Damsel, I say unto thee, arise."

Instantly a tremor quivered through the entire body. The pulses of life beat again in the blue-veined temples, the pallid lips opened with a smile, the bosom heaved with returning breath, the waxen lids opened widely as if from sleep, and the dark eyes looked out wonderingly. The girl arose, weak from her long illness, but free from disease. She walked slowly across the room, while the parents wept for joy. Jesus bade them give her food, and charged all the household to tell no one what had been done there. But notwithstanding his injunction to secrecy, the news spread far and near that he had raised the dead to life. A large number were present when the child died, and when they again beheld her alive and well, it was impossible to prevent them from reporting the wonderful deed done by the great Physician.

CHAPTER XXVIII.

THE TRANSFIGURATION.

As the time drew near when Jesus was to suffer and die, he was more frequently alone with his disciples. After teaching the people all day, he would repair with his disciples to a retired place and pray and commune with them. He was weary, yet he had no time to rest, for his work on earth was hastening to a close, and he had much to do before the final hour arrived. He had declared to his disciples that he would establish his kingdom so firmly on earth that the gates of hell should not prevail against it. Jesus, in view of his approaching trial, gathered his disciples about him and opened their minds regarding his future humiliation and shameful death at the hands of his persecutors. The impulsive Peter could not for a moment endure the thought, and insisted that it could not be. Jesus solemnly rebuked Peter's unbelief in suggesting that prophecy would not be fulfilled in the sacrifice of the Son of God.

Jesus then proceeded to explain to his disciples that they also must suffer for his name, bear the cross in following him, and endure a corresponding humiliation, reproach, and shame with that of their Master, or they could never share his glory. His sufferings must be followed by theirs, and his crucifixion must teach them that they should be crucified to the world, resigning all hope of its pomp and pleasure. Previous to this declaration, Jesus had frequently spoken to his disciples of his future humiliation, and he had resolutely discouraged all their hopes of his temporal aggrandizement; but they had so long been accustomed to look upon Messiah as one who would reign as a mighty king, that it had been impossible for them to relinquish entirely their glowing expectations.

But now the words of Jesus were unmistakable. He was to live, a humble, homeless wanderer, and to die the death of a malefactor. Sadness oppressed their hearts, for they loved their Master; but doubt also harassed their minds, for it seemed incomprehensible that the Son of God should be subjected to such cruel humiliation. They could not understand why he should

voluntarily go to Jerusalem to meet the treatment which he told them he should there receive.
They were deeply grieved that he should resign
himself to such an ignominious fate, and leave
them in greater darkness than that in which
they were groping before he revealed himself to
them. The thought suggested itself to their
minds that they might take him by force to a
place of security, but they dared not attempt
this as he had repeatedly denounced all such
projects as the suggestions of Satan. In the
midst of their gloom they could not refrain from
comforting themselves occasionally with the
thought that some unforeseen circumstance might
avert the fearful doom that awaited their Lord.
Thus they sorrowed and doubted, hoped and
feared, for six long, gloomy days.

Jesus was acquainted with the grief and perplexity of his disciples, and he designed to give
them additional proof of his Messiahship, in order that their faith might not utterly fail them
in the severe ordeal to which they were soon to
be subjected. As the sun was setting he called
his three most devoted disciples to his side, and
led them out of the noisy town, across the fields,
and up the steep side of a mountain. Jesus was
weary from toil and travel. He had taught the
people and healed the sick throughout the entire
day; but he sought this high elevation because
he could there find retirement from the crowds
that continually sought him, and time for meditation and prayer. He was very weary, and was
much fatigued in toiling up the steep ascent.

The disciples were also tired, and, although they
were accustomed to this practice of retiring into
the solitudes for prayer, they could not help won-

dering that Jesus should attempt to climb this rugged mountain, after such a day of fatigue. But they asked no questions as to his purpose, and patiently accompanied him. As they are ascending the mountain, the setting sun leaves the valleys in shadow, while the light still lingers on the mountain tops, and gilds with its fading glory the rugged path they are treading. But soon the golden light dies out from hill as well as valley, the sun disappears behind the western horizon, and the solitary travelers are wrapt in the darkness of night. And the gloom of their surroundings seems in harmony with their sorrowful lives, around which the clouds are gathering and thickening.

Having gained the place he sought, Jesus engaged in earnest prayer to his Father. Hour after hour, with tears and importunity, he supplicated for strength to bear his afflictions and for grace to be bestowed upon his disciples that they might bear the terrible trials that awaited them in the future. The dew was heavy upon his bowed form, but he heeded it not; the shadows of night gathered thickly about him, but he regarded not their gloom. So the hours passed slowly by. At first the disciples united their prayers with his in sincere devotion; but as the hours dragged slowly on, they were overcome with weariness and loss of sleep, and even while endeavoring to retain their interest in the scene, they fell asleep. Jesus had told them of his future sufferings, he had taken them with him that they might watch and pray with him while he was pleading with his Father; even then he was praying that his disciples might have strength to endure the coming test of his humiliation and death. He especially plead that they might witness such a manifestation of his divinity as would forever remove from their minds all unbelief and lingering doubts; a manifestation that would comfort them in the hour of his supreme agony with the knowledge that he was of a surety the Son of God, and that his shameful death was a part of the divine plan of redemption.

God hears the petition of his Son, and angels prepare to minister unto him. But God selects Moses and Elijah to visit Christ and converse with him in regard to his coming sufferings at Jerusalem. While Jesus bows in lowliness upon the damp and stony ground, suddenly the heavens open, the golden gates of the City of God are thrown wide, and holy radiance descends upon the mount, enshrouding the kneeling form of Christ. He arises from his prostrate position, and stands in God-like majesty; the soul-agony is gone from his countenance, which now shines with a serene light, and his garments are no longer coarse and soiled, but white and glittering like the noon-day sun.

The sleeping disciples are awakened by the flood of glory that illuminates the whole mount. They gaze with fear and amazement upon the shining garments and radiant countenance of their Master. At first their eyes are dazzled by the unearthly brilliancy of the scene, but as they become able to endure the wondrous light, they perceive that Jesus is not alone. Two glorious figures stand engaged in conversation with him. They are Moses, who talked with God face to face amid the thunder and lightnings of Sinai, and Elijah, that prophet of God who did not see death, but was conducted to Heaven in a chariot of fire. These two, whom God had seen fit to favor above all others who ever lived upon earth, were delegated by the Father to bring the glory of Heaven to his Son, and comfort him, talking with him concerning the completion of his mission, and especially of his sufferings to be endured at Jerusalem.

The Father chose Moses and Elijah to be his messengers to Christ, and glorify him with the light of Heaven, and commune with him concerning his coming agony, because they had lived upon earth as men; they had experienced human sorrow and suffering, and could sympathize with the trial of Jesus, in his earthly life. Elijah, in his position as a prophet to Israel, had represented Christ, and his work had been, in a degree, similar to that of the Saviour. And Moses, as the leader of Israel, had stood in the place of Christ, communing with him and following his directions; therefore, these two, of all the hosts that gathered around the throne of God, were fittest to minister to the Son of God.

When Moses, enraged at the unbelief of the children of Israel, smote the rock in wrath and furnished them the water for which they called, he took the glory to himself; for his mind was so engrossed with the ingratitude and waywardness of Israel that he failed to honor God and magnify his name, in performing the act which He had commanded him to do. It was the plan of the Almighty to frequently bring the children of Israel into straight places, and then, in their great necessity, to deliver them by his power, that they might recognize his special regard for them, and glorify his name. But Moses, in yielding to the natural impulses of his heart, appropriated to himself the honor due to God, fell under the power of Satan, and was forbidden to enter the promised land. Had Moses remained steadfast, the Lord would have brought him to the promised land, and would then have translated him to Heaven without his seeing death.

As it was, Moses passed through death, but the Son of God came down from Heaven and resurrected him before his body had seen corruption. Though Satan contended with Michael for the body of Moses, and claimed it as his rightful prey, he could not prevail against the Son of God, and Moses, with a resurrected and glorified body, was borne to the courts of Heaven, and was now one of the honored two, commissioned by the Father to wait upon his Son.

By permitting themselves to be so overcome by sleep, the disciples had lost the conversation between the Heavenly messengers and the glorified Redeemer. But as they suddenly awake from profound slumber, and behold the sublime vision before them, they are filled with rapture and awe. As they look upon the radiant form of their beloved Master, they are obliged to shield their eyes with their hands, not being able otherwise to endure the inexpressible glory that clothes his person, and which emits beams of light like those of the sun. For a brief space the disciples behold their Lord glorified and exalted before their eyes, and honored by the radiant beings whom they recognize as the favored ones of God.

They believe that Elias has now come, according to prophecy, and that the kingdom of Christ is to be set up on earth. Even in the first glow of his amazement, Peter plans for accommodating Christ and the ancient worthies. As soon as he can command his voice he addresses Jesus thus: "Master, it is good for us to be here; and let us make three tabernacles; one for thee, and one for Moses, and one for Elias." In the joy of the moment, Peter flatters himself that the two messengers from Heaven have been sent to preserve the life of Jesus from the fate that threatens him at Jerusalem. He is overjoyed at the thought that these glorious attendants, clothed in light and power, are to protect the Son of God, and establish his kingly authority upon earth. He forgets for the time the frequent explanations given by Jesus himself of the plan of salvation, which could only be perfected through his own suffering and death.

While the disciples were overwhelmed with rapture and amazement, "a bright cloud overshadowed them, and behold, a voice out of the cloud which said, This is my beloved Son, in whom I am well pleased; hear ye him." When the disciples beheld the awful cloud of glory, brighter than that which went before the tribes of Israel in the wilderness, and when they heard the voice of God peal from the cloud, in accents of majesty that caused the mount to tremble as if shaken from its foundation, they could not endure the grandeur that oppressed their senses, and fell smitten to the ground.

Thus they remained upon their faces, not daring to look up, till Jesus approached and raised them from the ground, dispelling their fears with his well-known, cheering voice, saying, "Arise, and be not afraid." Venturing to lift up their eyes, they see that the heavenly glory has passed away, the radiant forms of Moses and Elijah have disappeared, the Son of God is no longer clothed with a divine radiance so bright that the eyes of man can not endure it,—they are upon the mount alone with Jesus.

The entire night had been passed in the mountain, and as the sun rose and chased away the shadows with its cheering rays, Jesus and his disciples descended the mountain. Gladly would they have lingered in that holy place which had been touched with the glory of Heaven, and where the Son of God had been transfigured before the eyes of his disciples; but there was work to be done for the people who were already searching far and near for Jesus.

At the foot of the mountain a large crowd had gathered, led there by the disciples who had remained behind, and who knew of the favorite resorts of Jesus for meditation and prayer. As they approached the waiting multitude, Jesus charged his disciples to keep secret what they had witnessed, saying, "Tell the vision to no man until the Son of Man be risen again from the dead." Jesus knew that neither the people nor the disciples who had led them to the place, were prepared to appreciate or understand the wonderful event of the transfiguration upon the mount. After his resurrection, the testimony of those who had witnessed it, was to be given to substantiate the fact that he was indeed the Son of God.

Now the three chosen disciples have evidence which they cannot doubt that Jesus is the promised Messiah. A voice from the excellent glory has declared his divinity. Now they are strengthened to endure the humiliation and crucifixion of their Lord. The patient Teacher, the meek and lowly One, who, for nearly three years, has wandered to and fro, from city to city, a Man of sorrows, homeless, having no place to rest, no bed upon which to stretch his weary form at night, has been acknowledged by the voice of God as his Son, and Moses and Elijah, glorious ones in the courts of Heaven, have paid him homage. The favored disciples can doubt no longer. They have seen with their eyes, and heard with their ears, things that are beyond the comprehension of man.

Jesus now returned to his work of ministering to the people. As the throng caught sight of the Saviour, they ran to meet him, greeting him with much reverence. But he perceived that they were in great perplexity. This was because of a circumstance that had just transpired : A man had brought his son to the disciples to be delivered of a dumb spirit that tormented him exceedingly. But the disciples had been unable to relieve him, and therefore the scribes had seized upon this opportunity to dispute with them as to their power of working miracles. These men were now triumphantly declaring that a devil was here found whom neither the disciples nor their Master could conquer.

As Jesus approached the scene he inquired the cause of the trouble ; the afflicted father replied : "Master, I have brought unto thee my son, which hath a dumb spirit ; and wheresoever he taketh him, he teareth him ; and he foameth, and gnasheth with his teeth, and pineth away ; and I spake to thy disciples that they should cast him out, and they could not." Jesus listened attentively to this narration, and then met the failure of his disciples, the doubts of the people, and the boasting of the scribes, with these words : " O faithless generation ! how long shall I be with you ? how long shall I suffer you ? Bring him unto me."

The father obeyed the command of Jesus ; but no sooner was his son brought into the divine presence than the evil spirit attacked him with violence, and he fell upon the ground in agony, and writhed, and foamed at the mouth. Jesus permitted Satan to exercise his power thus over his victim, in order that the people might better understand the nature of the miracle he was about to perform, and be more deeply impressed with a sense of his divine power. Jesus proceeded to inquire of the father how long his son had thus been afflicted by the demon. The father answered :—

" Of a child. And ofttimes it hath cast him into the fire, and into the water, to destroy him ; but if thou canst do anything, have compassion on us, and help us." The failure of the disciples to heal this deplorable case had sadly discouraged the father, and the sufferings of his son now wrung his soul with anguish. The question of Jesus brought to his mind the long years of suffering endured by his son, and his heart sank within him. He feared that what the scribes asserted was true, and that Jesus himself could not overcome so powerful a devil. Jesus perceived his dispirited condition and sought to inspire him with faith. He addressed him thus : " If thou canst believe, all things are possible to him that believeth." Hope was immediately kindled in the father's heart, and he cried, "Lord, I believe; help thou mine unbelief."

The distressed father realized his immediate need of help, and that no one could furnish that help but the merciful Saviour, and he relied alone upon him. His faith was not in vain; for Jesus, before the whole multitude, that flocked about to witness the scene, "rebuked the foul spirit, saying unto him, Thou dumb and deaf spirit, I charge thee, come out of him, and enter no more into him." And immediately the demon left him, and the boy lay as one dead. The action of the evil spirit upon him had been so violent that it had overcome all his natural strength; and when it left him he was powerless and unconscious. The people, who had witnessed with awe the sudden change that came over the lad, now whispered among themselves, "He is dead." But Jesus stooped and with tender pity "took him by the hand, and lifted him up; and he arose."

Great was the father's joy over his son, and great was the joy of the son in his freedom from the cruel demon that had so long tormented him. Both father and son praised and magnified the name of their Deliverer, while the people looked on with unbounded astonishment, and the scribes, crest-fallen and defeated, turned sullenly away.

Jesus had conferred upon his disciples the power to work miracles of healing; but their failure in this case, before so many witnesses, had deeply mortified them. When they were alone with Jesus they asked him why it was that they were unable to cast out the devil. Jesus answered that it was because of their unbelief, and the carelessness with which they regarded the sacred work that had been committed to them. They had not fitted themselves for their holy office by fasting and prayer. It was impossible for them to vanquish Satan except as they received power from God; they should go to him in humiliation and self-sacrifice and plead for strength to conquer the enemy of souls. Nothing but entire dependence upon God, and perfect consecration to the work, would insure their success. Jesus encouraged his disappointed followers in these words: "If ye have faith as a grain of mustard seed, ye shall say unto this mountain, Remove hence to yonder place, and it shall remove; and nothing shall be impossible unto you."

In a brief space of time the favored disciples had beheld the extremes of glory and of grief. Jesus, descending the mount where he had been transfigured by the glory of God, where he had talked with the messengers of Heaven, and been proclaimed the Son of God by the Father's voice issuing from the radiant glory, meets a revolting spectacle, a lunatic child, with countenance distorted, gnashing its teeth in spasms of agony which no mortal could relieve. And this mighty Redeemer, who but a few short hours before stood glorified before his wondering disciples, stoops to lift this victim of Satan from the ground where he is wallowing, and restores him to his father, freed forever from the demon's power.

Previous to his transfiguration, Jesus had told his disciples that there were some then with him who should not see death until they should see the kingdom of God come with power. In the transfiguration on the mount, this promise was fulfilled, for they there saw the kingdom of Christ in miniature. Jesus was clothed with the glory of Heaven, and proclaimed by the Father's voice to be the Son of God. Moses was present, representing those who will be raised from the dead at the second coming of Christ; and Elijah, who was translated to Heaven without seeing death, represented those who will be living on earth at the time of Christ's second appearing, and who will be changed from mortal to immortal, and be translated to Heaven without seeing death.

CHAPTER XXIX.

FEAST OF TABERNACLES.

THREE times a year, all the Jews were required to assemble for religious purposes at Jerusalem. Jesus had not attended several of these gatherings because of the enmity of the Jews. When he declared in the synagogue that he was the bread of life, many of those who had followed him apostatized and united with the Pharisees to watch him and spy upon his movements in the hope of finding cause to condemn him to death.

The sons of Joseph, who passed as brothers of Jesus, were very much affected by this desertion of so many of his disciples, and, as the time approached for the Feast of Tabernacles, they urged Jesus to go up to Jerusalem, and, if he was indeed the Messiah, to present his claims before the rulers, and enforce his rights.

Jesus replied to them with solemn dignity: "My time is not yet come; but your time is always ready. The world cannot hate you; but

me it hateth, because I testify of it that the
works thereof are evil.   Go ye up unto this feast;
I go not up yet unto this feast, for my time is not
yet full come."   The world loved those who were
like itself; but the contrast between Christ and
the world was most marked; there could be no
harmony between them.   His teachings, and his
reproofs of sin, stirred up its hatred against him.
The Saviour knew what awaited him at Jerusalem, he knew that the malice of the Jews would
soon bring about his death, and it was not his
place to hasten that event by prematurely exposing himself to their unscrupulous hatred.   He
was to patiently await his appointed time.

At the commencement of the Feast of Tabernacles, the absence of Jesus was commented upon.
The Pharisees and rulers anxiously looked for
him to come, hoping that they might have an
opportunity to condemn him on account of something he might say or do.   They anxiously inquired, "Where is he?" but no one knew.   Presently a dispute rose among the people in regard
to Jesus, many nobly defending him as one sent
of God, while others bitterly accused him as a
deceiver of the people.

Meanwhile, Jesus had quietly arrived at Jerusalem.   He had chosen an unfrequented route by
which to go, in order to avoid the travelers who
were making their way to the city from all quarters.   In the midst of the feast, when the dispute
concerning himself was at its height, Jesus walked
calmly into the court of the temple, and stood
before the crowd as one possessed of unquestionable authority.   The sudden and unexpected appearance of one whom they believed would not
dare to show himself among them in the presence

of all the chief priests and rulers, astonished the people so that a sudden hush succeeded the excited discussion in which they had been engaged. They were astonished at his dignified and courageous bearing in the midst of many powerful men who were thirsting for his life.

Standing thus, with the eyes of all the people riveted upon him, he addressed them as no man had ever done. His knowledge was greater than that of the learned priests and elders, and he assumed an authority which they had never ventured to take. Those very men who had so lately been wrought up to a frenzy of hate, and were ready to do violence to Christ at the first opportunity, now listened spell-bound to his words, and felt themselves powerless to do him harm. He was the attraction of the hour; all other interests were forgotten for the time. The hearts of the people thrilled with awe as they listened to his divine words.

His discourse showed that he was well acquainted with the law in all its bearings, and was a clear interpreter of the Scriptures. The question passes from one to another, "How knoweth this man letters, having never learned?" Some, less acquainted with his former life, inquire among themselves in what school he has been instructed. Finally, the rulers recover their presence of mind sufficiently to demand by what authority he stands so boldly teaching the people. They seek to turn the attention of the multitude from Jesus to the question of his right to teach, and to their own importance and authority. But the voice of Jesus answers their queries with thrilling power:—

"My doctrine is not mine, but His that sent me.

If any man will do his will, he shall know of the doctrine, whether it be of God, or whether I speak of myself. He that speaketh of himself seeketh his own glory; but he that seeketh his glory that sent him, the same is true, and no unrighteousness is in him." Jesus here declares that his Heavenly Father is the source of all strength, and the foundation of all wisdom. No natural talent nor acquired learning can supply the place of a knowledge of the will of God. A willingness to obey the requirements of the Lord opens the mind and heart to candid inquiry, and diligent searching for the doctrine of truth. He declares that, with a mind thus open, men can discern between him who speaks in the cause of God and him who speaks for his own glory for selfish purposes. Of this latter class were the haughty priests and Pharisees.

Jesus spoke upon the subject of the law. He was in the presence of the very men who were great sticklers for its exactions, yet failed to carry out its principles in their lives. These persons persecuted Jesus, who taught so pointedly the sanctity of God's statutes, and freed them from the senseless restrictions which had been attached to them. Since Jesus had healed the paralytic on the Sabbath day, the Pharisees had a determined purpose to compass his death, and were eagerly watching for an opportunity to accomplish their design. Jesus, penetrating their purposes, inquired of them :—

"Did not Moses give you the law, and yet none of you keepeth the law? Why go ye about to kill me?" This pointed accusation struck home to the guilty consciences of the Pharisees and rulers, but only increased their rage. That this humble man should stand up before the people and expose the hidden iniquity of their lives, seemed a presumption too great to be believed. But the rulers wished to conceal their evil purposes from the people, and evaded the words of Jesus, crying out, "Thou hast a devil; who goeth about to kill thee?" In these words they would insinuate that all the wonderful works of Jesus were instigated by an evil spirit. They also wished to direct the minds of the people from the words of Jesus revealing their purpose of taking his life.

But "Jesus answered and said unto them, I have done one work, and ye all marvel. Moses therefore gave unto you circumcision; not because it is of Moses, but of the fathers; and ye on the Sabbath day circumcise a man." Jesus referred to his act of healing the man on the Sabbath, and showed that it was in accordance with the Sabbath law. He alluded also to the custom among the Jews of circumcising on the Sabbath. If it was lawful to circumcise a man on the Sabbath, it must certainly be right to relieve the afflicted, "to make a man every whit whole on the Sabbath day." He bade them "judge not according to appearance, but judge righteous judgment." The boldness with which Jesus defended himself, and interpreted the spirit of the law, silenced the rulers and led many of those who heard him to say, "Is not this he whom they seek to kill? But lo, he speaketh boldly, and they say nothing unto him. Do the rulers know indeed that this is the very Christ?" Many of those who lived at Jerusalem, and were not ignorant of the designs of the Sanhedrim council against Jesus, were charmed with the doctrine that he taught and with his pure and dignified bearing, and were inclined to accept him as the Son of God.

They were not filled with the bitter prejudice and hatred of the priests and rulers; but Satan was ready to suggest doubts and questions in their minds as to the divinity of this man of humble origin. Many had received the impression that Messiah would have no natural relationship to humanity, and it was not pleasant for them to think of him, whom they had hoped would be a mighty King of Israel, as one who sprung from poverty and obscurity. Therefore they said among themselves, "Howbeit we know this man whence he is; but when Christ cometh, no man knoweth whence he is." The minds of these men were closed to the prophecies, which pointed out how and when Christ was to come.

While their minds were balancing between doubt and faith, Jesus took up their thoughts and answered them thus: "Ye both know me, and ye know whence I am; and I am not come of myself, but He that sent me is true, whom ye know not. But I know him; for I am from him, and he hath sent me." They claimed a knowledge of what the origin of Christ should be, while they were in reality utterly ignorant of it, and were locked in spiritual blindness. If they had lived in accordance with the will of the Father, they would have known his Son when he was manifested to them.

The words of Jesus convinced many of those who listened; but the rage of the rulers was increased by this very fact, and they made an attempt to seize him; "but no man laid hands on him, because his hour was not yet come.

And many of the people believed on him, and said, When Christ cometh will he do more miracles than these which this man hath done ?"

Jesus stood before his enemies with calm and dignified mien, declaring his mission to the world, and revealing the hidden sins and deadly designs of the Pharisees and rulers. Though these lofty persons would gladly have sealed his lips, and though they had the will to destroy him where he stood, they were prevented by an invisible influence, which put a limit to their rage and said to them, "Thus far shalt thou go, and no farther."

The words of Jesus found a place in many hearts, and, like seed sown in goodly soil, they afterward bore abundant harvests. The spies scattered throughout the throng now report to the chief priests and elders that Jesus is gaining great influence among the people and that many are already acknowledging their belief in him. The priests therefore secretly lay their plans to arrest Jesus; but they arrange to take him when he is alone, for they dare not risk the effect upon the people of seizing him while in their presence. Jesus, divining their malevolent intents, declares in words of solemn pathos :—

"Yet a little while am I with you, and then I go unto Him that sent me. Ye shall seek me, and shall not find me; and where I am, thither ye cannot come." Soon the Saviour of the world will find a refuge from the persecution of his enemies, where their scorn and hate will be powerless to harm him. He will ascend to his Father, to be again the Adored of angels; and thither his murderers can never come.

The Feast of Tabernacles was celebrated to

commemorate the time when the Hebrews dwelt in tents during their sojourn in the wilderness. While this great festival lasted, the people were required to leave their houses and live in booths made of green branches of pine or myrtle. These leafy structures were sometimes erected on the tops of the houses, and in the streets, but oftener outside the walls of the city, in the valleys and along the hill-sides. Scattered about in every direction, these green camps presented a very picturesque appearance.

The feast lasted one week, and during all that time the temple was a festal scene of great rejoicing. There was the pomp of the sacrificial ceremonies; and the sound of music, mingled with hosannas, made the place jubilant. At the first dawn of day, the priests sounded a long, shrill blast upon their silver trumpets; and the answering trumpets, and the glad shouts of the people from their booths, echoing over hill and valley, welcomed the festal day. Then the priest dipped from the flowing waters of the Kedron a flagon of water, and, lifting it on high, while the trumpets were sounding, he ascended the broad steps of the temple, keeping time with the music with slow and measured tread, chanting meanwhile: "Our feet shall stand within thy gates, O Jerusalem!"

He bore the flagon to the altar which occupied a central position in the temple court. Here were two silver basins, with a priest standing at each one. The flagon of water was poured into one basin, and a flagon of wine into the other; and the contents of both flowed into a pipe which communicated with the Kedron, and was conducted to the Dead Sea. This display of the consecrated water represented the fountain that flowed from the rock to refresh the Hebrews in the wilderness. Then the jubilant strains rang forth:—

"The Lord Jehovah is my strength and song;" "therefore with joy shall we draw water out of the wells of salvation!" All the vast assembly joined in triumphant chorus with musical instruments and deep-toned trumpets, while competent choristers conducted the grand harmonious concert of praise.

The festivities were carried on with an unparalleled splendor. At night the temple and its court blazed so with artificial light that the whole city was illuminated. The music, the waving of palm-branches, the glad hosannas, the great concourse of people, over which the light streamed from the hanging lamps, the dazzling array of the priests, and the majesty of the ceremonies, all combined to make a scene that deeply impressed all beholders.

The feast was drawing to a close. The morning of the last, crowning day found the people wearied from the long season of festivity. Suddenly Jesus lifted up his voice in tones that rang through the courts of the temple:—

"If any man thirst, let him come unto me, and drink. He that believeth on me, as the Scripture hath said, out of his belly shall flow rivers of living water." The condition of the people made this appeal very forcible. They had been engaged in a continued scene of pomp and festivity, their eyes had been dazzled with light and color, and their ears regaled with the richest music; but there had been nothing to meet the wants of the spirit, nothing to satisfy the thirst of the soul

for that which perishes not. Jesus invited them
to come and drink of the fountain of life, of that
which should be in them a well of water springing up into everlasting life.

The priest had that morning performed the
imposing ceremony which represented the smit-
ing of the rock in the wilderness and the issuing
therefrom of the water. That rock was a figure
of Christ. His words were the water of life. As
Jesus spoke thus to the people, their hearts
thrilled with a strange awe, and many were ready
to exclaim, with the woman of Samaria, "Give
me of this water, that I thirst not."

The words of the Divine Teacher presented
his gospel in a most impressive figure. More
than eighteen hundred years have passed since
the lips of Jesus pronounced those words in the
hearing of thousands of thirsty souls; but they
are as comforting and cheering to our hearts to-
day, and as full of hope, as to those who accepted
them in the Jewish temple. Jesus knew the
wants of the human soul. Hollow pomp, riches
and honor, cannot satisfy the heart. "If any
man thirst, let him come unto me." The rich, the
poor, the high, the low, are alike welcomed. He
promises to relieve the burdened mind, to comfort the sorrowing, and give hope to the despond-
ent. Many of those who heard Jesus were
mourners over disappointed hopes, some were
nourishing a secret grief, some were seeking to
satisfy the restless longing of the soul with the
things of this world and the praise of men; but
when all this was gained, they found that they
had toiled to reach only a broken cistern, from
which they could not quench their fever thirst.
Amid all the glitter of the joyous scene they

stood, dissatisfied and sad. That sudden cry, "If any man thirst—" startles them from their sorrowful meditation, and as they listen to the words that follow, their minds kindle with a new hope. They look upon the Lifegiver standing in majesty before them, divinity flashing through his humanity, and revealing his heavenly power in words that thrill their hearts.

The cry of Christ to the thirsty soul is still going forth. It appeals to us with even greater power than to those who heard it in the temple on that last day of the feast. The weary and exhausted ones are offered the refreshing draught of eternal life. Jesus invites them to rest in him. He will take their burdens. He will give them peace. Centuries before the advent of Christ, Isaiah described him as a "hiding-place from the wind," a "covert from the tempest," as "the shadow of a great rock in a weary land." All who come to Christ receive his love in their hearts, which is the water that springs up unto everlasting life. Those who receive it impart it in turn to others, in good works, in right examples, and in Christian counsel.

The day was over, and the Pharisees and rulers waited impatiently for a report from the officers whom they had set upon the track of Jesus, in order to arrest him. But their emissaries return without him. They are angrily asked, "Why have ye not brought him?" The officers, with solemn countenances, answer, "Never man spake like this man." Dealing with violence and crime had naturally hardened the hearts of these men; but they were not so unfeeling as the priests and elders, who had resolutely shut out the light, and given themselves up to envy and malice.

The officers had heard the words of Jesus in the temple, they had felt the wondrous influence of his presence, and their hearts had been strangely softened and drawn toward him whom they were commanded to arrest as a criminal. They were unequal to the task set them by the priests and rulers; they could not summon courage to lay hands upon this pure Being who stood, with the light of Heaven upon his countenance, preaching a free salvation. As they stand excusing themselves for not obeying their orders, and saying, "Never man spake like this man," the Pharisees, enraged that even these tools of the law should be influenced by this Galilean peasant, cry out angrily:—

"Are ye also deceived? Have any of the rulers or of the Pharisees believed on him? But this people, who knoweth not the law, are cursed." They then proceed to lay plans to condemn and execute Jesus immediately, fearful that if he is left free any longer he will gain all the people. They decide that their only hope is to speedily silence him. But Nicodemus, one of the Pharisees, and he who had come to Jesus in the night and had been taught of him concerning the new birth, speaks out boldly:—

"Doth our law judge any man, before it hear him, and know what he doeth?" For a moment silence falls on the assembly. Nicodemus was a rich and influential man, learned in the law, and holding a high position among the rulers. What he said was true, and came home to the Pharisees with startling emphasis; they could not condemn a man unheard. But this was not the only reason that the haughty rulers remained confounded, gazing at him who had so boldly spoken in favor of justice. They were startled and chagrined that one of their own number had been so impressed by the power of Jesus as to openly defend him in the council. When they recovered from their astonishment, they addressed him with cutting sarcasm :—

"Art thou also of Galilee ? Search and look; for out of Galilee ariseth no prophet." But they were nevertheless unable to carry their purpose, and condemn Jesus without a hearing. They were defeated and crest-fallen for the time, and "every man went unto his own house."

CHAPTER XXX.

GO AND SIN NO MORE.

EARLY on the following morning, Jesus " came again into the temple, and all the people came unto him; and he sat down, and taught them."

While Jesus was engaged in teaching, the scribes and Pharisees brought to him a woman whom they accused of the sin of adultery, and said to him, Master, " now Moses in the law commanded us that such should be stoned; but what sayest thou ? This they said, tempting him, that they might have to accuse him. But Jesus stooped down, and with his finger wrote on the ground, as though he heard them not."

The scribes and Pharisees had agreed to bring

this case before Jesus, thinking that whatever decision he made in regard to it, they would therein find occasion to accuse and condemn him. If he should acquit the woman, they would accuse him of despising the law of Moses, and condemn him on that account; and if he should declare that she was guilty of death, they would accuse him to the Romans as one who was stirring up sedition and assuming authority which alone belonged to them. But Jesus well knew for what purpose this case had been brought to him; he read the secrets of their hearts, and knew the character and life-history of every man in his presence. He seemed indifferent to the question of the Pharisees, and while they were talking and pressing about him, he stooped and wrote carelessly with his finger in the sand.

Although doing this without apparent design, Jesus was tracing on the ground, in legible characters, the particular sins of which the woman's accusers were guilty, beginning with the eldest and ending with the youngest. At length the Pharisees became impatient at the indifference of Jesus, and his delay in deciding the question before him, and drew nearer, urging the matter. But as their eyes fell upon the words written in the sand, fear and surprise took possession of them. The people, looking on, saw their countenances suddenly change, and pressed forward to discover what they were regarding with such an expression of astonishment and shame. Many of those who thus gathered round also read the record of hidden sin inscribed against these accusers of another.

Then Jesus "lifted up himself, and said unto them, He that is without sin among you, let him first cast a stone at her. And again he stooped down, and wrote on the ground." The accusers saw that Jesus not only knew the secrets of their past sins, but was acquainted with their purpose in bringing this case before him, and had in his matchless wisdom defeated their deeply laid scheme. They now became fearful lest Jesus would expose their guilt to all present, and they therefore "being convicted by their own conscience, went out one by one, beginning at the eldest, even unto the last; and Jesus was left alone, and the woman standing in the midst."

There was not one of her accusers but was more guilty than the conscience-stricken woman who stood trembling with shame before him. After the Pharisees had hastily left the presence of Christ, in their guilty consternation, he arose and looked upon the woman, saying, "Woman, where are those thine accusers? hath no man condemned thee? She said, No man, Lord. And Jesus said unto her, Neither do I condemn thee. Go, and sin no more."

Jesus did not palliate sin nor lessen the sense of crime; but he came not to condemn; he came to lead the sinner to eternal life. The world looked upon this erring woman as one to be slighted and scorned; but the pure and holy Jesus stooped to address her with words of comfort, encouraging her to reform her life. Instead of to condemn the guilty, his work was to reach into the very depths of human woe and degradation, lift up the debased and sinful, and bid the trembling penitent to "sin no more." When the woman stood before Jesus, cowering under the accusation of the Pharisees and a sense of the enormity of her crime, she knew that her life was trembling in the balance, and that a word from Jesus would add fuel to the indignation of the crowd, so that they would immediately stone her to death.

Her eyes droop before the calm and searching glance of Christ. Stricken with shame, she is unable to look upon that holy countenance. As she thus stands waiting for sentence to be passed upon her, the words fall upon her astonished ears that not only deliver her from her accusers, but send them away convicted of greater crimes than hers. After they are gone, she hears the mournfully solemn words: "Neither do I condemn thee. Go, and sin no more." Her heart melts with penitential grief; and, with gratitude to her Deliverer, she bows at the feet of Jesus, sobbing out in broken accents the emotions of her heart, and confessing her sins with bitter tears.

This was the beginning of a new life to this tempted, fallen soul, a life of purity and peace, devoted to the service of God. In raising this woman to a life of virtue, Jesus performed a greater act than that of healing the most grievous bodily malady; he cured the sickness of the soul which is unto death everlasting. This penitent woman became one of the firmest friends of Jesus. She repaid his forgiveness and compassion, with a self-sacrificing love and worship. Afterward, when she stood sorrow-stricken at the foot of the cross, and saw the dying agony on the face of her Lord, and heard his bitter cry, her soul was pierced afresh; for she knew that this sacrifice was on account of sin; and her responsibility as one whose deep guilt had helped to bring about this anguish of the Son of God, seemed very heavy indeed. She felt that those

pangs which pierced the Saviour's frame were for
her; the blood that flowed from his wounds was
to blot out her record of sin; the groans which
escaped from his dying lips were caused by her
transgression. Her heart ached with a sorrow
past all expression, and she felt that a life of self-
abnegating atonement would poorly compensate
for the gift of life, purchased for her at such an
infinite price.

In his act of pardoning, and encouraging this
fallen woman to live a better life, the character
of Jesus shines forth in the beauty of a perfect
righteousness. Knowing not the taint of sin
himself, he pities the weakness of the erring one,
and reaches to her a helping hand. While
the self-righteous and hypocritical Pharisees denounce, and the tumultuous crowd is ready to
stone and slay, and the trembling victim waits
for death—Jesus, the Friend of sinners, bids her,
" Go, and sin no more."

It is not the true follower of Christ who turns
from the erring with cold, averted eyes, leaving
them unrestrained to pursue their downward
course. Christian charity is slow to censure,
quick to detect penitence, ready to forgive, to
encourage, to set the wanderer in the path of
virtue, and stay his feet therein.

The wisdom displayed by Jesus on this occasion, in defending himself against the designs of
his enemies, and the evidence which he gave them
that he knew the hidden secrets of their lives, the
conviction that he pressed home upon the guilty
consciences of the very men who were seeking to
destroy him, were sufficient evidence of his divine character. Jesus also taught another important lesson in this scene: That those who are

ever forward to accuse others, quick to detect
them in wrong, and zealous that they should be
brought to justice, are often guiltier in their own
lives than those whom they accuse. Many who
beheld the whole scene were led to compare the
pardoning compassion of Jesus with the unrelent-
ing spirit of the Pharisees, to whom mercy was a
stranger; and they turned to the pitying Saviour
as unto One who would lead the repentant sinner into peace and security.

"Then spake Jesus again unto them, saying,
I am the light of the world; he that followeth
me shall not walk in darkness, but shall have
the light of life." Jesus had represented himself, in his relation to fallen man, as a fountain
of living water, to which all who thirst may
come and drink. The brilliant lights in the
temple illuminated all Jerusalem, and he now
used these lights to represent his relation to the
world. In clear and thrilling tones he declared:
"I am the light of the world." As the radiant
lamps of the temple lit up the whole city, so
Christ, the source of spiritual light, illuminated
the darkness of a world lying in sin. His manner was so impressive, and his words carried
with them such a weight of truth, that many
were there convicted that he was indeed the Son
of God. But the Pharisees, ever ready to contradict him, accused him of egotism, saying,
"Thou bearest record of thyself; thy record is
not true." Jesus, answering their objections, asserted again his divine commission:—

"Though I bear record of myself, yet my record
is true; for I know whence I came, and whither
I go; but ye cannot tell whence I come and
whither I go." They were ignorant of his divine

character and mission because they had not
searched the prophecies concerning the Messiah,
as it was their privilege and duty to do. They
had no connection with God and Heaven, and
therefore did not comprehend the work of the
Saviour of the world, and, though they had received the most convincing evidence that Jesus
was that Saviour, yet they refused to open their
minds to understand. At first they had set their
hearts against him, and refused to believe the
strongest proof of his divinity, and, as a consequence, their hearts had grown harder until they
were determined not to believe nor accept him.

"Ye judge after the flesh; I judge no man.
And yet, if I judge, my judgment is true; for I
am not alone, but I and the Father that sent
me." Thus he declared that he was sent of God,
to do his work. He had not consulted with
priests nor rulers as to the course he was to pursue; for his commission was from the highest authority, even the Creator of the universe. Jesus,
in his sacred office, had taught the people, had
relieved suffering, had forgiven sin, and had
cleansed the temple, which was his Father's
house, and driven out its desecraters from its
sacred portals; he had condemned the hypocritical lives of the Pharisees, and reproved their
hidden sins; and in all this he had acted under
the instruction of his Heavenly Father. For
this reason they hated him and sought to kill
him. Jesus declared to them: "Ye are from beneath; I am from above. Ye are of this world;
I am not of this world."

"When ye have lifted up the Son of Man,
then shall ye know that I am he, and that I do
nothing of myself, but as my Father hath taught

me." "And he that sent me is with me; the Father hath not left me alone; for I do always those things that please him." These words were spoken with thrilling power, and, for the time, closed the lips of the Pharisees, and caused many of those who listened with attentive minds to unite with Jesus, believing him to be the Son God. To these believing ones he said, "If ye continue in my word, then are ye my disciples indeed. And ye shall know the truth, and the truth shall make you free." But to the Pharisees who rejected him, and who hardened their hearts against him, he declared: "I go my way, and ye shall seek me, and shall die in your sins; whither I go, ye cannot come."

But the Pharisees took up his words, addressed to those who believed, and commented upon them, saying, "We be Abraham's seed, and were never in bondage to any man; how sayest thou, Ye shall be made free?" Jesus looked upon these men,—the slaves of unbelief and bitter malice, whose thoughts were bent upon revenge,—and answered them, "Verily, verily, I say unto you, Whosoever committeth sin, is the servant of sin." They were in the worst of bondage, ruled by the spirit of evil. Jesus declared to them that if they were the true children of Abraham, and lived in obedience to God, they would not seek to kill one who was speaking the truth that was given him of God. This was not doing the works of Abraham, whom they claimed as their father.

Jesus, with startling emphasis, denied that the Jews were following the example of Abraham. Said he, "Ye do the deeds of your father." The Pharisees, partly comprehending his meaning,

said, "We be not born of fornication; we have
one Father, even God." But Jesus answered
them : "If God were your Father, ye would love
me; for I proceeded forth and came from God;
neither came I of myself, but he sent me." The
Pharisees had turned from God, and refused to
recognize his Son. If their minds had been open
to the love of God, they would have acknowledged the Saviour who was sent to the world by
him. Jesus boldly revealed their desperate condition :—

"Ye are of your father the devil, and the lusts
of your father ye will do. He was a murderer
from the beginning, and abode not in the truth,
because there is no truth in him. When he speaketh a lie, he speaketh of his own; for he is a liar,
and the father of it. And because I tell you the
truth, ye believe me not." These words were
spoken with sorrowful pathos, as Jesus realized
the terrible condition into which these men had
fallen. But his enemies heard him with uncon-
trollable anger; although his majestic bearing,
and the mighty weight of the truths he uttered,
held them powerless. Jesus continued to draw
the sharp contrast between their position and
that of Abraham, whose children they claimed
to be :—

"Your father Abraham rejoiced to see my day;
and he saw it, and was glad." The Jews listened
incredulously to this assertion, and said, sneering-
ly, "Thou art not yet fifty years old, and hast
thou seen Abraham ?" Jesus, with a lofty dignity that sent a thrill of conviction through their
guilty souls, answered, "Verily, verily, I say unto
you, Before Abraham was, I am." For a moment, silence fell upon all the people, as the

grand and awful import of these words dawned upon their minds. But the Pharisees, speedily recovering from the influence of his words, and fearing their effect upon the people, commenced to create an uproar, railing at him as a blasphemer. "Then took they up stones to cast at him; but Jesus hid himself, and went out of the temple, going through the midst of them, and so passed by."

CHAPTER XXXI.

RESURRECTION OF LAZARUS.

JESUS had often found the rest that his weary human nature required at the house of Lazarus, in Bethany. His first visit there was when he and his disciples were weary from a toilsome journey on foot from Jericho to Jerusalem. They tarried as guests at the quiet home of Lazarus, and were ministered unto by his sisters, Martha and Mary. Notwithstanding the fatigue of Jesus, he continued the instruction which he had been giving his disciples on the road, in reference to the qualifications necessary to fit men for the kingdom of Heaven. The peace of Christ rested upon the home of the brother and sisters. Martha had been all anxiety to provide for the comfort of her guests, but Mary was charmed by the words of Jesus to his disciples, and, seeing a golden opportunity to become better acquainted with the doctrines of Christ, quietly entered the room where he was sitting, and, taking her place

at the feet of Jesus, drank in eagerly every word
that fell from his lips.

The energetic Martha was meanwhile making
ample preparations for the entertainment of her
guests, and missed her sister's help. Finally she
discovered that Mary was sitting at the feet of
Jesus, and listening with rapt attention to what
he was saying. Martha, wearied with many cares,
was so vexed to see her sister calmly listening
thus, that she forgot the courtesy due to her
guests, and openly complained of Mary's idleness,
and appealed to Jesus that he would not permit
all the domestic duties to fall upon one.

Jesus answered these complaints with mild and
patient words : " Martha, Martha, thou art careful
and troubled about many things ; but one thing is
needful, and Mary hath chosen that good part,
which shall not be taken away from her." That
which Jesus indicated that Martha needed, was
a calm, devotional spirit, a deeper anxiety to learn
more concerning the future immortal life, and the
graces necessary to spiritual advancement. She
needed less anxiety for earthly things, which
pass away, and more for heavenly things, which
affect the eternal welfare of the soul. It is necessary to faithfully perform the duties of the
present life, but Jesus would teach his children
that they must seize every opportunity to gain
that knowledge which will make them wise unto
salvation.

One of the dangers of the present age is devot-
ing too much time to business matters and to unnecessary cares, which we create for ourselves,
while the development of Christian character is
neglected. Careful, energetic Marthas are needed
for this time, who will blend with their prompt,

decisive qualities that "better part" of which Christ spoke. A character of such combined strength and godliness is an unconquerable power for good.

A dark cloud now hung over this quiet home where Jesus had rested. Lazarus was stricken with sudden illness. The afflicted sisters sent a message to Jesus: "Lord, behold, he whom thou lovest is sick." They made no urgent requirement for the immediate presence of Jesus, for they believed that he would understand the case and relieve their brother. Lazarus was a firm believer in the divine mission of Jesus; he loved him ardently and was in turn beloved by the blessed Master, whose peace had rested on his quiet home. The faith and love which the brother and sisters felt toward Jesus encouraged them to believe that he would not disregard their distress. Therefore they sent the simple, confiding message: "He whom thou lovest is sick."

When Jesus received the message, he said, "This sickness is not unto death, but for the glory of God, that the Son of God might be glorified thereby." He accordingly remained where he was for two days. After the messenger was sent, Lazarus grew rapidly worse. The sisters counted the days and hours that must intervene between the sending of the message and the arrival of Jesus to their aid. As the time approached when they should expect him, they anxiously watched the travelers who appeared in the distance, hoping to discover the form of Jesus. All their efforts for the recovery of their brother were in vain, and they felt that he must die unless divine help interposed to save him. Their constant prayer was,

Oh ! that Jesus would come ! He could save our beloved brother !

Presently their messenger returns, but unaccompanied by Jesus. He bears to the sorrowing sisters the words of the Saviour, " This sickness is not unto death." But the hearts of the sisters fail them, for lo, their brother is already wrestling with the fierce destroyer, and soon closes his eyes in death.

Jesus, at the end of the two days, proposed to go to Judea, but his disciples endeavored to prevent him from doing so. They reminded him of the hatred manifested toward him when he was last there. Said they, " The Jews of late sought to stone thee ; and goest thou thither again ? " Jesus then explained to them that he must go, for Lazarus was dead, adding, " And I am glad for your sakes that I was not there, to the intent ye may believe." Jesus did not delay going to the relief of Lazarus through want of interest in the stricken family ; but he designed to make the sorrowful event of the death of Lazarus an occasion to give undoubted proof of his divine power, and unite his disciples to him in a faith that could not be broken. Already some among them were questioning in their minds if they had not been deceived in the evidences of his divine power ; if he was really the Christ would he not have saved Lazarus whom he loved ? Jesus designed to work a crowning miracle that would convince all who would by any means be convinced that he was the Saviour of the world.

The danger attaching to this expedition into Judea was great, since the Jews were determined to kill Jesus. Finding it was impossible to dissuade him from going, Thomas proposed to the disciples that they should all accompany their Master, saying, "Let us also go, that we may die with him." Therefore the twelve accompanied the Saviour. On the way, Jesus labored for the needy, relieving the suffering and healing the sick as was his custom. When he reached Bethany he heard from several persons that Lazarus was dead, and had been buried four days. While still at a distance from the house, he heard the wailing of the mourners. When a Hebrew died it was customary for the relatives to give up all business for several days, and live on the coarsest food while they mourned for the dead. Professional mourners were also hired, and it was they whom Jesus heard wailing and shrieking in that house which had once been his quiet, pleasant resting place.

Jesus did not desire to meet the afflicted sisters in such a scene of confusion as their home then presented, so he stopped at a quiet place by the road-side, and sent a messenger to inform them where they could find him. Martha hastened to meet him; she told him of her brother's death, saying, "Lord, if thou hadst been here, my brother had not died." In her disappointment and grief she had not lost confidence in Jesus, and added, "But I know, that even now, whatsoever thou wilt ask of God, God will give it unto thee."

Jesus encouraged her faith by declaring to her, "Thy brother shall rise again." Martha, not comprehending the full meaning of Jesus, answered that she knew he would arise in the resurrection, at the last day. But Jesus, seeking to give a true direction to her faith, said, "I am the resurrection, and the life; he that believeth in me, though he were dead, yet shall he live; and whosoever liveth and believeth in me, shall never die. Believest thou this?" Jesus would direct the thoughts of Martha to himself, and strengthen her faith in regard to his power. His words had a double meaning; not only did they refer to the immediate act of raising Lazarus, but they also referred to the general resurrection of all the righteous, of which the resurrection of Lazarus which he was then about to perform, was but a representation. Jesus declared himself the Author of the resurrection. He who himself was soon to die upon the cross, stood with the keys of death, a conqueror of the grave, and asserted his right and power to give eternal life.

When Jesus asked Martha: "Believest thou?" she answered by a confession of her faith: "Lord, I believe that thou art the Christ, the Son of God, which should come into the world." Thus Martha declared her belief in the Messiahship of Jesus, and that he was able to perform any work which it pleased him to do. Jesus bade Martha call her sister, and the friends that had come to comfort the afflicted women. When Mary came she fell at the feet of Jesus, also crying, "Lord, if thou hadst been here, my brother had not died." At the sight of all this distress, Jesus "groaned in the spirit, and was troubled, and said, Where have ye laid him? They said unto him, Lord, come and see." Together they all proceeded to the grave of Lazarus, which was a cave with a stone upon it.

It was a mournful scene. Lazarus had been much beloved, and his sisters wept for him with breaking hearts, while those who had been his friends mingled their tears with those of the bereaved sisters. Jesus had also loved Lazarus, whose faith had ever been strong in him, never wavering nor failing for a moment. In view of this human distress, and of the fact that these afflicted friends could mourn over the dead, when the Saviour of the world stood by, who had power to raise from the dead,—"Jesus wept." His grief was not alone because of the scene before him. The weight of the grief of ages was upon his soul, and, looking down the years that were to come, he saw the suffering and sorrow, tears and death, that were to be the lot of men. His heart was pierced with the pain of the human family of all ages and in all lands. The woes of the sinful race were heavy on his soul, and the fountain of his tears was broken up, as he longed to relieve all their distress.

Seeing the tears and hearing the groans of Jesus, those who stood about said, "Behold, how he loved him!" Then they whispered among themselves, "Could not this man, which opened the eyes of the blind, have caused that even this man should not have died?" Jesus groaned within himself at the unbelief of those who had professed faith in him. They thought his tears were because of his love for Lazarus, and that he who had done such mighty works had been unable to save Lazarus from death. Burdened by the blind infidelity of those who should have had faith in him, Jesus approached the grave, and in tones of authority commanded that the stone should be rolled away. Human hands were, on their part, required to do all that it was possible

for them to do, and *then* divine power would finish the work.

But Martha objected to the stone being removed, and reminded Jesus that the body had
been buried four days, and that corruption had
already commenced its work. Jesus answered
her reproachfully : " Said I not unto thee, that,
if thou wouldest believe, thou shouldest see the
glory of God ?" The stone was then taken away,
and the dead was revealed to sight. It was evident to all that putrefaction had really commenced. All is now done that lies in the power
of man to do. The friends gather round with
mingled curiosity and awe to see what Jesus is
about to do. Lifting up his eyes, the Saviour
prayed :—

"Father, I thank thee that thou hast heard
me. And I knew that thou hearest me always;
but because of the people which stand by I said
it, that they may believe that thou hast sent me."
The hush that followed this prayer was broken
by Jesus crying out with a loud voice, " Lazarus, come forth." Instantly life animates that
form which had been so changed by decay that
the friends of the deceased recoiled from looking upon it. Lazarus, bound hand and foot
with grave-clothes, and with a napkin about his
face, rises, obedient to the command of his Saviour, and attempts to walk, but is impeded by
the winding-sheet. Jesus commands his friends
to " loose him, and let him go."

Human hands are again brought into requisi-
tion to do the work which it is possible for them
to do. The burial clothes which bear evidence
of the corruption of the body are removed, and
Lazarus stands before them, not as one emaciated

from disease, and with feeble, tottering limbs, but as a man in the prime of life, and in the vigor of a noble manhood, his eyes beaming with intelligence and love for his Saviour. He bows at the feet of Jesus and glorifies him. A dumb surprise at first seizes all present; but now succeeds an inexpressible scene of rejoicing and thanksgiving. The sisters receive their brother back to life as the gift of God, and with joyful tears, brokenly express their thanks and praise to the Saviour. But while brother, sisters, and friends are rejoicing in this reunion, Jesus retires from the exciting scene, and when they look for the Lifegiver, he is nowhere to be found.

This crowning miracle of Christ caused many to believe on him. But some who were in the crowd about the grave, and heard and saw the wonderful works performed by Jesus, were not converted, but steeled their hearts against the evidence of their own eyes and ears. This demonstration of the power of Christ was the crowning manifestation offered by God to man as a proof that he had sent his Son into the world for the salvation of the human race. If the Pharisees rejected this mighty evidence, no power in Heaven nor upon earth could wrest from them their Satanic unbelief.

The spies hurry away to report to the rulers this work of Jesus, and that the "world is gone after him." In performing this miracle, the Saviour took a decisive step toward the completion of his earthly mission. The grandest evidence of his life was now given that he was the Son of God, and had control of death and the grave. Hearts that had long been under the power of sin, in rejecting this proof of the divinity of Jesus, locked themselves in impenetrable darkness and came wholly under the sway of Satan, to be hurried by him over the brink of eternal ruin.

The mighty miracle wrought at the grave of Lazarus intensified the hatred of the Pharisees against Jesus. This demonstration of divine power, which presented such unquestionable proof that Jesus was the Son of God, was sufficient to convince any mind under the control of reason and enlightened conscience. But the Pharisees, who had rejected all lesser evidence, were only enraged at this new miracle of raising the dead in the full light of day, and before a crowd of witnesses. No artifice of theirs could explain away such evidence. For this very reason their hate grew deadlier, and they watched every opportunity of accomplishing their secret purpose to destroy him. In heart they were already murderers.

The Jewish authorities counseled together as to what course they should pursue to counteract the effect of this miracle upon the people; for the news spread far and wide that Jesus had raised Lazarus from the dead, and the reality of the event was established by many eye-witnesses. Still the enemies of Jesus sought to circulate lying reports, perverting the facts in the case as far as they were able, and endeavoring to turn the people away from one who had dared to rob the grave of its dead.

In this council of the Jews were some influential men who believed on Jesus; but their wishes were overruled by the malignant Pharisees, who hated Jesus because he had exposed their hypo-

critical pretensions, and had torn aside the cloak
of precision and rigorous rites under which their
moral deformity was hidden.   The pure religion
that Jesus taught, and his simple, godly life, condemned their hollow professions of piety.   They
thirsted for revenge, and nothing short of taking
his life would satisfy them.   They had tried to
provoke him to say or do something that would
give them occasion to condemn him, and several
times they had attempted to stone him, but he
had quietly withdrawn and they had lost sight
of him.

The miracles performed by Jesus on the Sabbath were all for the relief of the afflicted, but
the Pharisees had sought to use these works of
mercy as a cause by which they might condemn
him as a Sabbath-breaker.   They endeavored to
arouse the Herodians against him; they represented that Jesus was seeking to set up a rival kingdom among them, and consulted with them how
they should destroy him.   They had sought to
excite the Romans against him, and had represented him to them as one who was trying to
subvert their authority.   They had tried every
pretext to cut him off from influencing the people, but they had so far been foiled in their attempts; for the multitudes who witnessed the
works of mercy and benevolence done by Jesus,
and heard his pure and holy teachings, knew
that these were not the words and deeds of a
Sabbath-breaker and a blasphemer.   Even the
officers sent by the Pharisees had been so influenced by the divine presence of the great Teacher
that they could not lay hands upon him.   In
desperation the Jews had finally passed an edict

that if any man confessed that he believed on Jesus he should be cast out of the synagogue.

So, as the priests, the rulers, and the elders gathered together for consultation, it was their fixed determination to silence this man who did such marvelous works that all men wondered. Nicodemus and Joseph had, in former councils, prevented the condemnation of Jesus, and for this reason they were not summoned on this occasion. Caiaphas, who acted as high priest that year, was a proud and cruel man; he was by nature overbearing and intolerant; he had studied the prophecies, and, although his mind was shrouded in darkness as to their true meaning, he spoke with great authority and apparent knowledge.

As the priests and Pharisees were consulting together, some of them said, "If we let him thus alone, all men will believe on him; and the Romans shall come, and take away both our place and nation." Then Caiaphas spoke out loftily: "Ye know nothing at all, nor consider that it is expedient for us that one man should die for the people, and that the whole nation perish not." The voice of the high priest decided the matter; even if Jesus was innocent, let him die; he was troublesome, drawing the people to himself, and lessening the authority of the rulers. He was only one, it was better that he should die, even though he was guiltless, than that the power of the rulers should diminish. Caiaphas, in declaring that one man should die for the nation, indicated that he had some knowledge of the prophecies, although it was very limited; but John in his account of this scene takes up the prophecy, and shows its broad and deep significance in these words: "And not for that nation only, but that also he should gather together in one the children of God that were scattered abroad." How blindly did the haughty Caiaphas acknowledge the mission of Jesus as a Redeemer!

Nearly all the council agreed with the high priest that it was the wisest policy to put Jesus to death. This decision having been made, the question was still to be determined how it should be carried out. They feared to take rash measures lest the people should become incensed and the violence meditated toward Jesus should be visited upon themselves. The Saviour was continually benefiting and teaching the people, they knew him to be one without blame, and his influence over them was very strong; it was on this account that the Pharisees delayed to execute the sentence which they had pronounced against him.

The Saviour understood the plottings of the priests against him; he knew that they longed to remove him from their midst, and that their wishes would soon be accomplished; but it was not his place to hasten the culminating event, and he withdrew from that region, taking his disciples with him. Jesus had now given three years of public labor to the world. His example of self-denial and disinterested benevolence was before them. His life of purity, of suffering, and devotion, was known to all. Yet this short period of three years was as long as the world could endure the presence of its Redeemer.

His life had been one of persecution and insult. Driven from Bethlehem by a jealous king, rejected by his own people at Nazareth, condemned to death without a cause at Jerusalem, Jesus, with his few faithful followers, finds a temporary asylum in a strange city. He who was ever touched by human woe, who healed the sick, restored sight to the blind, hearing to the deaf, and speech to the dumb, who fed the hungry and comforted the sorrowful, was driven from the people whom he had labored to save. He who walked upon the heaving billows and by a word silenced their angry roaring, who cast out devils that in departing acknowledged him to be the Son of God, who broke the slumbers of the dead, who held thousands entranced by the words of wisdom which fell from his lips, was unable to reach the hearts of those who were blinded by prejudice and insane hatred, and who resolutely rejected the light.

It is not the plan of God to compel men to yield their wicked unbelief. Before them are light and darkness, truth and error. It is for them to decide which to accept. The human mind is endowed with power to discriminate between right and wrong. God designs that men shall not decide from impulse, but from weight of evidence, carefully comparing scripture with scripture. Had the Jews laid by their prejudice, and compared written prophecy with the facts characterizing the life of Jesus, they would have perceived a beautiful harmony between the prophecies and their fulfillment in the life and ministry of the lowly Galilean.

It was nearing the time of the passover, and many came to Jerusalem from various parts of the country to purify themselves according to the ceremonial custom of the Jews. There was much talk and speculation among these people concerning Jesus, and they wondered if he would not be present at the feast. "Now both the chief priests and the Pharisees had given a commandment, that if any man knew where he were, he should show it, that they might take him."

CHAPTER XXXII.

MARY'S OFFERING.

SIX days before the passover, Jesus stopped at the house of Lazarus in Bethany. He was on his way from Jericho to attend the feast of the passover at Jerusalem, and chose this retreat for rest and refreshment. Crowds of people passed on to the city, bearing the tidings that Jesus was on his way to the feast, and that he would rest over the Sabbath at Bethany. This information was received with great enthusiasm by the people; for the news had spread everywhere of the wonderful works wrought by Jesus, the last and most astonishing of which was the resurrection of Lazarus from the dead. Many flocked to Bethany, some from curiosity to see one who had been raised from the dead, and others because their hearts were in sympathy with Jesus, and they longed to look upon his face and hear his blessed words.

They returned with reports that increased the excitement of the multitude. All were anxious to see and hear Jesus, whose fame as a prophet had spread over all the land. There was a gen-

eral buzz of inquiry as to who the wonderful
Teacher was, from whence he had come, if Lazarus who had been raised from the dead would
accompany him to Jerusalem, and if it was likely
that the great prophet would be crowned king
at the feast. The attention of the people was
entirely engrossed in the subject of Jesus and his
wondrous works. The priests and rulers saw
that they were losing their hold upon the minds
of the people, and their rage against Jesus was
increased; they could hardly wait for him to
come and give them the desired opportunity of
gratifying their revenge and removing him forever from their way. As the time passed, they
became excited and restless, fearing that after all
Jesus might not come to Jerusalem. They were
fearful that he had read their purposes against
him, and would therefore remain away. They
remembered how often he had divined their
thoughts, exposed their hidden motives, and baffled their murderous designs. They could illy
conceal their anxiety, and questioned among
themselves, "What think ye, that he will not
come to the feast?"

A hasty council of the priests and Pharisees
was called to determine how to proceed with regard to Jesus, in view of the excitement and enthusiasm of the people on his account. They decided that it would be dangerous to seize upon
him openly on any pretext, for since the raising
of Lazarus the sympathies of the people were
greatly in favor of Jesus. So they determined
to use craft and take him secretly, avoiding all
uproar or interference, carry on the mockery of a
trial as quietly as possible, and trust to the fickle

tide of public opinion to set in their favor when it was known that Jesus was condemned to death.

But another consideration came up: If they should execute Jesus, and Lazarus should remain as a witness of his miraculous power to raise from the dead, the very fact that a man existed who had been four days in the grave, and whose body had begun to decay, yet had been called to life and health by a word from Jesus, would sooner or later create a reaction and bring disaster upon themselves for sacrificing the life of Him who could perform such a miracle for the benefit of humanity. They therefore decided that Lazarus must also die. They felt that if the people were to lose confidence in their rulers, the national power would be destroyed.

To such lengths do envy and bitter prejudice lead their slaves. In rejecting Christ, the Pharisees placed themselves where darkness and superstition closed around them, until, continually increasing in hatred and unbelief, they were ready to imbrue their hands in blood to accomplish their unholy ends, and would even take the life of one whom Infinite power had rescued from the grave. They placed themselves where no power, human or divine, could reach them; they sinned against the Holy Spirit, and God had no reserve power to meet their case. Their rebellion against Christ was settled and determined; he was a stumbling-block and a rock of offense to them; they would not have this man Jesus to reign over them. While all this plotting was going on at Jerusalem, Jesus was quietly resting from his labors at the house of Lazarus. Simon of Bethany, whom Jesus had healed of leprosy,

wishing to show his Master special honor, made
a supper and invited him and his friends as
guests. The Saviour sat at the table, with Simon,
whom he had cured of a loathsome disease, on
one side, and Lazarus, whom he had raised from
the dead, on the other. Martha served at the
table, but Mary was earnestly listening to every
word that fell from the lips of Jesus. She saw
that he was sad; she knew that immediately
after raising her brother from the dead, he was
obliged to seclude himself in order to escape the
persecution of the leading Jews. As she looked
upon her brother in the strength of perfect health,
her heart went out in gratitude to Jesus who had
restored him to her from the grave.

Jesus in his mercy had pardoned the sins of
Mary, which had been many and grievous, and
her heart was full of love for her Saviour. She
had often heard him speak of his approaching
death, and she was grieved that he should meet
so cruel a fate. At great personal sacrifice she
had purchased an alabaster box of precious ointment with which to anoint the body of Jesus at
his death. But she now heard many express an
opinion that he would be elevated to kingly
authority when he went to Jerusalem, and she
was only too ready to believe that it would be
so. She rejoiced that her Saviour would no longer be despised and rejected, and obliged to flee
for his life. In her love and gratitude she wished
to be the first to do him honor, and, seeking to
avoid observation, anointed his head and feet
with the precious ointment, and then wiped his
feet with her long, flowing hair.

Her movements had been unobserved by the

others, but the odor filled the house with its fragrance and published her act to all present. Some of the disciples manifested displeasure at this act, and Judas boldly expressed his disapprobation at such a wasteful extravagance. Simon the host, who was a Pharisee, was influenced by the words of Judas, and his heart filled with unbelief. He also thought that Jesus should hold no communication with Mary because of her past life. Judas, the prime instigator of this disaffection among those who sat at the table, was a stranger to the deep devotion and homage which actuated Mary to her deed of love. He had been appointed treasurer of the united funds of the disciples, and had dishonestly appropriated to himself the means which were designed for the service of God.

He had indulged a spirit of avarice until it had overpowered every good trait in his character. This act of Mary was in such marked contrast with his selfishness that he was ashamed of his avarice, and sought to attribute his objection to her gift, to a worthier motive. Turning to the disciples he asked, " Why was not this ointment sold for three hundred pence, and given to the poor ?" Thus he sought to hide his covetousness under apparent sympathy for the poor, when, in reality, he cared nothing for them.

He longed to have the avails of the expensive ointment in his own hands to apply to his own selfish purposes. By his professed sympathy for the poor he deceived his fellow-disciples, and by his artful insinuations caused them to look distrustfully upon the devotion of Mary. Whispered hints of prodigality passed round the table : " To

what purpose is this waste? for this ointment
might have been sold for much, and given to the
poor." Mary was abashed as the eyes of the disciples were bent sternly and reproachfully upon
her. She felt that her deed of devotion must
have been wrong, and tremblingly expected Jesus
to condemn it also.

But the Saviour had observed all that had
transpired, and knew the motives of all who were
there assembled. He read the object of Mary in
her costly offering. Though she had been very
sinful, her repentance was sincere, and Jesus,
while reproving her guilt, had pitied her weakness and forgiven her. Mary's heart was filled
with gratitude at the compassion of Jesus. Seven
times she had heard his stern rebuke to the demons which then controlled her heart and mind,
and she had listened to his strong cries to his
Father in her behalf. She knew how offensive
everything impure was to the unsullied mind of
Christ, and she overcame her sin in the strength
of her Saviour. She was transformed, a partaker
of the divine nature.

Mary had offered her gift in the grateful homage of her heart, and Jesus explained her motive
and vindicated her deed. "Let her alone," he
said. "Why," he asked, "trouble ye the woman?
for she hath wrought a good work upon me."
He justified her work to all present as evincing
her gratitude to him for lifting her from a life of
shame to one of purity, and teaching her to believe
in him. Said he, "Against the day of my burying hath she kept this." The ointment so sa-
credly kept to anoint the dead body of her Lord
she had poured upon his head in the belief that

he was about to be lifted to a throne in Jerusalem.

Jesus might have pointed out Judas to the disciples as the cause of such severe judgment being passed on Mary. He might have revealed to them the hypocrisy of his character; he might have made known his utter want of feeling for the poor, and his embezzlement of money appropriated to their relief. He could have raised their indignation against him for his oppression of the widow, the orphan, and the hireling; but he refrained from exposing the true character of Judas. He reproached him not, and thus avoided giving him an excuse for his future perfidy.

But he rebuked the disciples, saying, "Ye have the poor with you always, and whensoever ye will ye may do them good; but me ye have not always. She hath done what she could. She is come aforehand to anoint my body to the burying. Verily, I say unto you, wheresoever this gospel shall be preached throughout the whole world, this also that she hath done shall be spoken of for a memorial of her." Jesus, looking into the future, spoke with certainty concerning his gospel: That it was to be preached throughout the whole world. Kingdoms would rise and fall; the names of monarchs and conquerors would be forgotten; but the memory of this woman's deed would be immortalized upon the pages of sacred history.

Had the disciples rightly appreciated the exalted character of their Master, they would have considered no sacrifice too costly to offer to the Son of God. The wise men of the East understood more definitely his true position, and the honor due him, than his own followers, who had received his instruction and beheld his mighty miracles. They brought precious gifts to the Saviour, and bent in homage before him, while he was but a babe, and cradled in a manger.

The look which Jesus cast upon the selfish Judas convinced him that the Master penetrated his hypocrisy and read his base, contemptible character. He was stirred with resentment. His heart burned with envy that Jesus should be the recipient of an offering suitable to the monarchs of earth. He went directly from that supper to the chief priests, and agreed to betray him into their hands. The priests were greatly rejoiced at this, and " they covenanted with him for thirty pieces of silver, and from that time he sought opportunity to betray him."

In the case of Judas we see the fearful result of covetousness and unholy anger. He begrudged the offering made to Jesus, and although not personally rebuked, he was irritated to combine revenge with his avarice, and sell his Lord for a few pieces of silver. Mary showed how highly she prized the Saviour when she accounted the most precious gift none too costly for him; but Judas valued Jesus at the price for which he sold him; his niggardly soul balanced the life of the Son of God against a paltry sum of money. The same cold, calculating spirit is manifested by many who profess Christ to-day. Their offerings to his cause are grudgingly bestowed or withheld altogether under various plausible excuses. A pretense of wide philanthropy, un-limited by church or creed, is not unfrequently one of them, and they plead, like Judas, It is better to give it to the poor. But the true Christian shows his faith by investing in the cause of truth; he is known by his works, for "faith without works is dead."

Jesus read Simon's heart, and knew how he had been ·influenced by the insinuations of Judas, and that he had questioned in his mind, saying, "This man, if he were a prophet, would have known who and what manner of woman this is that toucheth him; for she is a sinner." When Judas had left the house, Jesus turned to his host and said, "Simon, I have somewhat to say unto thee." Simon replied, "Master, say on." Then Jesus proceeded to speak a parable, which illustrated the contrast between the gratitude of his host, who had been healed of the leprosy, and that of Mary, whose sins had been pardoned. Said he, "There was a certain creditor which had two debtors; the one owed five hundred pence, and the other fifty. And when they had nothing to pay, he frankly forgave them both. Tell me, therefore, which of them will love him most?"

Simon did not discern the application which Jesus designed to make, but he answered him, "I suppose that he to whom he forgave most." Jesus replied, "Thou hast rightly judged." This answer condemned Simon. He had been a great sinner, and also a loathsome leper, avoided by all. He had come to Jesus piteously imploring his help, and He who never turned a deaf ear to human woe, had cleansed him from sin and from the terrible disease that was upon him. Simon was humbled, but he had been a proud Pharisee, and he did not look upon himself as being so great a sinner as he really was, and he had now become self-sufficient and lifted up in his own estimation. He had exalted himself as far superior to the poor woman who anointed the feet of her Lord. In entertaining Jesus at his house, he thought he was paying him marked respect; but the Saviour was lowered in his estimation when he permitted the devotion of Mary, who had been so great a sinner. He overlooked the miracle which Jesus had wrought upon him in saving him from a living death,. and coldly reasoned with himself if Jesus could be the Messiah, and yet stoop to receive the gift of this woman. He thought that if he were the Christ, he would know that a sinner had approached him and repel her. He did not realize that he himself had been a greater sinner than she, and that Christ had forgiven him as well as Mary. He was ready to doubt the divine character of his Master because he imagined that he detected in him a want of discernment.

On the other hand, Mary was thoroughly penitent and humbled because of her sins. In her gratitude for his pardoning mercy she was ready to sacrifice all for Jesus, and no doubt as to his divine power troubled her mind for a moment. It was not the comparative degrees of obligation which should be felt by the two persons, which Jesus designed to illustrate by this parable, for both were unable to cancel their debt of gratitude; but he took Simon on his own ground, as feeling himself more righteous than the woman, and showed him that though the sins which had been forgiven him were great, he had not repaid his Benefactor with that respect and love which casts out all unbelief. His sense of obligation to his Saviour was small, while Mary, prizing the gift of mercy bestowed upon her, was filled with gratitude and love.

Jesus drew the contrast sharply between the two. Said he: "Seest thou this woman? I entered into thine house, thou gavest me no water for my feet; but she hath washed my feet with tears, and wiped them with the hairs of her head. Thou gavest me no kiss; but this woman, since the time I came in, hath not ceased to kiss my feet. My head with oil thou didst not anoint; but this woman hath anointed my feet with ointment."

The proud Pharisee had considered that he had sufficiently honored Jesus by inviting him to his house; and in his self-consequence had neglected to show him the proper regard due to so exalted a guest, and to one who had wrought upon him a miracle of mercy. Jesus encouraged acts of heart-felt courtesy, and the woman, whose gratitude and love was expressed in her act of attention, was highly commended by the Saviour: "Wherefore I say unto thee, Her sins, which are many, are forgiven; for she loved much; but to whom little is forgiven, the same loveth little."

Simon's eyes were opened to his neglect and unbelief. He was touched by the kindness of Jesus in not openly rebuking him before all the guests. He perceived that Jesus did not wish to exhibit his guilt and his want of gratitude to others, but desired to convince his mind by a true statement of his case, and to subdue his heart by pitying kindness. Stern denunciation would have closed the heart of Simon against repentance; but patient admonition convinced him of his error and won his heart. He saw the magnitude of the debt which he owed his Lord, and became a humble, self-sacrificing man.

When we realize the full debt of obligation to our Saviour, we are united to him by closer bonds, and our love will be expressed in all our acts. Jesus will remember every good work done by his children. The self-sacrificing and benevolent will live in his memory and be rewarded. No act of devotion to his cause will be forgotten by him. There is no sacrifice too costly to be offered on the altar of our faith.

CHAPTER XXXIII.

RIDING INTO JERUSALEM.

On the first day of the week, Jesus resumed his journey to Jerusalem to join in the feast of the passover. Multitudes who had flocked to Bethany to see him, accompanied him, eager to witness his entry into Jerusalem. All nature seemed to rejoice; the trees were clothed in verdure, and blossoms which shed their delicate fragrance upon the air. Many people were on their way to the city to keep the feast of the passover. These companies were continually joining the multitude attending Jesus. He sent two of his disciples to bring "a colt, the foal of an ass," that he might ride into Jerusalem. It was but a short distance, and as he had always chosen to travel

on foot, his disciples were puzzled to know why
he should prefer to ride. But hope brightened
in their hearts with the joyous thought that
Jesus was about to enter the capital and proclaim himself King of the Jews, and assert his
royal power. While on their errand, the disciples communicated their glowing anticipations to
the friends of Jesus, and the excitement spread
far and near, raising the expectations of the people to the highest pitch.

Jesus selected for his use a colt upon which
never man had sat. The disciples in glad enthusiasm spread their garments upon the colt and
placed their Master upon him. No sooner was
he seated than a loud shout of triumph rent the
air, and the multitude hailed him as Messiah, their
King. Jesus now accepted the homage which he
had never before permitted, and his disciples received this as a proof that their glad hopes were
to be realized by seeing him acknowledged at
Jerusalem as the King of Israel. All were happy
and excited; the people vied with each other in
paying him homage. They could not display outward pomp and splendor, but they gave him the
worship of happy hearts. They were unable to
present him with costly gifts, but they spread
their outer garments as a carpet in his path, and
they also strewed the leafy branches of the olive
and palm in the way. They could lead the triumphal procession with no royal standards, but
they cut down the spreading palm boughs, Nature's emblem of victory, and waved them aloft,
while their loud acclamations and hosannas rent
the air.

As they proceeded, the multitude was continually increased by those who had heard of the coming of Jesus and hastened to join the procession. Spectators were constantly mingling with the throng and asking, Who is this? What does all this commotion signify? They had all heard of Jesus and were expecting him to go to Jerusalem, but they knew that he had heretofore refused to receive kingly honors, and they were greatly astonished to learn that this was he. They wondered what could have wrought this change in him who had declared that his kingdom was not of this world.

While they are wondering and questioning, the eager crowd silence their queries with a shout of triumph that is repeated again and again, and is echoed from the surrounding hills and valleys. And now the joyful procession is joined by crowds from Jerusalem, that have heard of the grand demonstration, and hasten to meet the Saviour and conduct him to Jerusalem. From the great gathering of the Hebrews to attend the passover, thousands go forth to welcome Jesus to the city. They greet him with the waving of palm branches and a burst of sacred song. The priests at the temple sound the trumpet for evening service, but there are few to respond, and the rulers say to each other in alarm, "The world has gone after him."

The Saviour during his earthly life had hitherto refused to receive kingly honor, and had resolutely discouraged all attempts to elevate him to an earthly throne; but this occasion was intended by Jesus to call public attention to him as the world's Redeemer. He was nearing the period when his life was to be offered a ransom for guilty man. Although he was soon to be betrayed and to be hanged upon the cross like a malefactor, yet he would enter Jerusalem, the scene of his approaching sacrifice, attended by demonstrations of joy and the honor belonging to royalty, to faintly prefigure the glory of his future coming to the world as Zion's King.

It was the purpose of Jesus to draw attention to the crowning sacrifice that was to end his mission to a fallen world. They were assembling at Jerusalem to celebrate the passover, while he, the antitypical Lamb, by a voluntary act set himself apart as an oblation. Jesus understood that it was needful in all future ages that the church should make his death for the sins of the world a subject of deep thought and study. Every fact connected with it should be verified beyond a doubt. It was necessary, then, that the eyes of all people should be directed to him, that the demonstrations which preceded his great sacrifice should be such as to call the attention of all to the sacrifice itself. After such an exhibition as that attending his entry into Jerusalem, all eyes would follow his rapid progress to the final end.

The startling events connected with this triumphal ride were calculated to be the talk of every tongue, and bring Jesus before every mind. After his crucifixion these events would be connected with his trial and death; prophecies would be searched and would reveal the fact that this was indeed the Messiah; and converts to the faith of Jesus would be multiplied in all lands. In this one triumphant scene of his earthly life, the Saviour might have appeared escorted by

heavenly angels and heralded by the trumps of
God; but he remained true to the life of humiliation he had accepted, bearing the burden of humanity till his life was given for the life of the
world.

This day, which seemed to the disciples the
crowning day of their lives, would have been
shadowed with gloomy clouds had they known
that this scene of rejoicing was but a prelude to
the suffering and death of their Master. Although he had repeatedly told them of his certain sacrifice, yet in the glad triumph of the
present they forgot his sorrowful words, and
looked forward to his prosperous reign on the
throne of David. New accessions were being
made continually to the procession, and, with few
exceptions, all who joined it caught the glad inspiration of the hour, and helped to swell the hosannas that echoed and re-echoed from hill to hill
and from valley to valley. The shouts went up
continually, "Hosanna to the Son of David!
Blessed is He that cometh in the name of the
Lord! Hosanna in the highest!" It was as if
all that vast multitude were seeking to excel one
another in responding to the call from a prophetic past.

Many Pharisees witnessed the scene, and, burning with envy and malice, sought to turn the
popular current. They exercised all the authority which they could command to repress the enthusiasm of the people; but all their appeals
and threatenings were in vain. Fearful that this
multitude, in the strength of their numbers,
would lift Jesus to the position of king, they,
as a last resort, pressed through the crowd and,

accosted him with reproving and threatening words: "Master, rebuke thy disciples." They declared that such noisy and excited demonstrations were unlawful and would not be permitted by the authorities. But the reply of Jesus silenced their haughty commands: "I tell you that, if these should hold their peace, the stones would immediately cry out."

God himself had, in his special providence, arranged the order of the events then transpiring, and if men had failed to carry out the divine plan, He would have given a voice to the inanimate stones and they would have hailed his Son with acclamations of praise. This scene had been revealed in prophetic vision to the holy seers of old, and man was powerless to turn aside the purposes of Jehovah. As the silenced Pharisees drew back, the words of Zechariah were taken up by hundreds of voices: "Rejoice greatly, O daughter of Zion; shout, O daughter of Jerusalem. Behold, thy King cometh unto thee; he is just, and having salvation; lowly, and riding upon an ass, and upon a colt, the foal of an ass."

The Pharisees were forced to desist from their efforts to calm the enthusiasm of the people. All their expostulations only served to increase their ardor. The world had never before seen such a triumphal procession. It was not like that of the earth's famous conquerors. No train of mourning captives, as trophies of kingly valor, made a feature of that imposing pageant. But about the Saviour were the glorious trophies of his labors of love for sinful man. There were the captives whom he had rescued from Satan's

cruel power, praising God for their deliverance.
The blind to whom he had restored sight pressed
on, leading the way. The dumb, whose tongues
he had loosed, shouted the loudest hosannas.
The cripples whom he had healed bounded
freely on, the most active in breaking the palm-
branches and in waving them before the Saviour.
Widows and orphans were among the multitude
exalting the name of Jesus for his works of
mercy to them. The lepers who had been
cleansed by a word from him, and rescued from
a living death, spread their untainted garments
in his path and hailed him as the King of Glory.
Those who had been awakened by his magic
voice from the sleep of death were in that
throng. Lazarus, whose body had seen corruption in the grave, now restored to the full
strength of glorious manhood, guided the humble
beast upon which his Liberator rode.

When the procession arrived at the summit of
the hill and was about to descend into the city, Jesus halted, and all the multitude with him. Jerusalem in all its glory lay before them, bathed
in the light of the declining sun. The temple
attracted all eyes. In stately grandeur it tow-
ered above all else, seeming to point toward
Heaven as if directing the people upward to the
only true and living God. This temple in its
splendid majesty had long been the pride and
glory of the Jewish nation. The Romans also
prided themselves in it as an unequaled monu-
ment of magnificence. Their king had united
with the Jews in embellishing it, and together
they had spared no pains nor expense to furnish
it with the most costly and beautiful decorations
both without and within.

A portion of the wall of the building had withstood the siege of armies, and, in its perfect masonry, appeared like one solid stone dug entire from the quarry. While the westering sun was tinting and gilding the heavens, its resplendent glory lit up the pure white marble of the temple and sparkled on its gold-capped pillars. From the crest of the hill where Jesus and his followers stood, it had the appearance of a massive structure of snow studded with flashing jewels. At the entrance to the temple was a vine composed of gold and silver, with green leaves and massive clusters of grapes, all executed at an enormous expense by the most skillful artists. This design represented Israel in the character of a prosperous vine. The gold, silver, and living green were all combined with such rare taste and exquisite workmanship, that, as it twined gracefully about the white and glistening pillars, clinging with shining tendrils to their golden ornaments, it was a wonderful thing of beauty, catching the splendor of the setting sun, and shining as if with a glory borrowed from Heaven.

Jesus gazes upon the enchanting scene before him, and the vast multitude hush their shouts, spell-bound by this sudden vision of beauty. All eyes turn instinctively upon the Saviour, expecting to see in his countenance the admiration which they themselves feel. But instead of this they behold a cloud of sorrow gathering upon his countenance. They are surprised and disappointed to see the eyes of the Saviour fill with tears, and his body rock to and fro like a tree before the tempest, while a wail of anguish bursts from his quivering lips as if from the depths of a broken heart. What a sight was this for angels to behold! Their loved Commander in an agony of tears! What a sight was this for that glad throng who had accompanied him with shouts of triumph and waving of palm-branches to that summit overlooking the glorious city where they fondly hoped he would reign! Their acclamations were now silenced, while many tears flowed in sympathy with the grief they could not comprehend.

Jesus had wept at the grave of Lazarus, but it was in a God-like grief in harmony with the occasion. But this sudden sorrow is like a note of wailing in a grand triumphal chorus. In the midst of a scene of rejoicing, where all were paying him homage, Israel's King was in tears; not silent tears of gladness, but tears and groans of insuppressible agony. The multitude are struck with a sudden gloom while they look upon this grief which is incomprehensible to them. The tears of Jesus were not in anticipation of physical suffering as he contemplated his crucifixion, though just before him was the garden of Gethsemane where he knew that soon the horror of a great darkness would overshadow him. The sheep gate was also in sight through which for centuries the beasts for sacrificial offerings had been conducted. This gate was soon to open for him, the great Antitype toward whose sacrifice for the sins of the world all these offerings had pointed. Near by was Calvary, the scene of his approaching agony.

Yet it is not because of these reminders of his cruel death that the Redeemer weeps and groans in anguish of spirit. His is no selfish sorrow.

The thought of physical pain does not intimidate that noble, self-sacrificing soul. It is the sight of Jerusalem that pierces the heart of Jesus with anguish,—Jerusalem that had rejected the Son of God and scorned his love, who refused to be convinced by his mighty miracles and is about to take his life. He sees what she is in her guilt of rejecting her Redeemer, and what she might have been had she accepted Him who alone could heal her wound. He had come to save her; how can he give up the child of his care!

He raised his hand,—that had so often blessed the sick and suffering,—and waving it toward the doomed city, in broken utterances of grief exclaimed: "If thou hadst known, even thou, in this thy day the things which belong to thy peace—" Here the Saviour paused and left unsaid what might have been the condition of Jerusalem had she accepted the only help that God could give her,—the gift of his beloved Son. If Jerusalem had known what it was her privilege to know, and had acted according to the light bestowed upon her by God, she might have stood forth in the pride of prosperity, the queen of kingdoms, free in the strength of her God-given power. There would then have been no armed soldiers waiting at her gates, no Roman banners waving from her walls. The glorious destiny which might have blessed Jerusalem, had she accepted her Redeemer, rose before the Son of God. He saw that she might through him have been healed of her grievous malady, liberated from bondage, and established as the mighty metropolis of the earth. From her walls the dove of peace would have gone forth to all nations.

She would have been the world's diadem of glory.

But the bright picture of what Jerusalem might have been had she accepted the Son of God, fades from the Saviour's sight as he realizes what she is under the oppressive Roman yoke, bearing the frown of God, doomed to his retributive justice. He takes up the broken thread of his lamentations: "But now they are hid from thine eyes. For the days shall come upon thee, that thine enemies shall cast a trench about thee, and compass thee round, and keep thee in on every side, and shall lay thee even with the ground, and thy children within thee; and they shall not leave in thee one stone upon another; because thou knewest not the time of thy visitation."

Christ came to save Jerusalem with her children from the consequences of her former sins; but the unholy expectations of the Pharisees were not answered in the manner of his appearing. Pharisaical pride, hypocrisy, jealousy, and malice had prevented him from accomplishing his purpose. Jesus knew the terrible retribution which would be visited upon the doomed city. He sees Jerusalem encompassed with armies, the besieged inhabitants driven to starvation and death, mothers making a repast on the dead bodies of their own children, and both parents and children snatching the last morsel of food from one another, natural affection being destroyed through the gnawing pangs of hunger. He sees that the stubbornness of the Jews, as evinced in their rejection of his salvation, will also lead them to refuse their only remaining chance of safety, submission to the invading armies. He sees the wretched inhabitants suffering torture on the rack, and crucifixion, the beautiful palaces destroyed, the temple where God had revealed his glory, in ruins, and of all its pure and spotless walls, decorated with lofty pillars and gilded devices, not one stone left upon another, while the city is plowed like a field. Well may the Saviour weep in agony in view of such a fearful picture!

Jerusalem had been the child of his care, and as a tender father mourns over a wayward son, so Jesus wept over Jerusalem. How can I give thee up! How can I see thee devoted to destruction and desolation! Must I let thee go to fill up the cup of thine iniquity! One soul is of such value that, in comparison with it, worlds sink into insignificance; but here was a whole nation to be lost. When the fast westering sun should pass from sight in the heavens, Jerusalem's day of grace would be at an end. While that vast procession was halting on the brow of Olivet, it was yet not too late for Jerusalem to repent and be saved. The Angel of Mercy was then folding her wings to step down from the golden throne and give place to Justice and swift-coming judgment. But Christ's great heart of love still pleads for Jerusalem, which had scorned all his mercies, despised his warnings, and was about to finish her iniquitous work by imbruing her hands in his blood. If Jerusalem would but repent, it is not yet too late. While the last rays of the setting sun are lingering on temple, tower, and flashing minaret, will not some good angel lead her to the Saviour's love, and avert the fearful doom that awaits her!

Beautiful and unholy city, that had stoned the prophets, that had rejected the Son of God, that was locking herself, by her impenitence, in fetters of bondage,—thy day of mercy is almost spent!

Here had lived a favored people; God made their temple his habitation; it was "beautiful for situation, the joy of the whole earth." The record of more than a thousand years of Christ's guardian care and tender love, such as a father bears his only child, was there. In that temple had the prophets uttered their solemn warnings. There had the burning censers waved, while incense, mingled with the prayers of the worshipers, had ascended to God. There the blood of beasts had flowed, typical of the blood of Christ. There Jehovah had manifested his glory above the mercy-seat. There the priests had officiated in flowing robes and jeweled breast-plates, and the pomp of symbol and ceremony had gone on for ages. But all this must have an end; for Jerusalem has sealed her own doom, and her destruction is at hand.

Contemplating the fate of the city he had loved, the soul of Jesus yearned over the child of his care. Unrequited love broke the heart of the Son of God. Little did the multitude know of the grief that weighed upon the spirit of Him whom they worshiped. They saw his tears and heard his groans, and for a brief space a mysterious awe interrupted their joyful demonstrations; but they could not understand the meaning of his lamentation over Jerusalem. Meanwhile, reports were brought to the rulers that Jesus was approaching the city attended by a great concourse of people. In trepidation they go out to meet him, hoping to disperse the crowd by means of their authority. As the procession is about to descend the Mount of Olives, it is intercepted by the rulers. They inquire who and what is the cause of all this tumultuous rejoicing. As they, with much authority, repeat their question,—Who is this? the disciples, filled with a spirit of inspiration, are heard above all the noise of the crowd, repeating in eloquent strains the prophecies which answered this question. Adam will tell you, It is the seed of the woman that shall bruise the serpent's head. Ask Abraham, he will tell you, It is Melchisedek, King of Salem, King of Peace. Jacob will tell you, He is Shiloh of the tribe of Judah. Isaiah will tell you, Immanuel, Wonderful, Counsellor, the Mighty God, the everlasting Father, the Prince of Peace. Jeremiah will tell you, The Branch of David, the Lord, our righteousness. Daniel will tell you, He is the Messiah. Hosea will tell you, He is the Lord God of Hosts, the Lord is his memorial. John the Baptist will tell you, He is the Lamb of God who taketh away the sin of the world. The great Jehovah has proclaimed from his throne, This is my beloved Son. We, his disciples, declare, This is Jesus, the Messiah, the Prince of Life, the Redeemer of the world. And even the Prince of the powers of darkness acknowledges him, saying, " I know thee who thou art, the Holy One of God."

CATALOGUE

Of Books, Pamphlets, Tracts, &c., Issued by the Seventh-Day Adventist Publishing Association, Battle Creek, Mich.

———

THE ADVENT REVIEW & HERALD OF THE SABBATH, weekly. Terms, $2.00 a year, in advance.

THE YOUTH'S INSTRUCTOR, monthly, devoted to moral and religious instruction. Terms, 50 cts. a year, in advance.

THE HEALTH REFORMER, monthly, devoted to an exposition of the laws of life. etc. Terms, $1.00 a year, in advance.

THE ADVENT TIDENDE, a religious monthly in the Danish language. Terms, $1.00 a year, in advance.

THE SVENSK ADVENT HAROLD, a religious monthly in the Swedish tongue. Terms, $1.00 a year, in advance.

HYMN AND TUNE BOOK.—536 hymns—147 tunes. $1.00.

THE HISTORY OF THE SABBATH AND FIRST DAY OF THE WEEK. By J. N. Andrews. 528 pp., $1.25.

THE CHRISTIAN LIFE AND PUBLIC LABORS OF WM. MILLER, the noted Lecturer and Writer upon the Prophecies. $1.00.

THOUGHTS ON THE BOOK OF DANIEL, critical and practical. By U. Smith. Bound, $1.00; condensed edition, paper, 35 cts.

THOUGHTS ON THE REVELATION, critical and practical. By U. Smith. 328 pp., $1.00.

THE NATURE AND DESTINY OF MAN. By U. Smith. 384 pp., bound, $1.00, paper, 40 cts.

THE CONSTITUTIONAL AMENDMENT: or a Discussion between W. H. Littlejohn and the editor of the *Christian Statesman* on the Sabbath question. $1.00.

THE SPIRIT OF PROPHECY; or, the Great Controversy between Christ and his angels, and Satan and his angels, in three volumes, by Mrs. Ellen G. White. These volumes cover the time from the fall of Satan to the destruction of sin and sinners at the close of the one thousand years of Rev. 20.

Vol.   I.   OLD TESTAMENT FACTS TO CHRIST.   Price, $1.00.

"   II.   LIFE AND MINISTRY OF CHRIST.   Price, $1.00.

" III.   REACHES TO THE END OF SIN.   Price, $1.00.

LIFE OF ELDER JOSEPH BATES. $1.25.

THE GAME OF LIFE, with notes. Three illustrations, 5x6 inches each, representing Satan playing with man for his soul. In board, 50 cts., in paper, 30 cts.

(POEM.) A WORD FOR THE SABBATH: or False Theories Exposed. By U. Smith. 3d ed. revised and enlarged. 40 cts.

THE UNITED STATES IN PROPHECY. By U. Smith. Bound, 50 cts. ; paper, 25 cts.

PROGRESSIVE BIBLE LESSONS for Youth, in boards,   50 cts.
         "   "   "   Children,   "   35 cts.

THE ADVENT KEEPSAKE; a daily text of Scripture on the Second Advent, etc. 25 cts.

SERMONS ON THE SABBATH AND LAW; embracing an Outline of the Biblical and Secular History of the Sabbath for 6000 years. By J. N. Andrews. 25 cts.

FACTS FOR THE TIMES; a Collection of Valuable Extracts from Eminent Authors. 30 cts.

HISTORY of the Doctrine of the Immortality of the Soul. By D. M. Canright. 25 cts.

THE STATE OF THE DEAD. By U. Smith. 224 pp., 25 cts.

OUR FAITH AND HOPE. Sermons on the Second Coming of Christ. By James White. 25 cts.

REFUTATION OF THE AGE TO COME. By J. H. W. 20 cts.

THE ATONEMENT. By J. H. Waggoner. 20 cts.

THE NATURE AND TENDENCY OF MODERN SPIRITUALISM. By J. H. Waggoner. 20 cts.

MIRACULOUS POWERS. 20 cts.

Lightning Source UK Ltd.
Milton Keynes UK
UKHW022356090223
416721UK00001B/206